THE BULLY

THE BULLY

YEARS

David Instone

THOMAS PUBLICATIONS

ISBN 0 9512051 6 1

Printed by: Precision Colour Printing Ltd., Haldane, Halesfield 1, Telford,
Shropshire TF7 4QQ

INDEX

ACKNOWLEDGEMENTS

My sincere thanks go to the Express & Star, especially editor Warren Wilson and sports editor Steve Gordos, for their permission and encouragement to write this book.

The photographs have been supplied by kind permission of the Express & Star, all but one or two of them by chief photographer David Bagnall, whom I consistently and accidentally manage to avoid as we cover 50 or more Wolves games each per season. David's son Sam took the front-cover picture, which shows Steve Bull just after scoring his 200th Football League goal - Wolves' winner at Southend in April, 1995.

The front and back covers have been designed by artist John Hackney while picture scanner Paul Wilson and my good friend Peter Creed have been invaluable go-betweens. The expertise and cooperation of all are much appreciated.

Also, for the loan of scrapbooks and videos, I thank supporters Clive Smith, Gwilym Machin and Phil Murphy. Clive and Gwilym probably will miss a Wolves match one day. But maybe not in my lifetime. Phil now has another "team" at home to support and has cut back on his away trips accordingly. But he has followed Wolves from the heart for more than a quarter of a century.

My deepest thanks, though, are extended to my wife and occasional "sports widow" Liz, who has not only designed every page of this book except for the covers, but also made me a little less computer illiterate. The latter task, she tells me, was much more difficult.

FOREWORD
By Sir Jack Hayward OBE

I am very honoured to have been asked to write the foreword to this book by David Instone, extolling the feats of Steve Bull.

Steve is one of the all-time "greats" in the long and illustrious history of Wolverhampton Wanderers Football Club. His records are already enshrined in Wolves' roll of honour.

He has become renowned throughout the football world as someone who must be diligently marked at all times in the matches in which he appears.

This so well explains his frequent injuries. He has, however, a tough physique and dauntless spirit and is always anxious to get back into the team and play when others might not consider themselves fully fit.

No wonder he is known as the Tipton Terror. Or should that be Tipton Terrier? I never really know!

I am pleased that Steve's deeds are being recorded for posterity. This is only right for one of Wolves' greatest stars and servants.

INTRODUCTION

It could probably all have been said in the one simple sentence: Stephen George Bull, 250-plus goals from not many more than 400 Wolves appearances (friendlies not included). After all, that's the hub of the whole story.

More than 250 goals for one club. Wow! That's the equivalent of 25 goals a season for a full decade and only the precious few through the ages and through the divisions have produced a stronger statistical case with which to support their dedication to a single cause in the game.

Even John Richards - King John to those who revered him in his hey-day two decades ago - has now been left well over half a century of goals behind by Bully at the top of the all-time Molineux scoring charts.

It's a phenomenal tale, not only of loyalty to one club, but also of longevity and hero worship of a character who could easily have descended on to Centre Stage from up on the South Bank terraces. HE is very much one of THEM.

We're talking of a man who has been God around Molineux; the most loved human being in and around Wolverhampton for nearly ten years, although the writer of the foreword to this book has his own massive legion of admirers.

So, how do you start to tell the story of the Bully Years? With the international highs he attained with his England debut goal at a stunned Hampden Park and his trip to the 1990 World Cup finals 12 months later?

Or what about the avalanche of scoring records and wonder-goals with which he has lifted a club who were dying on their feet the day he first walked through the door?

I have decided to recount the story as it has unfolded and in the order in which it has unfolded. With a slow trawl through the Express & Star and Sporting Star pages of the last nine years, the written description of each and every one of his 251 Wolves goals in League and cup up to the end of 1994-95 is reproduced here for posterity. (Those not marked as being in other competitions are League matches).

The padding alongside those bare, glorious facts comes from a detailed journey through some of the most traumatic and eventful years in the club's highly distinguished history....the horrors of Chorley, the last brush with extinction, the renaissance seasons, the Sir Jack Hayward takeover and the replacement of Graham Turner with Graham Taylor.

But the common theme is the goal-scoring brilliance of one man. A man who, remember, hit the target 52 times for his club in 1987-88 and on 50 occasions the following season, with a few thrown in for England teams for good measure. No wonder chapters two and three are the longest. What golden days they were!

Sadly, there have been communication problems between Bully and the media in recent seasons, and we have had to respect his wishes to keep his counsel. But I hope this piece of work, which concentrates on nothing but his on-field heroics, reminds the adoring masses of how the legend grew and grew - and survived the passing of the seasons.

The Bully Years reveals the player's thoughts along his dream journey from factory floor to World Cup star and is liberally sprinkled with the comments through a nine-year passage of time of the likes of Graham Turner, Graham Taylor, Bobby Robson, Alex Ferguson, Andy Mutch, Sir Jack Hayward and the late Billy Wright CBE.

I saw Bully make his Wolves debut and have witnessed well over 200 of his goals for the club. What a magnificent story it has been to watch and to report. Throughout the compilation of this tribute, I have wondered whether I would be able to take a fresh vantage point in the upper reaches of the Premiership in a couple of years' time and compose the sequel, perhaps entitled "300 and still going strong."

But time waits for no man and, when the day eventually comes for someone else to fill his famous gold No 9 shirt, I hope this book will serve in some modest way as a testimony to his wonderful career.

Above all, I trust it will provide happy memories for those who have savoured his every step, and knowledge for those - perhaps the children and grandchildren of the 1980s and 1990s Molineux faithful - of what he was all about.

This is not, or at least hasn't been intended as, the epitaph; it's the story over the first eight and a half years of the common working man who stepped out of the builder's yard and into the hearts of tens of thousands with his lung-busting efforts. The most loved human being in his territory for nearly a decade.

Turner swoops for two

By David Instone

Wolves today made a surprise £70,000 move into the transfer market for Albion duo Steve Bull and Andy Thompson.

The two players had talks at Molineux this morning and were immediately sent for a medical in an attempt to rush the deals through in time for Saturday's home game with Wrexham.

Bull's fee is £50,000, Thompson's is £20,000 and Wolves manager Graham Turner predicted: "It's a big investment, but we'll get a long-term return — there's no doubt about that.

"They're two bright young players with a lot of potential. They'll prove a wise investment. The deals will also prove to supporters that the people who have taken over the club, mean business."

The two clubs quickly reached agreement today, leaving the players to discuss personal terms before going through the formalities.

Tipton-born striker Bull, 21, made his debut last season and has added another six appearances this term, scoring three goals.

Midfielder Thompson, from Featherstone, has made more than 20 first-team appearances, playing or lining up as sub in most games this season.

On-loan keeper Eric Nixon plays his last game for Wolves on Saturday. The third and final month of his temporary move from Manchester City ends on Saturday and City are unwilling to let him go permanently.

Wolves are also resigned to losing midfielder Ian Handysides after Saturday, the Blues player not relishing a full-time drop into the Fourth Division.

Meanwhile peace was finally declared between Albion striker Garth Crooks and manager Ron Saunders today when the player asked to come off the transfer list.

It was the final step towards harmony after a stormy nine months which had seen Crooks dropped, transfer-listed and fined more than £1,000.

The breakthrough came with the former Stoke and Spurs striker agreeing to spend three or four nights a week in the Midlands, rather than commuting daily from his London home.

"That was the big bone of contention, but he's agreed to spend more time up here," Saunders said.

"We never twist players' arms here — he wanted to come off the list."

Crooks only broke back into the side in early October, scoring in his comeback game against Oldham and since adding further goals against Portsmouth, Birmingham

Turkey offer for Big Ron

Ron Atkinson has been offered the national coaching job in Turkey.

Atkinson, sacked as manager of Manchester United two weeks ago, said today: "They have been in touch with me, and will be sending me some details to browse through.

"There are lots of things to consider at the moment and this is just one of them."

Rose in charge

Brian Rose, the former Somerset cricket captain who led the team to six cup successes in six seasons, will be the club's first team manager.

Windies suffer

West Indies were 212-7 in their first innings at the close of the first day of the third and final Test against Pakistan today.

Tony Laing (Nottingham) is to meet West Germany's Tony Habermayer for the vacant European light-welterweight title.

Hobson's ch

STEVE WHO?

1986-87

"Turner swoops for two" read the main headline on the back page of the
Express & Star on Thursday, November 20, 1986. Two reserves, that is,
from across the Black Country at West Bromwich Albion; Steve Bull and
Andy Thompson.

It was still B.C. (before Chorley). Or at least before the fateful third
meeting with the team of tinkers, tailors and candlestick makers who were
to sweep the little-known Multipart Northern Premier League club to a
famous FA Cup victory and leave Wolves - the scourge of Europe in floodlit
football's famous pioneering friendlies in the 1950s - at the lowest ebb in
their 109-year history.

The spectacular gold and black nosedive, therefore, still had a little way
to go to bottom out. But £70,000 was no mean amount for a club who had
almost gone bankrupt earlier that year.

"It's a big investment but we'll get a long-term return," said Graham
Turner on signing day, having marked his seventh week as Wolves manager
by persuading directors Dick Homden and Jack Harris to splash out from
their own pockets an initial £50,000 on Bull and £20,000 on Thompson.
"They're two bright young players with a lot of potential. They'll prove a
wise investment. The deals will also prove to supporters that the people who
have taken over the club mean business."

They were bold words by a man not given to over-statement and, in the
case of Bull particularly, no-one could have known how prophetic Turner's
statements were. At the zenith of the striker's career four years later, Wolves
could have been offered 100 times the initial payment and still been
undecided about selling him. Such were the heights he touched and the peaks
of popularity he attained and has retained with an adoring public.

As the first journalist to interview the new arrivals - so high was the
turnover of players in those days that a revolving door might have been more
appropriate than an entrance and an exit - I was led by secretary Keith
Pearson into Molineux's decaying boardroom. And there they were. Fresh-
faced, hopeful and not a little bewildered.

A couple of hours earlier they had turned up for training at Albion, only
to be told not to get changed but to speak instead to manager Ron Saunders.
He had a proposition. It was a proposition they might easily have rejected out

1

Day One ... Steve Bull and Andy Thompson; the way they were.

of hand because one respected member of the Molineux playing staff told me some time later it had become standard practice in the higher divisions in the mid-1980s for players to rib struggling team-mates in training with the line: "Buck up or Wolves will be in for you." Such were the depths now being trawled by a club who had inspired and thrilled the world three decades earlier.

Well, crisis or not, Wolves were in for the young duo, who were sufficiently dissatisfied with their first-team opportunities at The Hawthorns as to jump at the chance to speak to Turner. Each was startled, however, to be told they were not travelling along the A41 alone.

"I was waiting in the office at Albion when Steve came in," Thompson revealed. "And I was very surprised they let him go because of the amount of goals he scored in the second team."

The duo made the short journey across the Black Country in Bull's modest car, an already firm friendship about to be cemented by their decision to say yes to Wolves in double-quick time. The striker went in first and Turner said later: "He agreed in five minutes to join us. It was the quickest deal I've ever done. Until Andy Thompson came in straight afterwards, that is, and said yes in about three minutes!"

2

Debut day just over 48 hours later was, in football terms, something of a disaster. At the end of a week in which Garry Pendrey and physio Paul Darby had been added to the Molineux backroom team, a Wolves side languishing in the middle of the table crashed 3-0 at home to Wrexham.

Two days after Wolves fans' first glimpse of a man I predicted "should prove a muscular ally in time to Andy Mutch," Bull was back on the sidelines with Thompson as the club entered a little unfinished business with the part-timers who gathered once or twice a week under the name of Chorley Football Club.

The duo were in the stands at neutral Bolton as Wolves sought to bring a winning end to an FA Cup first-round saga that had already heaped quite enough embarrassment on them. At both Burnden Park and Molineux, the result between one of European football's most famous clubs and an outfit from the rank and file of the Multipart League had been the same: 1-1. Now, it was D-Night.

Bull and Thompson had been signed too late to play in the tie and were among a 5,421 crowd who watched in disbelief as Wolves were systematically taken apart. The 3-0 scoreline was no misrepresentation of the game, either; it was an accurate summary of another match that prompted calls for the dismissal of Turner.

But the manager hit back at the terrace snipers who were clinging pointlessly to the coat-tails of the brief Brian Little era, and blamed four or five years of bad management for the club's predicament. That, in turn, brought an angry retort from some of Wolves' former directors, leaving a bewildered Bull to admit later: "I wondered what I had stepped into."

Things got worse before they had any chance of improving as Wolves lost their way in the Lincoln fog and slumped to a third successive 3-0 defeat. All Bull had to show for his return to the side on the day Barry Powell launched his second stint with the club was his first booking - for ungentlemanly conduct.

Because they had gone out of the FA Cup, as well as the Littlewoods Cup, at the first hurdle, Wolves were left with a fortnight to stew on their slide down the Fourth Division. But the gap between League fixtures was bridged by a Tuesday night Freight Rover Trophy trip to South Wales that severely tested the loyalty of their fans.

The attendance for the preliminary round tie at Cardiff was a miserable 1,201 but, for the gold and black faithful in attendance, it was to become an historic night. It was the evening on which Bull scored the first of his avalanche of Wolves goals - an effort later described in print as "an unlikely winner."

3

His 75th minute shot, after he had accidentally poked an opponent in the eye, came in a much-maligned competition and had little apparent significance at the time. But the ever-professional Turner detected a possible launch-pad to greater things. "It was a good win and, hopefully, a starting point for a revival," he said. And, of the match-winner, which followed a shot blazed over from seven yards by the same player, he added: "Steve's goal will help him a great deal." Stephen George Bull was on his way.

It was to another outpost that Wolves travelled for their next game and that, too, brought a collector's item of a goal. Again, though, there weren't many collectors as a gate of 1,689 witnessed the side's first visit to Hartlepool for 62 years. But the long trip up the A1 to a ground overlooking the North Sea docks was made worthwhile by the sight of Bull scoring his first League goal for Wolves and bringing about a second 1-0 win in a row.

GOAL-COUNT

1 - *There seemed to be nothing on for Wolves as Bull challenged Cardiff skipper Terry Boyle in the air but the defender sank to his knees holding his face and the ball fell invitingly for the former Albion striker. Bull gladly accepted the chance, slamming the ball past surprised Cardiff keeper Graham Moseley.*

Dec 2, 1986: Cardiff 0 Wolves 1, Freight Rover Trophy preliminary round.

WOLVES: Barratt, Stoutt, Barnes, Clarke, Powell, Zelem, Purdie, Thompson, Bull, Mutch, Dougherty. Subs: Oldroyd, Holmes. Goal: Bull (75). Att: 1,201.

GOAL-COUNT

2 - *Purdie pounced and pushed the ball forward for Bull to charge through a huge gap in the home defence and go round goalkeeper Eddie Blackburn before scoring into an empty net from the edge of the box.*

Dec 13, 1986: Hartlepool 0 Wolves 1

WOLVES: Barratt, Stoutt, Barnes, Powell, Zelem (Holmes 22), Clarke, Purdie, Thompson, Bull, Mutch, Dougherty. Goal: Bull (25). Att: 1,689.

Steve Bull, WBA.

4

Hard on the heels of the player's first Wolves goal and first League goal for Wolves came his first Molineux goal. Or rather goals. Bournemouth were the visitors on a freezing Freight Rover Trophy night nine days before Christmas and braces from both Bull and the soon-to-depart Paul Dougherty set up an exciting 4-3 win that warmed another meagre crowd.

It would be an exaggeration to say Bull was making the football world sit up and take notice. But a few Fourth Division watchers were starting to look a little more closely as he obliged again in the following Saturday's home game against Southend, albeit with an effort that came too late to prevent another Molineux defeat.

If the football public at large had any doubts about who this fresh upstart was, the player himself had crystal-clear targets and showed a bold front as he challenged himself on Christmas Eve to chalk up 25 for his club before the end of the season. "It's a tall order but I should already have had more than five," he said. "I've missed more than I've scored at Wolves but nobody remembers the misses as long as you take a few of your chances. I've had a couple of bets to say I'll score 25 for Wolves this season - and I'm determined to do it." Confidence was not in short supply.

Bull's first Christmas with his new club proved a best-forgotten one, although, after a Boxing Day lunchtime defeat at Hereford, both he and Thompson scored in the first 16 minutes at home to Exeter the following day before a commanding lead was frittered away. Wolves were still languishing below half-way in the table and Peterborough's first-ever League visit to Molineux rang in an equally depressing start to 1987, particularly for debutant

---

GOAL-COUNT

3 - *Bull slipped the unhappy Whitlock and gave Peyton no chance from close range.*

4 - *Purdie set up the chance with a cross to Dougherty, Mutch miskicked when the ball was turned back into the middle and sharp-shooter Bull made sure.*

Dec 16, 1986: Wolves 4 Bournemouth 3, Freight Rover Trophy preliminary round.

WOLVES: Barratt, Oldroyd, Barnes, Powell, Stoutt, Clarke, Purdie, Thompson, Bull, Mutch, Dougherty. Subs: Brindley, Holmes.
Goals: Dougherty (26, 81), Bull (38, 55).
Att: 1,923.

GOAL-COUNT

5 - *Bull was finally rewarded for his efforts when he turned in a centre from Dougherty but the goal came too late to save Wolves.*

Dec 20, 1986: Wolves 1 Southend 2

WOLVES: Barratt, Oldroyd, Barnes, Powell, Stoutt, Clarke, Purdie, Thompson, Bull, Mutch, Dougherty. Sub: Holmes.
Goal: Bull (86).
Att: 4,129.

5

Mark Kendall. The jovial on-loan keeper was beaten three times without reply.

Bull, having hit the bar while firing blanks in the subsequent trips to Wrexham and Cambridge, rediscovered the way to goal in a late-January return trip to Cardiff, this time in the League. It was a victory that meant Wolves had won more away games than virtually every other side in the country - and lost more at home than the vast majority.

The raw recruit's strike at Ninian Park represented only partial success because he muscled past his markers on several other occasions, only to squander clear chances. It was probably the first indication that, while his finishing sometimes left much to be desired, he had few equals as a chaser and a creator of his own opportunities.

"My head never goes down," Bull said. "All I want to do if I miss

> ## GOAL-COUNT
> **6** - *Bull seized possession and ran on to get past Taylor before cutting in from the left to hit a fierce shot low past Shaw.*
>
> *Dec 27, 1986: Wolves 2 Exeter 2*
>
> *WOLVES: Barratt, Stoutt, Barnes, Powell, Brindley, Clarke, Purdie, Thompson, Bull, Mutch (N Edwards 77), Holmes.*
> *Goals: Bull (8), Thompson (16).*
> *Att: 4,626.*

> ## GOAL-COUNT
> **7** - *Two minutes later, the rampaging Bull charged through for the second time and Wolves had secured their second win at the ground in two months.*
>
> *Jan 24, 1987: Cardiff 0 Wolves 2*
>
> *WOLVES: Kendall, Stoutt, Barnes, Streete, Clarke, Robertson, N Edwards, Caswell, Bull, Mutch, Thompson. Sub: Forman.*
> *Goals: Thompson (40, pen), Bull (42).*
> *Att: 3,331.*

a chance is go looking for another one. I know I should have scored a lot more already for Wolves and certainly should have had more at Cardiff. But the manager here just keeps telling me not to worry about how many I miss - only about how many I score."

Turner, understandably becoming excited at the form of his costliest signing so far, was in no doubts. "Steve's young and, if he could acquire a bit more composure in front of goal, who knows how many he would score?" he said. "He has got the heart of a lion and he chases everything. He is doing what he was bought for by getting into scoring positions and, because he is inexperienced, it's fair to assume he is only going to get better. Sometimes, you wish he would pass rather than shoot but it's vital he doesn't lose that thirst for goals. Hitting the net is the only thing on his mind. And that's no bad thing for a striker."

Wolves signed off Bull's second full month at the club in a manner that had become depressingly familiar; with a defeat. They had unluckily gone out of the Freight Rover Trophy at home to Hereford in midweek, then all the striker's best efforts were in vain on the Saturday afternoon that a visiting Crewe player with the equally distinctive name of Peter Bodak helped himself to a match-winning hat-trick.

Molineux was still in a state of some despair and Bull's own spirits were not helped by the break-up of his first marriage after only a few months. There was no reason to believe the fortunes of player or club were about to change when a Stockport side standing 91st in the Football League led going into the closing stages of their visit to the decaying old stadium at the start of February.

Courtesy of a mixture of dreadful finishing and dreadful luck, Wolves found themselves staring at the prospect of their 11th home defeat of the season as they trailed to a second-half goal by the veteran Ernie Moss. Andy Mutch, the chirpy former refrigerator engineer who had not scored in 17 outings since Bull's arrival, summed up their efforts by hitting the post and missing from six yards. But, in the eyes of long-suffering supporters - and the gate was a typically pitiful 3,238 - this was to prove the day the club's fortunes finally began to turn.

> ## *GOAL-COUNT*
>
> *8 - Bull again missed two golden opportunities before lobbing in his eighth Wolves goal.*
>
> *Feb 7, 1987: Wolves 3 Stockport 1*
>
> *WOLVES: Kendall, Stoutt, Clarke, Thompson, Brindley, Robertson, Purdie, N Edwards, Bull, Mutch, Holmes. Sub: Forman.*
> *Goals: Thompson (79, pen), Holmes (87), Bull (88).*
> *Att: 3,238.*

It was still 1-0 with 11 minutes to go, then a foul on Jon Purdie enabled Thompson to drive home the equaliser with his third successful penalty in consecutive games. Grateful as they were for crumbs of comfort, the faithful few were content, it seemed, with half a loaf. But their drift towards the exits was dramatically reversed by two more goals in the final three minutes, first by Micky Holmes, then by Bull some 60 seconds later.

For a club in danger of being terminally gripped by failure, it was an astonishing comeback, and an appraisal of the post-match mood is perhaps enlightening bearing in mind the Molineux rebirth the game heralded. "I thought it was a case of here we go again when Stockport scored," said Turner at his Press conference. "The performance didn't please me very much but we were the better team, even if it took a long while to prove it."

After those honest words, I recall a determined Turner striding down one of Molineux's crumbling corridors afterwards with the prediction that a win at Burnley in the next game would mark a real turning of the corner. At first diagnosis, it appeared to be a major attack of delusion. But the manager - growing in popularity after a miserable start at the club - was to be proved correct.

The February 14 trip to Turf Moor was a Valentine's Day massacre, a 5-2 triumph giving Wolves the biggest win on their travels and all kinds of other records. It was their biggest victory for over two years, their biggest away win for more than five years and the first time they had hit five in an away match since the 5-1 romp at Bristol Rovers the small matter of 433 League games ago on December 27, 1976. As if that lot of milestones wasn't enough for the statisticians, the three points also gave Wolves the most away League wins (seven) they had managed in a season since their League Cup winning campaign of 1979-80.

Mutch took advantage of the rampage, which came after Wolves had trailed 2-1 at half-time, to return to the score-sheet for the first time in three months, but there was a down-side to the occasion as well. Young striker Neil Edwards broke a leg and ruptured ankle ligaments in what Turner described as a bad tackle by an opponent, and was destined not to fully recover. Amid the joy of three points, a promising career effectively died that day.

Bully on the prowl ... at home to Torquay in April, 1987.

8

When Aldershot were sent packing from Molineux on the end of a 3-0 beating three days later, Wolves were starting to look the part as a promotion force. After three and a half years of intense struggle, it was all very unusual, even in the context of their recent past, for the latest two high-scoring victories had come without Bull hitting the target.

He turned creator and made two of the three against Aldershot before drawing another blank when Fourth Division leaders Northampton escaped with a 1-1 draw in front of a 9,991 crowd. But, if his shooting boots were elsewhere when they might have been burying the Cobblers, Bull's performance bore certain encouraging pointers to the future, the Express & Star match report predicting: "A little more steadiness in his finishing and he could go goal-crazy."

The paper could claim another good observation when saying of the following Saturday's 2-2 draw on the Preston plastic: "If Steve Bull had a pound for every scoring opportunity that falls his way, he would soon be a millionaire. But, if he continues to squander them as he did at Deepdale, he will have to get used to comparative poverty."

The striker had actually been pushed into the goal-scoring shadows, first by his big pal Thompson and then by the popular journeyman midfielder, Micky Holmes. Thompson's goal at Burnley had made him the first Wolves player to score in four successive games since Derek Dougan in 1973 and, when that run ended, Holmes took over.

The quietly-spoken Yorkshireman, a survivor of the Bradford fire tragedy in 1985 before he moved to Wolves on a free transfer, had recently been on the sidelines for two months and had not scored in 26 appearances prior to his effort as sub against Crewe at the end of January. But he followed up with strikes against Stockport, Burnley, Aldershot, Northampton, Preston and Colchester in consecutive games to beg the question: Was club history being made?

The answer was yes, or, at least, partly so. Since the last war, only Jimmy Murray (in 1958-59) had matched Holmes' current feat of scoring in seven successive Wolves games, although the town's former mayor, Tom Phillipson, had

GOAL-COUNT

9 - *Four minutes from time, Bull ran on to a long through pass from Streete, swept the ball to Mutch and was in position at the far post to take the return and put the finishing touch.*

Mar 3, 1987: Wolves 2 Colchester 0

WOLVES: Kendall, Stoutt, Thompson, Streete, Brindley, Robertson, Purdie (Kelly 73), Forman, Bull, Mutch, Holmes. Goals: Holmes (42), Bull (86). Att: 5,715.

9

overshadowed both by rattling in goals in ten matches in a row in 1925-26. It was something of a dreamland for Holmes, who was flourishing in a big way after previously being one of the hapless figures in the club's decline.

"For a long time, we felt we couldn't win," he told me later. "Then, all of a sudden, we felt we couldn't lose. We always knew that, when we did turn the corner, we would take some stopping because of the club's potential. Sure enough, that's what happened and those few weeks were golden for me and very important in the recent history of Wolverhampton Wanderers."

As Holmes's goals started to dry up - he scored only once more in 1986-87 - so Bull set his sights again. On the night Turner's seventh Wolves signing, Robert Kelly, made his debut following a £20,000 move from Leicester, Bull broke a four-game drought with the killer second goal at home to Colchester. It was Wolves' 51st goal of a season that was now full of promise and helped the side to a sixth successive game without defeat - their best such run for nearly four barren years.

Bull then moved into double figures for the club with a goal in Wolves' first defeat at the hands of Orient since the war - the first time Turner's side had been beaten away since the turn of the year. But it proved only a temporary setback. Wolves were still hot on the heels of the top six and the signing of another player from neighbouring Albion - this time winger Robbie Dennison for an initial £15,000 rising to £27,500 - helped set up a crushing 4-0 win at home to Swansea.

When the dosage was repeated in a bizarre 4-3 win at Halifax three nights later, the side had hit four in successive matches for the first time since 1982. Surprisingly, Bull was on the mark in neither game, although he hit the post at The Shay, where Thompson missed a penalty for the first time in Wolves colours before scoring from the rebound.

GOAL-COUNT

10 - *Bull moved on to a loose ball in the Orient penalty area and then beat keeper Wells with a low shot from close range.*

Mar 7, 1987: Orient 3 Wolves 1

WOLVES: Kendall, Stoutt, Barnes, Streete, Clarke, Robertson, Kelly, Thompson, Bull, Mutch, Holmes. Sub: Forman.
Goal: Bull (57).
Att: 4,605.

Life at the Football League basement may have seemed strange for the supporters who had tasted Wembley success, FA Cup semi-final heartache and European participation in the previous seven years and who had stayed loyal through some trips to the darker corners of the football map. But these were happy days; the side were winning again and the feeling of renaissance was in the air wherever they played.

Dennison's first goal for the club brought maximum points in a Saturday lunchtime clash at Tranmere, where the two teams were reduced to ten men by the sendings-off of Nicky Clarke and ex-Molineux man John Morrissey. Wolves were sitting fifth as a result of completing their third double of the season.

Their position became healthier still after Bull's header on his 22nd birthday proved the only goal of the game at home to Scunthorpe and, although the emerging fans' favourite again showed his uncanny knack of hitting the woodwork at home to Torquay seven days later, Dennison's effort clinched a third consecutive 1-0 victory.

Despite the points buffer still enjoyed by Northampton and Preston in the top two slots, Wolves were snapping at the heels of Southend in the race for the automatic third promotion place as the season entered its final month.

Bull's scoring efforts weren't needed as Rochdale were put to the sword 3-0 on another trip to the backwaters but he struck early to delight a massive army of 4,000 fans who had followed Wolves to Peterborough on Easter Saturday. It wasn't the most fluent of performances but, against big promotion rivals, it was enough to secure an 11th away League win of the season and a seventh victory in a row - the first time the club had managed the feat since 1946-47.

> ## GOAL-COUNT
>
> *11* - *Dennison again proved his bargain value by picking up a through pass from Thompson and flighting the ball perfectly for his ex-Albion team-mate Bull to throw himself forward and head it powerfully past goalkeeper Ron Green.*
>
> *Mar 28, 1987: Wolves 1 Scunthorpe 0*
>
> *WOLVES: Kendall, Stoutt, Thompson, Streete, Clarke (Powell 10), Kelly, Purdie, Dennison, Bull, Mutch, Holmes.*
> *Goal: Bull (28).*
> *Att: 7,348.*

> ## GOAL-COUNT
>
> *12* - *From a long clearance by goalkeeper Kendall, Purdie headed on to send Bull storming in to score with a scorching volley from the edge of the area.*
>
> *Apr 18, 1987: Peterborough 0 Wolves 1*
>
> *WOLVES: Kendall, Stoutt, Thompson, Streete, Kelly, Robertson, Purdie, Dennison, Bull, Forman, Holmes. Sub: Powell.*
> *Goal: Bull (2).*
> *Att: 9,360.*

Kendall's £20,000 signing from Newport, after an initial loan period, had proved a master-stroke while Turner was also extracting excellent value from two of the players he had inherited, central defenders Alistair Robertson and Floyd Streete. All in the garden seemed relatively rosy.

Win No 8 and a sixth clean sheet in a row came at home to Hereford two days later in front of Wolves' biggest crowd for more than 18 months (10,730) but Jon Purdie's 37th minute decider was followed by a defeat in the crucial head-to-head at Southend the following weekend. Sadly, the club's Friday night exodus to the Essex coast became more memorable for the ensuing crowd trouble than the match as a single Martin Ling goal left Wolves facing a massive struggle for automatic promotion.

It was then, however, that Bull's goals, which had arrived at the relative trickle of six in 22 matches, suddenly came in a gush. Lincoln were on the end of two beauties in an emphatic defeat at Molineux and, despite the sending-off of inspirational skipper Robertson, Wolves - with Bull again among the scorers - followed up with a win at Exeter on May Day morning.

Wolves had already booked at least a place in the play-offs and that was confirmed as their fate when Southend won at Stockport at the start of the last weekend of the season. It seems unfair in hindsight that two promotion-chasing teams were allowed to play their last League matches on different days and the words of lifelong Wolves fan Mike Slater in his 1988 book "Molineux Memories" summed up the frustration as the club appoached the last-day visit of Hartlepool with little to play for.

"It was typical of Wolves' ill luck that they became the first club to occupy fourth place in Division Four and not automatically go up," he wrote. But Bull was in no mood to let the occasion pass quietly. He was back in form and showed it in the most

---

GOAL-COUNT

13 - *Nicholson's back-pass to Butler fell short and Bull nipped in, beat the keeper and calmly stroked his shot into the empty net.*

14 - *When Kelly played a through ball from midfield, the Lincoln defence was caught square and Bull raced through unchallenged before giving Butler no chance with a fierce drive.*

May 2, 1987: Wolves 3 Lincoln 0

WOLVES: Kendall, Stoutt, Thompson, Streete, Kelly, Robertson, Purdie, Dennison, Bull, Powell (Barnes 55), Holmes.
Goals: Bull (2, 12), Barnes (70).
Att: 7,285.

GOAL-COUNT

15 - *Bull fastened on to a knock-on by Thompson following Stoutt's free-kick and shot low past Exeter keeper John Shaw.*

May 4, 1987: Exeter 1 Wolves 3

WOLVES: Kendall, Stoutt, Barnes, Streete, Kelly, Robertson, Purdie (Mutch 77), Forman, Bull, Thompson, Holmes.
Goals: Bull (12), Forman (70), Kelly (89).
Att: 4,915.

GOAL-COUNT

16 - *Bull found himself sandwiched between two defenders chasing a through ball but his physique and gutsy determination won him the ball and a rasping shot into the roof of the net gave the keeper no chance.*

17 - *The stage belonged to Bull and his second goal, after 86 minutes, sparked the fans' first intrusion.*

18 - *Wolves won the ball, pushed it forward to Bull and the striker's calmly taken third signalled the end of proceedings as the players and officials dashed for safety a minute or so early.*

May 9, 1987: Wolves 4 Hartlepool 1

WOLVES: Kendall, Stoutt (Mutch 49), Barnes, Streete, Kelly, Clarke, Purdie, Forman, Bull, Thompson, Holmes.
Goals: Bull (30, 86, 88), Thompson (61, pen).
Att: 8,610.

appropriate way, crashing in his first hat-trick for the club and the first by any Wolves player since John Richards' treble had set up a 5-0 slaughter of visiting Newcastle in the relegation spring of 1976.

A king was born in the eyes of Wolves fans, some of whom marred the day with two invasions. Admittedly, they were of the friendly variety but the club held their collective breath as they went into the play-offs on a wave of hope and apprehension.

Crowd trouble was still an unfortunate part of Wolves' lives but, having finished nine points clear of their semi-final opponents Colchester and rounded off the season with seven home wins in a row, the club didn't seem to have a great deal to worry about on the pitch at least. And so it proved as goals by Kelly and Bull either side of the half-hour mark in the first leg at Layer Road subdued Colchester's biggest crowd for five years and turned the tie into something of a formality.

Thanks to a scrappy goalless draw in the second leg at Molineux in a match in which Bull was nursing an ankle injury, Wolves were two games from promotion as the end of May and the moment of truth approached. All their fans of the time will remember Aldershot as the club's final opponents in the days when such occasions were played over two legs and not on the lush acres of Wembley. But not too many will remember that the humble

GOAL-COUNT

19 - *Thompson's angled shot on the run beat Chamberlain, bounced back off the foot of the post and Bull was perfectly positioned to ram home the rebound.*

May 17, 1987: Colchester 0 Wolves 2, play-off semi-final first leg.

WOLVES: Kendall, Stoutt, Barnes, Streete, Kelly, Robertson, Purdie, Thompson, Bull, Mutch, Holmes. Sub: Forman.
Goals: Kelly (28), Bull (32).
Att: 4,829.

That will do nicely ... celebrating a goal against Lincoln
in the days when the North Bank was deserted.

Hampshire outfit had beaten Bolton in the other semi-final, the Lancashire
club having qualified for the play-offs by finishing three places off the bottom
of the Third Division.

Wolves had beaten Aldershot home and away in the season proper and
finished nine points and two places better than them, so hopes were high as
fans queued all night for tickets for the Friday evening first leg at the
Recreation Ground. But Robertson was ruled out of both legs by suspension
and it was all to go horribly wrong.

On a pitch heavily watered and then further saturated by a pre-match
downpour, the minnows put the skids under Wolves with a 25-yard cracker
from Ian McDonald after only four minutes - a lead they increased with a
Bobby Barnes penalty conceded by Streete a minute into the second half.

Undeterred, nearly 20,000 fans turned up at Molineux three days later on Whit Monday afternoon, but the anticipated lift-off in the club's revival never got off the ground. Wolves had pockets of pressure in a frantic game but there were precious few clear-cut chances as the dream of Third Division football gradually evaporated. It was left to Barnes to put Wolves out of their misery with the offside-looking killer goal seven minutes from the end and manager Turner gave Central TV a clip of film they were to play over and over again down the years as he left his crow's nest look-out high above the disused Waterloo Road Stand and angrily yanked open the door.

The march back to respectability was on hold and the frustration of that spring of 1987 took some shifting. But Wolves fans had found a new hero from amid the rubble of several seasons. And, although we weren't to know it at the time, the year's wait was to have a glorious pay-back.

BULLY'S 1986-87 STATISTICS:
Played 37 (30 League, 4 play-offs, 3 Freight Rover Trophy).
Goals 19 (15 League, 3 Freight Rover Trophy, 1 play-off).

On the ball ... an exhibition of close control from
the days when the Bull was little more than a calf.

15

Leading an unsuccessful charge ... Bull suffers a rare failure on the day Wolves' revival was surprisingly halted by Aldershot.

BULL'S EYE : PART ONE

1987-88

The epitaph of Wolves' failed promotion challenge had hardly been completed when their disappointment was compounded by an off-field departure. While Aston Villa had gone down - their nightmare 1986-87 season cost Graham Turner his job as early as September - neighbours Birmingham City took swift action after a close brush with the drop to the Third Division, sacking manager John Bond and targeting Garry Pendrey as his replacement.

Molineux chairman Dick Homden, a former boardroom colleague of Blues supremo Ken Wheldon at both Walsall and St Andrew's, vowed to hang on to Pendrey if at all possible but realised almost straightaway he was fighting a lost cause. Pendrey was a Blues man through and through and was quickly installed in his first managerial post.

Homden described the manner of Blues' approach as "terrible" but, for Turner's right-hand man, it was the dream move. "Three days ago, I was as choked as any of the players at missing promotion," Pendrey said. "Now, I'm manager of the club I've had in my blood since I was eight or nine. That's football."

Turner, left to recruit a new coach, was quickly approached by Kenny Hibbitt and the former Wolves favourite was more than a little peeved to be overlooked without so much as an interview. Ian Bowyer was another linked with the post but, for most of the summer, Turner put playing affairs first.

Russell Turley, Roger Eli, Derek Ryan and Barry Powell were given frees, the 33-year-old Powell describing himself as "disappointed and hurt" at missing out on one final season with the club he first joined as a 15-year-old. There was another virtual departure with midfielder Robert Kelly informed he had a disc problem that was to effectively end his playing career.

Turner also sold reserve keeper Scott Barrett to Stoke for £10,000 but got busy in the buying half of the transfer market as well by recruiting striker Jackie Gallagher from Peterborough for £8,000, midfielder Phil Robinson from Graham Taylor's Villa for £5,000, defender Gary Bellamy from Chesterfield for £17,000, utility man Keith Downing from Notts County on a free and young striker Mark Jones after his release from Albion.

17

There was a twist in the coach search for, after Derby keeper Eric Steele had said no to Wolves' approach, Barry Powell was offered an olive branch, and brushed aside his bruised feelings to take up a place in the backroom team with special responsibility for the youngsters.

Powell's third coming was announced on the day Bull and his colleagues compared tans and put a comb through their hair prior to the club's annual photo-call. And, in Bull's case, there wasn't much hair to comb. He had returned from the summer break with a crew-cut to replace the more formal look with which he had first entered Molineux.

> ## GOAL-COUNT
> **20** - *Robinson emerged from a midfield skirmish to play the ball through the middle and Bull produced an electrifying burst of speed to go past Bennyworth and fire hard and low just inside Blackwell's right-hand post.*
>
> *Aug 15, 1987: Scarborough 2 Wolves 2*
>
> *WOLVES: Kendall, Stoutt, Barnes, Streete, Robertson, Robinson, Thompson, Dennison (Downing 70), Bull, Mutch, Holmes. Sub: Gallagher.*
> *Goals: Bull (29), Stoutt (37).*
> *Att: 7,314.*

With memories of Bull's first few months fresh in the bookies' memory, Wolves were installed as 7-2 favourites for the Fourth Division title, although Turner retorted: "Our odds are ludicrous. There are so many unknown quantities that it's a very difficult division to get out of or to predict."

By an unfortunate quirk of the Football League computer, Wolves were despatched to Fourth Division newcomers Scarborough on kick-off day. And Bull quickly showed it was business as usual as he rifled in his club's first goal of the season in an entertaining 2-2 draw in the North Yorkshire sunshine. But the afternoon proved to be one of the blackest in Wolves' recent history.

Forty Wolves followers were arrested, a policeman was injured and one fan crashed to the terraces after falling through the stand roof on which he had been dancing. All told, a trail of damage reaching into thousands of pounds was inflicted on the seaside town and, inside the tiny ground, the violence became so bad that rival managers Graham Turner and Neil Warnock had to go on the pitch to appeal for calm at the start of the second half.

By huge irony, chairman Homden had missed the game to spend the day amid the tranquility of the Shrewsbury Flower Show, but he was to work overtime in the aftermath to repair the enormous damage to Wolves' reputation. Even as Wolves returned home to beat Notts County 3-0 in a Littlewoods Cup tie which left midfielder Micky Holmes with a broken arm, there was talk of all away games being made all-ticket and possibly an exclusion on fans travelling to away games.

And that quickly became reality with a six-match away ban on Wolves supporters and a £5,000 fine for the club. The Molineux board took their own decisive action by deciding no fans would travel to the two away matches - at Notts County and Hereford - before the exclusion took effect.

The early-season gloom deepened with a home defeat against Halifax in a game that fell between two more transfer deals - the departure of full-back David Barnes to Aldershot and the £11,000 signing of Cardiff midfielder Nigel Vaughan.

Although the cup taming of Third Division Notts County was comprehensively completed, it was not until the following Saturday's game against Hereford that Wolves recorded their first League victory. The trip to Edgar Street was marred by the sending-off of Downing, but

GOAL-COUNT

21 - *Downing skipped past two lunging tackles and found Mutch, who chested the ball into Bull's path and he at last provided the perfect finish after going close twice in the first half.*

22 - *Bull had the final word with a delicate lob that keeper Mick Leonard could only help into his net.*

Aug 25, 1987: Notts County 1 Wolves 2, Littlewoods Cup first round second leg.

WOLVES: Kendall, Stoutt, Clarke, Streete, Robertson, Robinson, Dennison (Gallagher 89), Thompson, Bull, Mutch, Downing. Sub: Bellamy. Goals: Bull (59, 80). Att: 2,730.

GOAL-COUNT

23 - *Bull chased a long through pass to the edge of the Hereford penalty area, outpacing Stevens and then letting fly on the run to beat Rose with a fierce shot into the roof of the net.*

Aug 29, 1987: Hereford 1 Wolves 2

WOLVES: Kendall, Stoutt, Clarke, Streete, Robertson, Robinson, Dennison, Thompson, Bull, Mutch, Downing. Subs: Bellamy, Gallagher. Goals: Bull (16), Mutch (22). Att: 2,628.

Keith Downing

19

Goal-scoring heroes ... Steve Bull and Micky Holmes, the midfielder whose regular appearances on the score-sheet in 1987 helped kick-start Wolves' revival.

his side made light of the matter thanks largely to a shot from their No 9 that flew in with all the power of a Hereford Bull. And they made it three wins in a row when Scunthorpe became the first Fourth Division side to lose at Molineux.

Against the Irons, Bull bagged two more to take his tally to six goals in six games and he followed up by hitting the target in the next two matches as well - away to Cardiff and at home to Crewe. The games marked a first goal in Wolves colours for Vaughan and Gallagher respectively but, with a points yield of only one out of six, the side were still stuck in mid-table.

GOAL-COUNT

24 - *Downing was lurking on the left to return the ball to the middle and Bull rose high above the defence to head firmly into the net.*

25 - *Bull latched on to a long pass from defence to give Green no chance from the edge of the penalty area.*

Aug 31, 1987: Wolves 4 Scunthorpe 1

WOLVES: Kendall, Stoutt, Clarke (Gallagher 74), Streete, Robertson, Robinson, Dennison, Thompson, Bull, Mutch, Downing. Sub: Bellamy.
Goals: Bull (9, 82), Mutch (21, 85).
Att: 6,672.

That was where they stayed despite a Mark Kendall penalty save and another Bull strike in a midweek draw at Peterborough but follow-up victories at Stockport and Manchester City - the latter a notable Littlewoods Cup first-leg triumph - brought the first words of real optimism from Turner. Andy Mutch had sprinted out of the starting blocks as well with six goals of his own and the manager said: "I have yet to see a more effective pair of strikers than Bull and Mutch. They complement one another and have begun the season extremely well."

While Wolves were modestly on the up, the month of September brought more upheaval at Albion. Ron Saunders was sacked as manager and there were no tears from Bull for the man who will forever have a place in Wolves fans' hearts for handing the player across the Black Country for only £64,000.

"I thought I was worthy of a better chance at Albion," Bull reflected. "But Ron Saunders saw me only as a stand-in while Stewart Evans was suspended. Now, I'm

GOAL-COUNT

26 - *Dennison fed Thompson on the right and he did well to beat his man and curl over a centre which had Cardiff's defence dithering and left Bull to stab home from close range.*

Sept 5, 1987: Cardiff 3 Wolves 2

WOLVES: Kendall, Stoutt, Clarke, Streete, Robertson, Robinson, Thompson, Dennison (Gallagher 81), Bull, Mutch, Downing (Vaughan 11).
Goals: Vaughan (35), Bull (54).
Att: 2,258.

having a good time at Wolves and Ron Saunders is out of a job."

Inevitably, Bull's name started to be linked with clubs higher up the Football League, and Turner, angered at one report suggesting Sunderland were interested, stated the Molineux case after the player had scored in front of scouts from Derby, Oxford, Villa, Manchester United and Liverpool in a surprise home defeat against Torquay.

"Steve is not for sale," he said. "We are ambitious and you can't be that if you are prepared to sell your best players." There was certainly no sign of itchy feet on Bull's part as he chipped in: "Wolves are a great club and I'm happy to stay here. We hit bad times but now we're on the way back and I hope I can play a big part in the revival."

Turner's dread was that the club - still under the ownership of a self-confessed non-football-fan in Birmingham builder Tony Gallagher - would take the matter out of his hands. But there was reassurance from the boardroom, where the increasingly supportive Homden said: "I won't sell unless it's for silly money - approaching seven figures. We have to hang on to our best players, not sell them. Steve is the sort of player we desperately need to keep and the same applies if we win promotion this season. We would want him to help us consolidate. He's unbelievably quick and his potential is outstanding. I would have to think hard if someone offered us a million but otherwise he's going nowhere."

Nowhere, that was, except towards the top of the goalscorers' list, and Bull reached a round dozen of goals for the campaign with the killer second that saw off visiting Rochdale and lifted Wolves four places up the table. But there was to be one more major detour before the side really set their sights on reaching the Fourth Division summit.

A poor performance back at the scene of their FA Cup humiliation against Chorley saw them beaten by Bolton, then Manchester City rode their luck to plunder an 88th minute goal to end Wolves' hopes of a sizeable Littlewoods Cup scalp. But, coinciding with Alistair Robertson's appointment as skipper after Floyd Streete had asked to stand down because of a contract wrangle with the club, the season took off spectacularly.

> ## GOAL-COUNT
>
> *30 - Bull finally broke through after the keeper had beaten down a point-blank shot from the lively Thompson.*
>
> *Sept 26, 1987: Wolves 1 Torquay 2*
>
> *WOLVES: Kendall, Bellamy, Thompson, Streete, Robertson, Robinson, Dennison, Vaughan, Bull, Mutch, Purdie (Gallagher 62). Sub: Downing.*
> *Goal: Bull (88).*
> *Att: 7,349.*

> ## GOAL-COUNT
>
> *31 - Vaughan's chip sent Downing away on the left for a cross which Mutch struck against the keeper before Bull hit the post with his first effort and the net with his second.*
>
> *Sept 29, 1987: Wolves 2 Rochdale 0*
>
> *WOLVES: Kendall, Bellamy, Thompson, Streete, Robertson, Robinson, Dennison (Downing 64), Vaughan, Bull, Mutch, Purdie. Sub: Gallagher.*
> *Goals: Mutch (2), Bull (77).*
> *Att: 5,553.*

On the day marked by the death of one of Wolves' all-time greats, Jimmy Mullen, the emerging present-day hero struck a characteristic winner at Carlisle and took his tally to 15 by scoring in 3-0 victories at home to both Tranmere and Cambridge in the space of four days. The two matches bore an uncanny resemblance to each other as they featured the same three scorers, at the same end (the North Bank) with all three goals coming on each occasion by the 23rd minute!

The difference was that Bull lasted barely an hour of the first game before suffering the first sending-off of his professional career. He was dismissed by Boreham Wood referee Roger Wiseman for a second bookable

23

offence - a challenge on Tranmere keeper Billy O'Rourke for which Turner later absolved him of any blame. "It was a 50-50 ball and Bull had to go for it," said the manager. "Put it this way, if he hadn't gone for it, he would have been in trouble with me."

As Bull contemplated the impending one-match ban that was to end his run of 56 successive appearances, two goals by Mutch earned Wolves a point at Darlington on the day the fans' away ban ended. A hundred or so supporters had regularly managed to breach the security clampdown anyway and there weren't too many more than that present as Bull signed off before his suspension with a tremendous late equaliser in a midweek Freight Rover Trophy draw at Swansea.

Bull, who had off-field problems as well with a one-year driving ban imposed by Aldridge magistrates for failing a breath test, was miffed that his suspension was for the home game with struggling Newport - a match that would have offered him every chance of further filling his scoring boots. And Wolves laboured without him, although the two goals they managed to put past Paul Bradshaw in the final 17 minutes - from ex-Newport man Vaughan

24

and Mutch - took them top of the table for the first time on October 31.

Bull's tally of 16 at this stage had him top of the country's goal charts by one from an up-and-coming Crewe starlet by the name of David Platt, whose total had included two efforts at Molineux back in early September. And there was a further revealing insight into the riches Albion had missed out on as new Wolves skipper Robertson recalled Bull's Hawthorns fortunes.

"Ron Saunders didn't fancy him as a player," Robertson said. "Steve is the first to admit his control is not the best in the world but, if someone has his ability to score goals, then the touch can come later. Admittedly, it took him some time to settle at Albion. He had come from non-League and players often find it difficult to adjust to training every day rather than a couple of nights a week. But, once he started to find his feet, he started to progress.

"He was creating countless chances in the reserves but was not taking them. However, since he joined Wolves, his finishing has become far more clinical and Albion's loss is certainly our gain. Most strikers would be happy with 25 goals a season but I don't think Steve would be happy even if he reached 35."

Bull's next game was back at the scene of his previous one - at Swansea's Vetch Field. And again he didn't disappoint with one of the goals in a 2-1 midweek win. Although he didn't make the score-sheet in the 3-0 victory that followed at home to promotion rivals Burnley, another red-letter day was just around the corner for him.

Wolves' FA Cup first-round pairing at home to Cheltenham had

GOAL-COUNT

35 - *Bull turned past one defender, nutmegged another and, from an angle where everybody was expecting a cross, unleashed a fierce right-foot shot which screamed between keeper Mike Hughes and his near post.*

Oct 27, 1987: Swansea 1 Wolves 1, Freight Rover Trophy preliminary round.

WOLVES: Kendall, Stoutt, Thompson, Streete, Robertson, Holmes, Dennison, Vaughan, Bull, Mutch, Downing (Gallagher 71). Sub: Clarke.
Goal: Bull (83).
Att: 2,886.

GOAL-COUNT

36 - *The bustling Bull held off a challenge from Alan Knill before beating Mike Hughes with a sweetly-struck shot just inside the keeper's right-hand post.*

Nov 3, 1987: Swansea 1 Wolves 2

WOLVES: Kendall, Stoutt, Thompson, Streete, Robertson, Gallagher, Dennison, Vaughan, Bull, Mutch, Downing. Subs: Powell, Clarke.
Goals: Bull (28), Gallagher (68).
Att: 5,293.

25

Window un-dressing ... a partly-attired Steve Bull witnesses
post-victory high jinks from midfielder Phil Robinson.

26

GOAL-COUNT

37 - Bull's first was the best of this and many other games - a powerful run through two inadequate challenges and a fierce 18-yarder into the top far corner of the net.

38 - Bull's second was a narrow-angled shot after Churchward had stopped but failed to hold a powerful header from Mutch.

39 - And Bull made it five, thundering home left-footed after another superb move involving Vaughan.

Nov 14, 1987: Wolves 5 Cheltenham 1, FA Cup first round.

WOLVES: Kendall, Stoutt, Thompson, Streete, Robertson (Clarke 81), Gallagher, Dennison, Vaughan, Bull, Mutch, Downing (Powell 81).
Goals: Vaughan (23), Bull (27, 60, 84), Downing (46).
Att: 10,541.

revived nightmare memories of the Chorley horrors 12 months ago, more so when the GM Conference club went ahead through Brett Angell after 20 minutes. But Bull bombed in his second hat-trick for the club in front of their second successive 10,000 crowd, and Wolves' seventh win in nine games had hoisted their star asset to the 20-goal mark in only 23 appearances.

Astonishingly, with the campaign barely a third spent, Bull had already become Wolves' highest scorer in a season for 12 years, passing the 19-goal mark established by Mel Eves in 1982-83 in the club's latest promotion year. And he was in sight of becoming their heaviest-ever scorer in a season as the best hauls of Derek Dougan (24), Ray Crawford (26), Ted Farmer (28), Jimmy Murray (33), John Richards (33), Tom Phillipson (37) and Dennis Westcott (43) lay ahead.

"The attributes Steve has are the right ones," said Richards, who had produced his best haul in the 1972-73 campaign. "He has courage, speed and strength - qualities you can't teach anyone. His weaknesses, like control and a bit of composure, can be taught. He is going to be quite a player."

And Farmer, the late 1950s and early 1960s counterpart whose career had been cruelly cut short by injury, offered: "The Fourth Division has been a good apprenticeship for Steve but I would like to see him in a higher division. His potential is enormous and, if he can calm down slightly and learn to come away from his markers rather than try to go through them, he could be worth a million."

27

Unfortunately, on the same day the tributes from the stars of yesteryear were appearing in the Sporting Star, Bull took another early bath, this time at Colchester for what Impington referee Michael Bailey spotted as a headbutt. Colchester's John Reeves also walked - for kicking the grounded Bull - and Turner said after his ten-man side had won thanks to Andy Thompson's 70th minute penalty: "Naturally, I'm concerned Bully has been sent off for a second time. But he is a player with a lot of aggression and that's what takes him into such situations."

A midweek Freight Rover Trophy win at home to Bristol City gave Bull the chance to remain on the boil with two more goals and Vaughan, as Micky Holmes had done a few months earlier, was proving a revelation as a goalscorer from midfield. When he pipped Bull to apply the finishing touch for Wolves' first in a competition the fans were slow to accept, it meant he had scored in six successive home matches.

But the run dried up four days later when lowly Wrexham stormed the Molineux fortress with a 2-0 victory that ended Wolves' 11-match unbeaten sequence and sent Bull into his two-match suspension on a frustrated note. But, in the wake of Barry Powell's decision to say no to the manager's job at Willenhall, the striker provided a quite extraordinary send-off by blasting five goals in an 8-1 Midland Intermediate League romp against Peterborough at a deserted Molineux - his hat-trick coming up in a mere half an hour.

> ## GOAL-COUNT
>
> **40** - *Mutch freed Dennison on the right and, when the cross came over, it was almost inevitable Bull would be on the end of it to guide a low angled shot past Prudhoe.*
>
> **41** - *Bull scored from close range 14 minutes from time with Mutch again the provider.*
>
> *Nov 24, 1987: Wolves 3 Bristol City 1, Freight Rover Trophy preliminary round.*
>
> *WOLVES: Kendall, Stoutt, Thompson, Streete, Clarke, Robinson, Dennison, Vaughan, Bull (Holmes 77), Mutch, Gallagher. Sub: Bellamy.*
> *Goals: Vaughan (19), Bull (40, 76).*
> *Att: 5,174.*

Wolves fared well in the absence of their guiding light, coming from behind to collect another Third Division scalp by winning impressively at Wigan in the FA Cup and then having the better of a goalless draw at Hartlepool that cost them their place at the top.

Bull showed he was ready for the pre-Christmas visit of new leaders Leyton Orient by warming up with two goals in the reserves at Chesterfield. And he didn't disappoint in the top-of-the-table clash against the East Londoners, scoring the only goals of the game in the second half to put his side back on top.

The brace kept Bull on target to become Wolves' highest scorer in a season and he said on Christmas Eve: "I'm aware of the record and would love to smash it. But I set myself a target of 35 at the start of the season and would consider anything above that as a bonus. The way the team are playing, who knows? I am converting more chances than last season and we're making good progress in the FA Cup and the Freight Rover Trophy."

Off the field, Molineux life was going along swimmingly compared with the hand-to-mouth existence of the previous few years. The club's first gate of 1987 had been a paltry 4,399 for the visit of Peterborough; the last was a staggering 15,588 - easily Wolves' biggest of the season - for the December 28 home game against Exeter. Equally as surprising as the turn-out was that Bull's name was absent from the score-sheet in a 3-0 victory.

Almost as many showed up as two more Bull specials saw off Hereford on New Year's Day and, when Mutch twice chipped in to settle the following lunchtime's clash at Crewe, Wolves were a point ahead of second-placed Colchester but, more significantly, four ahead, with a game in hand, on the Orient side then holding the third automatic promotion spot.

FA Cup dismissal away to Second Division high-fliers Bradford City was followed by a bizarre fog-ridden Molineux draw with Stockport before Bull plundered his second hat-trick of the season on the night Brentford were put to the sword in the Freight Rover Trophy.

The competition had been renamed the Sherpa Van Trophy by the time Wolves made their next appearance in it - a crushing of Peterborough by the

---

GOAL-COUNT

42, 43 - *Bull pounced with a fierce low drive to edge Wolves into the lead before wrapping it up with a deft header.*

Dec 19, 1987: Wolves 2 Leyton Orient 0

WOLVES: Kendall, Stoutt, Thompson, Streete, Robertson, Robinson, Dennison, Vaughan, Bull, Mutch, Downing. Subs: Gallagher, Holmes.
Goals: Bull (58, 80).
Att: 12,051.

GOAL-COUNT

44, 45 - *The phenomenal Bull broke the ice with a magnificent turn and shot on the run, then displayed his increasing composure by picking his spot and rifling past Kevin Rose for No 2.*

Jan 1, 1988: Wolves 2 Hereford 0

WOLVES: Kendall, Stoutt, Thompson, Streete, Robertson, Robinson, Dennison, Vaughan, Bull, Mutch, Downing. Subs: Gallagher, Holmes.
Goals: Bull (39, 84).
Att: 14,577.

GOAL-COUNT

46 - *Bull took his ninth minute opener well, shrugging off a challenge from defender Keith Millen to drive a shot home inside the near post.*

47 - *He fired home his second and his side's third after his initial close-range header from Dennison's centre had been parried by visiting keeper Gary Phillips.*

48 - *Then, Bull produced a fitting finale, scoring the type of stunning 20-yarder that more than warrants his Brazilian-style salute so reminiscent of a victorious jet fighter.*

Jan 19, 1988: Wolves 4 Brentford 0, Sherpa Van Trophy first round (previously the Freight Rover Trophy).

WOLVES: Kendall, Bellamy, Thompson, Streete, Robertson, Robinson, Dennison, Vaughan, Bull, Mutch, Downing (Holmes 74). Sub: Gallagher.
Goals: Bull (9, 77, 85), Dennison (46).
Att: 6,298.

Above: Crash ... another shot on the way.

Bang on target ... heading for the Bull's eye and a first half century of goals for Wolves.

30

same scoreline with Bull on target twice more. And the brace made the striker, with 14, the heaviest cup goalscorer in a season in Wolves' history. But, in the meantime, a home crash against promotion rivals Cardiff - described by manager Turner as an embarrassment - was every bit as alarming as the previous Saturday's win at Scunthorpe had been encouraging.

Bull left the field early against Peterborough because he was nursing a calf strain and Exeter's defenders were relieved when he failed to go the full distance on a mudbath pitch at St James's Park four days later. The trouble was for them that he had by then helped himself to the first away hat-trick of his Wolves career, a relatively straightforward affair that swept him to the 35-goal mark and left me saying in my Express & Star match report: "I, for one, certainly wouldn't back against him reaching 50 this season."

Turner subsequently revealed Bull had signed a new three-year contract several weeks earlier and the manager again underlined his determination to hang on to his star player. "I would like to think he will see out his contract with us," Turner said. "When we play a home game, a lot of clubs ring up asking for tickets, so we know the sort of interest being created. And several First Division clubs are among them."

Bull used the happy occasion to reiterate his loyalty to Wolves, saying: "I love the club and shall be happy to stay, even more so if we get promoted."

GOAL-COUNT

52 - *Downing did the spadework with a superb challenge in midfield, Mutch took a couple of strides forward, looked up and delivered a perfect far-post cross which Bull headed firmly past Gwinnett.*

53 - *Bellamy fed the ball in from the right, Mutch helped it on skilfully and Bull hooked a powerful low shot inside Gwinnett's left-hand post as he fell.*

54 - *Dennison played the ball into the area, Mutch produced a brilliant turn and a miscued cross and Bull bundled home from close range with Gwinnett stranded off his line.*

Feb 13, 1988: Exeter 2 Wolves 4

WOLVES: Kendall, Bellamy, Thompson, Streete, Robertson, Robinson, Dennison, Vaughan, Bull (Purdie 72), Mutch, Downing. Sub: Brindley.
Goals: Bull (7, 32, 61), Purdie (78).
Att: 3,483.

A shock midweek defeat in a rearranged game at Halifax was followed by two uneventful night-time goalless draws against Scarborough and Torquay, although the first of them was doubly significant. It carried them - on the strength of their mid-winter results - to Wembley for a special mid-April tournament to celebrate the Football League's centenary and it also marked a surprise appearance by Robbie Dennison, the winger having arrived back at Heathrow only that afternoon after being delayed by Greek air traffic control following his full Northern Ireland debut.

Turner, having set his side a 92-point target after he was named Fourth Division manager of the month for January, admitted they had hit a sticky patch, a development perhaps linked with the bug and bout of conjunctivitis through which Bull insisted on playing despite doctor's orders to the contrary. And it all came right again with two more goals in a Molineux mauling of Bolton after Turner had again spoken out, this time on the speculation surrounding his phenomenal marksman.

"Talk about Steve being sold is very annoying," he said. "But it's inevitable this sort of story will be banded around, simply because he has scored so many goals and we are top of the table. It would be betraying our supporters and destroying all that we are trying to build at this club if we sold him. We have had a few inquiries but no firm bids and I'm keeping him informed. All he should be doing at the moment is enjoying himself."

Chairman Homden put the matter into even sharper focus. "If we let him go and we failed to get promotion," he said, "everyone would point to his transfer as the cause and, if I was a paying fan, I would be saying exactly the same."

Bull's second goal in the 4-0 win over Bolton - a victory in which all the goals came in a scintillating first half - was the 150th of the Turner era. With

32

37 goals of his own in the bank since the start of the season, he was now the talking-point of the lower divisions, not that it made a jot of difference to his attitude or his lifestyle. He still enjoyed a game of pool and a pint of lager with the lads in Cannock on a Saturday night and Sunday lunchtime, and said: "They take the mickey if we lose and praise me up and buy me a couple of pints if we win."

But the former builder's yard labourer, who put his strength down to carrying bags of cement in his former career, couldn't conceal the satisfaction he felt at proving his former Hawthorns manager a little more wrong with every goal he rattled in. "He told me to go to Molineux and have a look round because I had no future at Albion," Bull recalled. "He said my first touch wasn't good enough but I couldn't understand how he could say that so I thought sod Ron Saunders!

"At the start of the season, a friend said he would pay me £1 for every goal I scored over 25 and £4 for every hat-trick, so I've made myself a few quid already."

Holmes' first goal of the season kept the bandwagon rolling with three midweek points at Rochdale and, although a miserable Friday night out in Tranmere emphatically ended a run of four successive clean sheets, Bull's Molineux header four evenings later took Wolves to within a round of Wembley in the Sherpa Van Trophy at the expense of a

---

GOAL-COUNT

55 - *Bull opened the scoring, angling home a fierce right-foot shot after Mutch had helped on a long clearance by on-loan full-back McDonald.*

56 - *Then, Bull made it two, blasting home a rebound after Mutch had had a goal-bound shot charged down by Mark Came.*

Feb 27, 1988: Wolves 4 Bolton 0

WOLVES: Kendall, Thompson, McDonald, Streete, Robertson, Robinson, Dennison, Vaughan (Downing 74), Bull, Mutch, Dennison. Sub: Gallagher.
Goals: Bull (6, 22), Dennison (34), Robinson (41).
Att: 12,430.

GOAL-COUNT

57 - *When Dennison supplied the cross from the right, Bull darted in to glance a header beyond Allen and just inside the far post.*

Mar 8, 1988: Wolves 1 Torquay 0, Sherpa Van Trophy, area semi-final.

WOLVES: Kendall, Stoutt, McDonald, Streete, Bellamy, Robinson, Dennison, Vaughan, Bull, Mutch, Holmes. Subs: Gallagher, Downing.
Goal: Bull (18).
Att: 11,039.

33

Happy Molineux times ... Andy Thompson, Ally Robertson, Phil Robinson, Steve Bull,

Torquay side containing a promising Black Country youngster called Lee Sharpe.

The tie marked the injury-enforced end of Thompson's sequence of 72 unbroken appearances but Wolves were nine points clear at the top of the table after unconvincingly overcoming visiting Carlisle in the full-back's continued absence.

The late cancellation of the following Friday's game at Newport gave Cardiff the chance to cut the gap and spelled disappointment not only for 200 Wolves fans who made a wasted journey, but also for new capture Mark Venus. Signed on loan from Leicester in time for the trip to desolate Somerton Park, the left-back was then confirmed as a £40,000 permanent arrival before an unhappy debut at home to Peterborough under the Molineux floodlights. A second-half goal from Mick Gooding put the skids under Wolves and prompted another £40,000 excursion into the transfer market, this time for Northampton midfielder Phil Chard.

Both new boys figured, Chard making it on to the score-sheet, as the nerves were eased by a 5-3 win at home to Darlington. But Bull was the hero yet again with a devastating hat-trick of right-foot shots that swept him past Dennis Westcott's post-war record of 39 goals in a season (achieved in 1946-47) and to within two of the former Stafford publican's all-time mark of 43.

Ironically, Turner had been sufficiently concerned with the striker's recent lethargy that he had persuaded his directors to finance a three-day recuperative visit to Torquay for his squad the following week. Maybe, in the light of the striker's re-emergence, the intake of sea air wasn't really needed but, just for good measure, Bull underlined his return to the rudest of health

GOAL-COUNT

58 - *Bull did the trick, cashing in on Morgan's hesitancy to reach Dennison's long through ball and hammering a low right-foot drive past the advancing Granger from near the edge of the area.*

59 - *Bull blasted home in characteristic style after Dennison's centre from the left had been headed down by Mutch.*

60 - *Wolves were again in full cry and Bull completed his hat-trick when he raced clear on to a long clearance and drilled another unstoppable shot past the advancing Granger.*

Mar 26, 1988: Wolves 5 Darlington 3

WOLVES: Kendall, Bellamy, Venus, Streete, Robertson, Robinson, Dennison, Chard, Bull, Mutch, Holmes. Subs: Vaughan, Gallagher.
Goals: Robinson (5), Bull (40, 67, 71), Chard (57).
Att: 9,349.

GOAL-COUNT

61 - *Bull settled the nerves of the Wolves followers by powering home a 15-yard volley when Burnley failed to clear a Bellamy free-kick.*

Apr 2, 1988: Burnley 0 Wolves 3

WOLVES: Kendall, Bellamy, Venus, Streete, Robertson, Robinson, Dennison (Thompson 81), Chard, Bull, Mutch, Holmes. Sub: Vaughan.
Goals: Holmes (10), Bull (61), Mutch (88).
Att: 10,341.

GOAL-COUNT

62 - *Mutch flicked on Chard's long throw and, while the Colchester defence hesitated for a split second, Bull was in like a flash to lash a low shot past keeper Craig Forrest.*

63 - *His record-breaker underlined his sheer strength. There seemed little on when Bull took a short pass from Vaughan but his persistence and endeavour whipped him past two defenders before a shot into the bottom corner left Forrest motionless.*

Apr 4, 1988: Wolves 2 Colchester 0

WOLVES: Kendall, Bellamy, Venus, Streete, Robertson, Robinson (Vaughan 45), Dennison, Chard, Bull, Mutch, Holmes. Sub: Thompson.
Goals: Bull (10, 75).
Att: 13,433.

in a very happy Easter for Wolves.

He bludgeoned home a volley in a big win at Burnley that was marked by another penalty save from Kendall, then breezed into Molineux two days later to rifle home the brace against Colchester that made him the club's highest-ever scorer in a season. The Westcott family, who had seen John Richards threaten the record a couple of times in the 1970s, made their own tribute when the late hero's son Peter presented the 1988 star with an inscribed tankard.

Bull was delighted to create a slice of history in front of a big holiday crowd that was slightly trimmed following the crack-of-dawn arrest of 66 suspected hooligans in Operation Growth. But he was in self-critical mood as he reflected: "I'm disappointed I didn't get at least a hat-trick."

A Sunday trip to Cambridge the following weekend brought the Bull family a first - Steve lining up against cousin Gary. Both had previously banged in the goals at different times for Black Country side Newey Goodman but were off target on an afternoon when Mutch scored Wolves' 100th goal of the season in Turner's 100th game as manager. The match at the tiny Abbey Stadium was an unwanted distraction two days before the biggest game of Wolves' season so far - the away first leg of the Sherpa Van Trophy Southern Area final against Third Division high-fliers Notts County. And Bull didn't disappoint the 4,000 travelling fans, duly coming up with his third Meadow Lane goal of the season.

A draw set Wolves nicely up for Wembley but they had another spot of business at the Twin Towers in the meantime with their appearance in the 16-club Mercantile tournament to celebrate the centenary of the Football League. Bull, like Kendall, Dennison and Holmes, had never been to the stadium and loved every minute despite the disappointment of a penalty shoot-out elimination in their first match against Everton.

"The game seemed to pass very quickly but it was a tremendous experience that has given us the taste for returning in the Sherpa Van Trophy," Bull said after witnessing a stunning Dennison goal. "It was great at the end to look up at the scoreboard and see Everton 1 Wolves 1 in lights."

The day was child's play, though, compared with the mass exodus set up when Wolves duly demolished John Barnwell's Notts County three nights later on the most memorable Molineux occasion for years. The club's biggest crowd of the season saw Bull drive in two more crackers and Wolverhampton partied long into the night as they savoured the prospect of a Wembley meeting with Burnley.

Plans for 30,000, 40,000 or even more tickets to be made available were in place by the time Wolves kicked off a trio of consecutive games against Welsh

---

GOAL-COUNT

64 - *Bull's 45th goal of the season owed much to a poor back-pass, Paul Smalley slicing badly into his path and the ball being despatched past Leonard a couple of touches and a scorching half-volley later.*

Apr 12, 1988: Notts County 1 Wolves 1, Sherpa Van Trophy area final first leg.

WOLVES: Kendall, Bellamy, Thompson, Streete, Robertson, Robinson, Dennison, Downing, Bull, Mutch, Holmes. Subs: Stoutt, Gallagher.
Goal: Bull (61).
Att: 10,941.

GOAL-COUNT

65 - *Holmes played a slide-rule pass through to Bull, who gave Leonard no chance with a right-foot shot into the bottom corner.*

66 - *Streete's long through ball was flicked on by the tireless Mutch, and Bull shrugged off the combined challenge of Hart and Withe before thumping another venomous shot past the bemused Leonard.*

Apr 19, 1988: Wolves 3 Notts County 0, Sherpa Van Trophy area final second leg.

WOLVES: Kendall, Bellamy, Thompson, Streete, Robertson, Robinson, Dennison, Downing, Bull, Mutch, Holmes. Subs: Gallagher, Vaughan.
Goals: Bull (8, 26), Downing (63).
Att: 18,413.

37

opposition with a routine disposal of visiting Swansea. The game gave Bull his 48th goal of the season and, at the other end of the field, keeper Kendall the 25th clean sheet that equalled Noel George's all-time club record.

More importantly, it meant promotion was a mere point away as Wolves and nearly 2,000 of their fans headed down the M5 for the rearranged Tuesday night game against a Newport outfit without a League point for a month and a half, and facing probable extinction. The game proved every bit as one-sided as expected, with two early goals from Bull - the second his 50th of a quite astonishing season - setting up an anti-climactic 11th away League win of the campaign.

GOAL-COUNT

67 - *Breaking from inside his own penalty area, Mutch ran out of defence before playing the perfect through ball for Bull to do the rest.*

Apr 23, 1988: Wolves 2 Swansea 0

WOLVES: Kendall, Bellamy, Thompson, Streete, Robertson, Robinson, Dennison (Purdie 81), Downing (Holmes 45), Bull, Mutch, Chard.
Goals: Robinson (38), Bull (50).
Att: 12,344.

Tuning up for the twin towers ... Steve Bull, Mark Kendall and Ally Robertson at rehearsal with composer David Tristram in the making of Wolves' Wembley record, "We're Back."

Former Wolves keeper Paul Bradshaw was the hapless figure on the end of Bull's latest heroics but the evening was more about celebrating the club's reawakening. "Our target has to be to go up again next season," Turner said straightaway. "Just being in the Third Division won't be enough. Supporters will be immediately looking for us to climb out. This is only the first step along the road to recovery."

Up in North Wales four days later, Turner had an unusual role to fulfill on the Wrexham pitch he used to play on. He had to urge Wolves

Farewell to the Fourth ... Clenched-fist celebrations from Kendall, Bull and Mutch after the promotion-securing win at Newport in April, 1988.

39

followers to make their way home after they had mistakenly and prematurely indulged in celebrating the winning of the title. Thinking their side were champions despite their 4-2 defeat at Racecourse Ground, the fans filed out only when informed that reports of nearest challengers Cardiff having lost to Hartlepool were incorrect.

The manager told them all to be at Molineux on May Day Monday for the real thing and nearly 18,000 of them took his advice to witness the two Bully goals that confirmed Wolves as the first club to win all four divisions of the Football League. Eighty minutes separated the striker's 51st and 52nd goals of the campaign and, before the division's highest crowd for six years saw skipper Ally Robertson stepping forward in the sunshine to receive the trophy, there was the drama of Kendall knocking himself out against his upright en route for his record-setting 26th clean sheet.

"Anybody who turned up expecting to see a good game will be disappointed," Turner said during the lap of honour. "But anybody who turned up to witness the celebration of the Wolves revival will have thoroughly enjoyed it. It has been the highlight of our season to be able to celebrate in front of our fans."

Victory had come in a repeat of the last home game of the previous season and, as the club waved farewell to the Fourth with a last-day victory at Orient, they headed the pile proudly by five points, their tally of 90 a club record by 11, albeit under the relatively new three-points-for-a-win format.

Bull received a special award at a Midland Soccer Writers dinner before returning to Albion to play, but not score, in a win over his former club in Robertson's testimonial game. Then, Turner was named Fourth Division Manager of the Year before taking his players away for a pre-Wembley week in Majorca that was marred by the tragic early return home of Floyd Streete. The popular defender flew back because of the serious illness that was to cost his baby daughter her life.

GOAL-COUNT

70 - *Bull's first came from a brilliant, angled overhead kick created and executed out of nothing.*

71 - *For an incredible 52nd time this season, Bull did what he likes doing best - leaving his markers in his wake, hitting the net and wheeling away to take the salutes of his admirers.*

May 2, 1988: Wolves 2 Hartlepool 0

WOLVES: Kendall, Bellamy, Thompson, Streete, Robertson, Robinson, Dennison, Chard, Bull, Mutch, Downing. Subs: Holmes, Purdie.
Goals: Bull (10, 90).
Att: 17,895.

40

At Molineux, the stampede for Sherpa Van Trophy final tickets reached historic proportions and, with Wolves' sales climbing to 45,000, it became clear their following would be one of the biggest in English football history. The lyrics of the club's Wembley record, We're Back, were highly appropriate and the stage was set for Bull to give the fans a fantastic send-off into summer.

His 52 goals left him two behind the highest figure ever managed in a Fourth Division season - the 54 by Peterborough's Terry Bly nearly 30 years earlier. But Bull played down the challenge by saying: "People keep telling me I need a Wembley hat-trick to break the record but those things don't worry me. I'll be happy with one if we win."

A massive 80,841 turned up - 10,000 more than had watched the previous weekend's England v Scotland Rous Cup match - but, for the first time in eight ties in the competition that season, Bull failed to score. He had to settle for an assist instead as his overhead kick from Dennison's corner teed up the first goal for Mutch, then Dennison himself secured a 2-0 victory with a spectacular free-kick early in the second half.

Former Wolves and England centre-half Bill Slater presented the trophy to Robertson who, lest the players forgot during their latest lap of honour, quickly handed it to Turner to ensure the manager took his share of the acclaim.

Bull, disappointed he didn't score, was nevertheless in high spirits the following day when, on the afternoon David Kelly hit the hat-trick that saw Walsall win the Third Division play-off final against Bristol City at Fellows Park, up to 50,000 fans saluted Wolves on their open-top bus tour of the town. It was a glorious end to a season illuminated by Bull's heroics - and there were more to come. A lot more.

BULLY'S 1987-88 WOLVES STATISTICS:
Played 58 (44 League, 4 League Cup, 8 Freight Rover/Sherpa Van Trophy, 2 FA Cup).
Goals 52 (34 League, 3 Littlewoods Cup, 12 Sherpa Van Trophy, 3 FA Cup).
CUMULATIVE WOLVES CAREER:
Played 95 (74 League, 4 League Cup, 11 Freight Rover/Sherpa Van Trophy, 2 FA cup, 4 play-off).
Goals 71 (49 League, 15 Freight Rover/Sherpa Van Trophy, 3 League Cup, 3 FA Cup, 1 play-off).

* For the sake of the cumulative statistics, the Littlewoods Cup, Rumbelows Cup and the Coca Cola Cup are referred to as the League Cup on this page and at the end of subsequent chapters.

41

Chapter 6 ... leading scorer and skipper get their hands on the title.

Beware! Bull with horns ... no goals but a Wembley
lap of honour with the Sherpa Van Trophy.

43

BULL'S EYE : PART TWO

1988-89

The Steve Bull-inspired 1987-88 season was described by Graham Turner as having provided him with his proudest moments in management. But the now popular boss had no thoughts of resting on his laurels as he planned for the Third Division.

While heads were still clearing from the Sherpa Van Trophy final celebrations at the end of May, he promptly handed free transfers to two of his Wembley side, Micky Holmes and 1986-87 Player of the Year Steve Stoutt. Jon Purdie and Matt Forman were also released, along with untried reserves Mark Freeman, Mark Smith and Mark Jones, while Jackie Gallagher and Nigel Vaughan were transfer-listed.

Happily, though, there was no stampede for Bull's services, despite several inquiries. He had already set himself a target of 25 goals for 1988-89 and was happy he would be trying to achieve the mark with Wolves. "No doubt some managers looked at my record last season and thought to themselves that it was only in the Fourth Division," he said. "But, to my mind, goals are goals whatever the level and I don't think I have anything to prove to anyone. I am confident I can keep it going in the Third Division."

With a tournament in the Isle of Man called off because of the hooligan risk, Wolves had to reshuffle their warm-up programme. But kick-off day couldn't come round quickly enough for Bull, who confessed to becoming homesick during a trip with girlfriend Julie to Corfu. The summer break was less than half-way through when the previous season's Golden Boot winner admitted: "I'm bored and raring to go again. After having a holiday and a couple of weeks to recover after Wembley, I've already started training on my own."

Wolves, having clinched a three-year £150,000 sponsorship with local paint and ink giants Manders, stayed out of the transfer market apart from picking up Tom Bennett on a free from Graham Taylor's Villa. But there was major disruption in the boardroom when Dick Homden was sacked as chairman following a personality clash with owner Tony Gallagher. Jack Harris was named chairman while he was in hospital with a minor chest complaint and the close friendship between he and Homden - football colleagues for 16 years - quickly came to a sad end, although Homden continued to support the club as a John Ireland Stand season ticket holder.

The upheaval did not prevent Turner speaking out in the Press on the eve of the season about having no contract. He demanded a meeting with Gallagher and solicitor Peter Glaister and finally got his way with a two-year deal after Wolves had made an early start to the campaign.

There was one common bond between the countdown to the season and the build-up to 1987-88. The bookies made Wolves title favourites! And Turner, having observed prices of 6-1 and 7-1, had a familiar quote of his own as he repeated: "The odds are ludicrous."

Lancashire Police insisted on an 11am kick-off to the opening game at Bury and it proved no time or place for Wolves to impress. In their first competitive game since Wembley, they crashed 3-1 and had their 2,500 followers chanting "What a load of rubbish" by half-time. Bull, having hit a hat-trick in a warm-up game at Halesowen Town, repaired some of the damage with a two-goal blast that set up a narrow first-leg lead at home to Birmingham in the Littlewoods Cup, and another odd-goal Molineux triumph against Reading got Wolves off the mark in the League.

But a frustrating cup second leg at St Andrew's spelled elimination against Garry Pendrey's Blues on the away goals rule and Bull was still looking for his first Third Division goal despite an emphatic 3-0 victory at Chesterfield. Even his old whipping boys, Notts County, kept him out as they left Molineux with a 0-0 draw but the ice was duly broken three days later by a toe-poked winner past Tony Lange at home to Aldershot.

For Bull, it was a fitting way to end his first hundred games for Wolves, a century made up of 51 home games, 49 away and an astonishing 73 goals, 49 of them at Molineux and 24 on the side's travels. Almost as amazingly, the run of four games without a goal that preceded the fixture equalled Bull's longest barren sequence as a Wolves player.

The Aldershot game, a repeat of the fateful play-off clash of 16 months

---

GOAL-COUNT

72 - *Bull found the target for the first time this season, heading home Robbie Dennison's cross - a perfectly-taken goal.*

73 - *A powerful shot by Dennison bounced back off the feet of Godden, thumped into the body of the advancing Bull and flashed into the empty net.*

Aug 30, 1988: Wolves 3 Birmingham 2, Littlewoods Cup first round first leg.

WOLVES: Kendall, Bellamy, Thompson, Streete, Robertson, Robinson, Chard, Vaughan, Bull, Mutch, Dennison. Subs: Venus, Clarke.
Goals: Bull (50, 81), Dennison (65).
Att: 11,007.

My Golden Boot ... Bully exhibits one of the rewards of his 1987-88 heroics.

earlier, also saw Wolves make their first changes of the season, one of them brought about by a debut for Mick Gooding, the midfielder arriving from Peterborough in a £70,000 deal following another public dispute between Turner and his board - this time over spending money.

Wolves were in the top three but Bull and Mutch were for once on the receiving end of some criticism as the manager said: "We weren't ruthless enough in front of goal. I was disappointed with our performance in the last third of the field and, if you don't take your chances, there's always going to be anxiety."

> ## GOAL-COUNT
>
> *74 - In fortunate circumstances, Bull reacted quickest to toe-poke his first Third Division goal after Mutch's intended pass had cannoned off a defender and into the danger area.*
>
> *Sep 20, 1988: Wolves 1 Aldershot 0*
>
> *WOLVES: Kendall, Bellamy, Thompson, Clarke, Robertson, Robinson, Gooding, Chard, Bull, Mutch, Dennison. Subs: Vaughan, Venus.*
> *Goal: Bull (27).*
> *Att: 8,991.*

There was particular concern over Bull, in the first week or two of the season because of his health and then because of the apparent struggle he was having getting through games in his old barnstorming style. The after-effects of a summer virus had prompted the club to have him thoroughly checked by the Molineux doctor and then sent to the human performance department at Lilleshall in an effort to rediscover his stamina of a few months earlier. Much to Wolves' relief, and not a little amusement, it finally transpired Bull's labours had nothing to do with illness or injury, but a change of boots that had altered his running style!

With the matter rectified, the goals started to flow again; two in a high-scoring win at one of his lucky grounds, Swansea, two more in a thrilling draw at home to second-placed Port Vale seven days later in the first League clash of two Midlands clubs for 56 years.

The trip to Fulham in the following midweek had a couple of amusing asides, although it took manager Turner some time to appreciate one of them. On the occasion of his 41st birthday, he

> ## GOAL-COUNT
>
> *75, 76 - Bull followed some remarkable ball control by slotting the first and got his second following a Dennison corner.*
>
> *Sep 24, 1988: Swansea 2 Wolves 5*
>
> *WOLVES: Kendall, Bellamy, Thompson, Venus, Clarke, Robinson, Gooding, Chard, Bull, Mutch, Dennison. Subs: Vaughan, Gallagher.*
> *Goals: Dennison (21), Robinson (37), Bull (42, 58), Chard (52).*
> *Att: 5,240.*

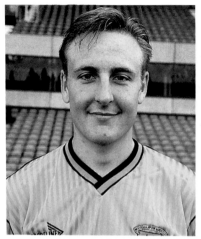

Mark Venus ... back in Wolves' starting
line-up after a spell as sub.

became so animated in his dressing-room lecture to a side guilty of a throwaway 2-2 draw that he sent a pot of tea flying all over his suit hanging on a peg. At least the trip to Craven Cottage enabled Mutch to break his scoring duck for the season, and there was an ironic twist to his feeling of relief. He was wearing the boots Bull had just discarded!

Wolves and Bull were about to click in a big way, though, their surge up the table starting after Mark Kendall's early penalty save had failed to stave off a defeat away to a high-riding Sheffield United side who had started with six home wins out of six.

The striker took his tally to eight goals in 12 games as Wigan were edged out at Molineux, then he hit late goals in victories at Bolton and Gillingham on successive Saturdays either side of a Mutch-inspired midweek win over Blackpool.

Wolves were up to second in the table and Turner's stock was so high that he attracted interest from Sheffield Wednesday and Albion as managerial vacancies cropped up at

Hillsborough and The Hawthorns. Wednesday were particularly keen and Turner asked his anxious board permission to personally say "Thanks, but no thanks." And, as he reflected on the satisfaction of the club's dramatic rise from the ashes, he said later: "It seems a long while ago now that I was sitting in my office with the tiles peeling off the ceiling and a bucket catching the drops of water." Wolves, top of the table for much of 1987-88, returned to familiar ground on a misty Bonfire

Night afternoon despite having seen Gooding and Phil Chard fall victim to a midfield injury jinx that had previously claimed Keith Downing and Paul Grainger, the latter having his nose broken in a training ground collision with the ever-competitive Bull.

Thankfully, Bull was back in the more acceptable habit of destroying opponents as was joined on the score-sheet by Floyd Streete and Downing in a 3-0 stroll at home to Southend - a match marked by the debut of Tom Bennett. Wolves were top, they had won five games on the trot and, after 14 League games, they had six more points than at the same juncture of the previous season.

Things got even better as a late Mutch winner on a Tuesday night at

49

GOAL-COUNT

83 - *Bull latched on to Venus's long through ball, toe-poked it round the hesitant Hardwick and joyfully blasted left-footed into an empty net.*

84 - *Then Bull scored his second, seconds from the end.*

Nov 12, 1988: Wolves 4 Huddersfield 1

WOLVES: *Kendall, Bellamy, Venus, Streete, Robertson, Robinson, Thompson, Downing, Bull, Mutch, Dennison. Subs: Gallagher, Bennett.*
Goals: *Mutch (39), Streete (57), Bull (65, 90).*
Att: *12,697.*

Bristol City enabled them to open a five-point lead, then Bull, on the day he finally picked up his Golden Boot, scored twice with his left foot as Huddersfield were put to the sword at Molineux. "We're starting to feel we can't be beaten," said the striker after taking his season's tally to 13.

But the side immediately learned to their cost they COULD be beaten after Turner's patience had finally snapped at a number of newspaper stories linking Bull with other clubs. Wimbledon manager Bobby Gould and owner Sam Hammam's recent presence at Molineux had fuelled one link, then Villa were splashed across the tabloid pages in a story that prompted the manager to let rip.

"I have reached the end of my tether with the rumours," he snarled. "I am fed up with hearing that Steve is leaving Molineux. This club are going well at the top of the Third Division, he is under contract for a long time here and he will be a Wolves player until we decide he leaves. There's very little chance of that happening and that's my last word on the subject."

The defeat that upset Wolves' momentum was an unlucky one in the first round of the FA Cup at Grimsby but Bull helped ensure it was only a minor blip as his scoring prowess touched new heights. His previous five Wolves hat-tricks had been of the usual variety - in other words, made up of three goals. But this one, in a slightly flattering 6-0 slaughter of Preston, contained four. Turner estimated it was a case of four goals from six chances and Preston manager John McGrath, a former centre-half of many years' standing, said: "I have never seen a better goal-scoring display."

The now phenomenal striker, already quoted as saying he couldn't wait to get at Second Division defences the following season, remained red-hot through a quite golden period up to Christmas. He struck again at Hereford in midweek as Wolves fought back from two down to draw the opening match in their defence of the Sherpa Van Trophy and, after a Sunday lunchtime bid to equal the club's record of nine successive League victories had ended in defeat and the dismissal of skipper Robertson at Northampton,

50

Scoring twins ... Andy Mutch and Steve Bull.

GOAL-COUNT

85 – *There seemed no danger when Mutch floated over a centre but, as quick as a flash, Bull was on to it to plant a fierce drive past Brown into the corner of the net.*

86 – *Mooney played a terrible back-pass to his keeper without spotting Bull behind him. Bull raced 40 yards, drew the advancing Brown and drove a perfect shot into the net.*

87 – *Mutch's persistence got the better of Atkins and teed up the ball for Bull, who kept calm and gave Brown no chance from ten yards.*

88 – *A brilliant one-two between Venus and Downing on the left unlocked the Preston defence, the ball ran free to Bull - and the result was almost inevitable as he slotted his fourth.*

Nov 26, 1988: Wolves 6 Preston 0

WOLVES: Kendall, Bellamy, Venus, Streete, Robertson, Vaughan (Bennett 73), Thompson, Downing (Gallagher 77), Bull, Mutch, Dennison.
Goals: Bull (13, 30, 59, 76), Mutch (35), Vaughan (69).
Att: 13,180.

GOAL-COUNT

89 – *Mutch stayed cool, centred low and accurately across an unguarded area and Bull produced a clinical right-foot finish for goal No 18.*

Nov 30, 1988: Hereford 2 Wolves 2, Sherpa Van Trophy, preliminary round.

WOLVES: Kendall, Bellamy, Venus, Streete, Robertson, Vaughan, Thompson, Downing, Bull, Mutch, Dennison. Subs: Gallagher, Robinson.
Goals: Thompson (62, pen), Bull (63).
Att: 4,215.

On the prowl.

Bull was up to familiar tricks.

He rained in another four goals - from four and a half chances - at home to Port Vale in the Sherpa Van Trophy and followed up against Mansfield in the last match before Christmas with a third hat-trick in successive home matches. Wolves' loyal fans were in dreamland after their club's 15th win in 17 Molineux fixtures and Bull - with

The day Wolves fans started to sense their hero was on to something big.....Bully "flies" away in celebration of his hat-trick against Mansfield in December, 1988, on the afternoon the supporters chanted his England claims.

five months of the season left - had already reached his pre-season goal target of 25 to establish himself as the country's leading marksman.

In many ways, it was a watershed occasion. Bull was looking a vastly improved player, not only producing one of the most spectacular scoring sprees in the club's glorious history, but converting a much higher percentage of his openings. Now, he was attracting big interest from the top flight and Wolves' ever-growing army of supporters recognised his rising to another notch of magnificence that December afternoon by singing for the first time: "Bully for England."

I wrote in my match report two days later: "The jubilant masses might not be far off. Any player who scores 77 League and cup goals in just over 16 months has to be worth close scrutiny by those at the very top of the English game." Bull had the football world at his feared feet but, from his mouth that day, came the words that everybody present wanted to hear: "I want to play in the First Division,

GOAL-COUNT

90 - Mutch, so often the tireless provider, flicked on Kendall's long kick for Bull to finish in the customary manner.

91 - Bull twisted to head home Thompson's 22nd minute cross after good work by Dennison.

92 - This time, it was a delicate right-foot chip which did the trick from Dennison's through ball......

93 - .....and a bullet-like close-range header rounded off his haul from Thompson's centre.

Dec 13, 1988: Wolves 5 Port Vale 1, Sherpa Van Trophy, preliminary round.

WOLVES: Kendall, Bellamy, Venus, Streete, Robertson, Robinson (Downing 67), Thompson (Vaughan 76), Gooding, Bull, Mutch, Dennison.
Goals: Bull (10, 22, 66, 74), Mutch (90).
Att: 9,734.

GOAL-COUNT

94 - Gooding's superb run and cross made way for Bull to send a delightful header low past Cox's right hand.

95 - Streete's deep ball into the area was chested down by Bull and there appeared little danger until the League's leading scorer recovered his balance and smashed a glorious rising drive into the top corner.

96 - Mutch helped on Bellamy's lofted through ball and Bull did the rest once more with a strong run and a neat right-foot shot past Cox and just inside the far post.

Dec 17, 1988: Wolves 6 Mansfield 2

WOLVES: Kendall, Bellamy, Venus, Streete, Robertson (Downing 64), Robinson, Thompson, Gooding, Bull, Mutch, Dennison (Vaughan 73).
Goals: Bull (26, 43, 58), Mutch (37), Gooding (40), Thompson (62).
Att: 12,134.

but WITH Wolves."

Two Christmas draws away to Bristol Rovers and Brentford, the second of them brought about by Bull's 100th goal with Albion and Wolves, gave everyone time to catch their breath again. Not least the player himself, who had been suffering from a virus and who said after his late point-saver at Griffin Park: "I was silly to play. I should have stayed at home."

If 1988 had been the Year of the Bull - he had scored no fewer than 54 goals - then the New Year dawned in familiar style as Chester became the first side to be gored by him in 1989. They were sent packing from Molineux in front of a 21,901 crowd that was the sixth biggest Bank Holiday crowd in the country and included Kenny Dalglish, the Anfield hero's presence prompting Turner to say: "Liverpool weren't that bad on Sunday, were they?"

There was, as usual, a Bully special (plus two assists) to cheer Wolves' highest gate for five and a half years while, at the other end, Kendall's hot-and-cold season continued with a penalty save from Steve Johnson.

Manchester United manager Alex Ferguson was a VIP Molineux visitor at around the same time and, in his Sporting Star column, joined in with the local comparisons being made between Bull and David Kelly. Ferguson held Kelly up as an example of a player who had done superbly in the lower divisions but was now struggling with West Ham in the top flight. The implication was that Bull still had to make the step-up, but the Old Trafford boss wrote: "I'm glad I don't have to mark him."

The Liverpudlian Mutch, unlike his more celebrated goal partner, was out of contract in the following summer and goals alongside Bull in the home

---

GOAL-COUNT

97 - *Bull chased a long pass from midfield, brushed aside a strong challenge from Millen and tucked his shot away inside the left-hand post.*

Dec 31, 1988: Brentford 2 Wolves 2

WOLVES: Kendall, Bellamy, Venus, Streete, Clarke, Robinson (Vaughan 63), Thompson, Gooding, Bull, Mutch, Downing. Sub: Bennett.
Goals: Mutch (42), Bull (88).
Att: 8,020.

GOAL-COUNT

98 - *Mutch highlighted his latest outstanding contribution by teeing up a spectacular overhead finish for Bull - who else?*

Jan 2, 1989: Wolves 3 Chester 1

WOLVES: Kendall, Bellamy, Venus, Streete, Robertson, Vaughan, Thompson, Gooding, Bull, Mutch, Downing. Subs: Bennett, R Kelly.
Goals: Gooding (12), Bull (18), Mutch (22).
Att: 21,901.

Mark Kendall ... penalty saves as follow-up
to his club record in 1987-88.

wins over Chester and Cardiff, followed by a match-winning brace at Reading, ensured he received his share of the plaudits and attention. Terry Venables was at Reading and Turner was later irritated at the Tottenham manager's extensive quotes in the Daily Mail which he believed almost constituted an illegal approach for the 14-goal Mutch.

Mutch had come a long way since being signed by Sammy Chapman for £5,000 of supporters' money in 1986 but Turner admitted: "I didn't fancy him at first as a striker. But it's a bit different now. He hunts well with Bull and is very positive in his approach to the job."

Victory at Elm Park had launched Wolves impressively into the second half of their League programme and they opened a ten-point lead at the top by following up with a scrappy success over Chesterfield. Then, Bully regained centre stage.

Maybe Sherpa Van Trophy visitors Bristol City should have known what might happen because he hadn't scored a hat-trick for all of five weeks. Having not scored at all for two and a half games, he even sounded an advance warning to Wolves' Southern Section first-round opponents on match-day morning by saying: "I have been stuck on 99 goals (for the club) long enough and don't intend to have to wait any longer. I'm due a goal tonight."

56

The rest, as they say, is history, the first goal of the striker's fourth hat-trick in two months taking him to his Wolves century in a mere 126 games. Dennis Westcott had managed the feat in 106 games in an era in which less emphasis was placed on defending, but the comparison with Tom Phillipson (100 goals in 128 matches), Billy Hartill (100 in 132), Jimmy Murray (100 in 163), Dennis Wilshaw (100 in 187) and Roy Swinbourne, John Richards and Derek Dougan - all of whom took more than 200 games to score their first 100 goals - was an apt endorsement of the 1980s favourite's heroics.

Bull's previous 86 appearances had brought 82 goals and he had marked his latest 44 outings at Molineux with a staggering 60 goals. He had scored 23 times in 14 ties in the competition but he was

still critical of himself. "I don't feel I played very well," he said. "I wasn't getting things together at all but the result was pretty good. In the last two or three games, I have been second to every ball. I have been on the heels of defenders instead of ahead of them."

It was a happy time for all concerned because Wolves had kicked off the year with five straight wins. But the sequence was halted by hard-fought draws at Notts County and Port Vale. Then the balloon went up yet again with another Molineux occasion and another Bull hat-trick, this time against Fulham.

A 12th game without defeat equalled Wolves' best run for six years and Fulham manager Ray Lewington had no words of consolation for the defenders increasingly likely to be confronting Bull higher up the League in 1989-90. "Why shouldn't he score goals higher?" he asked afterwards. "I can't see what a First Division defender is going to do so differently to my players today.

"He wears you down. He has got no tricks and doesn't try to be clever.

He just sticks to what he is good at and his ratio of shots on target is very high."

With 34 goals on the board from 34 League and cup matches, Bull was inevitably having to field questions about surpassing his monster 1987-88 haul of 52, and he said: "Yes, I think I can get there. I need virtually a goal a game but that's the rate I have managed so far this season anyway. If I can start scoring in away games as well as at Molineux, who knows what might happen?"

Only six of his goals so far had come on the side's travels but, after drawing a blank in an extra-time Sherpa Van win at home to Northampton, he started to put that right. As Mutch lined up his 101st consecutive game, Bull struck with a beauty in a vital victory on a filthy night at Blackpool, some complimentary words from Bobby Charlton preceding the 50th goal of the twin strikers' alliance in 1988-89.

The timing of the legendary former Manchester United and England player's tribute on a mid-February visit to Molineux was to prove uncanny as he pondered: "What's he worth to Wolves? The First Division, for he will take them there. They can't let him go."

Wolves fans had been singing "Bully for England" for several weeks now and, although their idol had been overlooked for the under-21 trip to Greece, the big call wasn't far away. It came at 3pm on a Thursday afternoon when Turner picked up the phone in his decaying Molineux office and heard Bobby Robson's voice.

Bull was in a group of half a dozen players at a crime prevention meeting at Wolverhampton Civic Hall shortly afterwards when the proud manager went over to him, shook his hand and said: "Congratulations." The player demanded to know what he had done to deserve such a greeting and received the news that he was off to Albania with his country as an over-age member of an under-21 squad also including Lee Sharpe, Michael Thomas, Stuart Ripley, Paul Merson, David Batty and Paul Ince.

"What can I say?" said the ever-modest subject of the now even more intense attention. "I'm delighted. It's every player's ambition to play at Wembley and win international honours and it looks like I will have done both in the space of a few months. I don't know where Albania is but I'll be finding out pretty soon. I thought I might be named in this squad some time but probably next season. I have not played against many of the other players and don't even bother to watch England's full internationals on TV. I'm not a great watcher of football, so I've got some learning to do."

Turner deflected some of the credit on to the club for giving Bull the platform for his magnificent deeds. And he could have had a double call-up to savour because under-21 coach Dave Sexton, who had watched the recent win at Reading, admitted he would like to have had Mutch in the party as well had there not been other similar players at the side's disposal.

The washing-out of a Friday night trip to Wigan was followed eight days later by the cancellation of the First Division programme prior to international week. That allowed many of Fleet Street's finest sports-writers to pay a rare visit to the Black Country to check out this barnstorming throwback of a centre-forward at the home game against Bolton - and they weren't to be disappointed.

A goal Bull was later to regard as one of his best three for the club

---

GOAL-COUNT

106 - *There was nothing else on, so Bull went into overdrive, skipped past three defenders on a high-speed run into the area and finished with a fierce shot into the far corner with the outside of his right foot.*

Feb 28, 1989: Blackpool 0 Wolves 2

WOLVES: Kendall, Bellamy, Venus, Streete, Downing, Vaughan, Thompson, Gooding, Bull, Mutch, Dennison. Subs: Robinson, Steele.
Goals: Bull (63), Vaughan (83).
Att: 6,482.

GOAL-COUNT

107 - *A long ball from Thompson was flicked on by Mutch to his partner 30 yards out and, with his back to goal, Bull took a stride to his left and let fly with a left-foot shot that tore past Felgate and into the top far corner.*

Mar 4, 1989: Wolves 1 Bolton 0

WOLVES: Kendall, Bellamy, Venus, Streete, Downing, Vaughan, Thompson, Gooding, Bull, Mutch, Dennison (Steele 73). Sub: Robinson.
Goal: Bull (34).
Att: 14,636.

earned three more points and many column inches more of praise, a fitting way to mark Turner's naming that day as Third Division Manager of the Month for February.

The boss, later to reveal that Leeds had been turned down in a big-money bid for Bull that weekend, set his side a 90-point 100-goal target to sweep themselves to promotion, and the man who would be in the front-line of that twin pursuit departed on international duty with a vote of confidence from Bolton manager Phil Neal. The experienced former international right-back said: "I think England have to give him a go. With better players around him playing to his strengths, there could be even more chances for him. And his ratio of goals per chances is remarkable."

Debut day came on Tuesday, March 7. Bull didn't score, returned home nursing a bruise or two but was still warmly complimented on his performance in a 2-1 win. "He had a fine game and gave our attack the sparkle that had been missing in Greece," said Sexton.

"This was the fourth time I had seen him play and, strangely, I have never seen him score. But he made an excellent start. His great thing is his determination to be on the end of things. He was mobile, he passed the ball well, he challenged and he got on the end of things. If it had been me, I would have been delighted."

Incredibly, Bull had not yet missed a single game for Wolves through injury or illness in two and a half years and was back to line up alongside Mutch for the 70th consecutive time in a Friday evening match at Southend three nights later.

Your country needs you ... Steve Bull finds another team worth putting his shirt on.

60

GOAL-COUNT

108 - *Bull belatedly joined in the rampage with a characteristic charge and shot after Mutch had flicked on Kendall's kick.*

Mar 14, 1989: Wolves 6 Gillingham 1

WOLVES: Kendall, Bellamy, Chard (Venus 26), Streete, Steele, Vaughan, Thompson, Gooding (Robinson 70), Bull, Mutch, Dennison.
Goals: Thompson (13, pen), Dennison (19), Steele (39), Mutch (42, 46), Bull (50).
Att: 12,574.

GOAL-COUNT

109 - *Dennison fed the ball inside from mid-way inside Bury's half, Gooding chipped forward first-time and Bull was there to seize control and hammer a glorious right-foot shot over Farnworth and into the roof of the net from just inside the area.*

110 - *Mutch shielded the ball superbly on the left-hand corner of the Bury area, released Dennison with a neat flick and the winger's centre was powerfully headed past Farnworth from six yards by the unstoppable Bull.*

111 - *Bull completed yet another hat-trick when the keeper fumbled Thompson's low cross and left him with an easy chance.*

Mar 18, 1989: Wolves 4 Bury 0

WOLVES: Stowell, Bellamy, Venus, Streete, Steele, Vaughan (Robinson 76), Thompson, Gooding, Bull, Mutch, Dennison (Downing 76).
Goals: Bull (36, 50, 86), Mutch (55).
Att: 14,828.

Bull had been further praised by Sexton for his coolness in the face of much provocation in Albania and must have thought he was back behind the Iron Curtain as Shane Westley and Paul Clark dished out some rough stuff Turner claimed added up to intimidation. But there could be no grumbles about an emphatic 3-1 defeat that ended, at the 16th and last hurdle, Wolves' hopes of equalling their longest unbeaten run for 30 years.

Refreshed by a weekend break in Cambridge, Wolves returned to take out their frustration on Keith Burkinshaw's bottom-of-the-table Gillingham side, the only surprise from the club's third six-goal haul of the season being that it figured only one entry on the score-sheet by Bull. The main honours in Wolves' club record 15th successive home victory was Tim Steele, a right-winger newly recruited for £80,000 from Shrewsbury.

Council-owned Molineux, albeit crumbling and horribly lop-sided because of the closure of two sides due to safety reasons, remained a very happy place as Wolves crushed Bury on the following Saturday to consolidate their status as the country's leading goalscorers and take their unbeaten home run beyond a year. Mike Stowell, signed on loan from Everton after Mark Kendall's 124-game run of successive appearances had been terminated by a knee operation, started with a clean sheet, but the honours went to a familiar recipient.

Bull blazed in with yet another hat-trick, his sixth of the season and all at home, to create novel problems. He was leaving Wolves with a serious shortage of match-balls by walking off with the customary spoils of his heroics, not that anyone was really complaining considering he had scored 40 goals in 40 games in 1988-89!

With Stowell not signed in time and goalkeeper-coach acquisition Eric Steele not properly match-fit, Turner swooped for his third keeper in less than a fortnight when he borrowed Roger Hansbury from Birmingham before his side's second Sherpa Van Trophy trip of the season to Hereford. Bull and Mutch did their stuff again to delight 6,000 travelling fans at Edgar Street and the No 9's popularity was underlined at the same time.

His eighth away goal of the season was his first since being signed by Dudley-based Quaser Sports to wear the same brand of boots as that endorsed by Gary Lineker. The 18-month deal was launched with a signing session in Wolverhampton that ran 45 minutes over-time and attracted at least 2,000 fans to a Wulfrun Centre store. "If we had not brought things to a halt, Bully could have been there all night," said Quaser managing director Kevan Broadhurst. "His pulling power amazed me."

GOAL-COUNT

112 - *Bull collected Mutch's pass, lost control for a moment, but, through sheer power and Crane's unfortunate rebound, ended up prodding a shot past Elliott.*

Mar 22, 1989: Hereford 0 Wolves 2, Sherpa Van Trophy, second round.

WOLVES: Hansbury, Bellamy, Venus, Streete, Steele, Vaughan, Thompson, Gooding, Bull, Mutch, Dennison. Subs: Robinson, Downing.
Goals: Mutch (35), Bull (42).
Att: 10,204.

In stark contrast to 1988, Easter was anything but happy for Wolves as they followed a tough draw at Chester with a surprise defeat that ended a magnificent home run of 24 wins and two draws in 26 games. If there had to be a side to break the sequence, though, Wolves fans would have chosen Bristol Rovers for the sake of the Pirates' assistant manager Kenny Hibbitt, who was applauded long and loud along the touchline before the game as he took his place in the visitors' dug-out.

The blueprint devised by Hibbitt and Gerry Francis for the game, which fell on the day before Bull's 24th birthday, was for their players to keep Wolves' fearsome strikers quiet. They did. But the hugely popular Hibbitt, veteran of 566 senior games and 114 goals in the Molineux cause, said: "This defeat is a one-off for Wolves. I don't think they will lose at home again this season and they will walk away with the championship. I said that

62

at Christmas and I'm sticking to it now."

Fortunately, second-placed Port Vale obliged Wolves by losing at home to Mansfield several hours later and the watching Turner was grateful for the sizeable lead his side had built up at the top of the table as they followed up with a defeat at Mansfield in a performance which had a Bully rocket and a Floyd Streete sending-off as its high and low points respectively.

A wasteful draw in a blizzard at Cardiff increased the apprehension and Terry Venables did nothing to lift Molineux spirits following a run of two defeats and two draws - the club's worst run for more than two years. The Spurs manager had despatched Bill Nicholson to watch the game at Mansfield and backed up his reasons for doing so by confirming: "It's quite correct to say we are watching Andy Mutch and are interested in buying him."

Turner was again irritated by Venables' decision to go public but wondered privately whether a smoke-screen was being constructed while Spurs' main target was Lineker.

In the meantime, skipper Ally Robertson's 600th Football League match brought a reassuring home win over Brentford as Bull provided the high spot of his own jaded contribution with the club's 100th goal of the season.

Wolves departed for the first leg of their Sherpa Van Trophy area final at Torquay in fine heart and, after a controversial 24-hour delay caused by a postponement over which Turner vowed to protest, two late Bully specials on a mudbath pitch teed them up perfectly for a return trip to Wembley.

GOAL-COUNT

113 - *Dennison released Bull with a clever chip over the defence and he didn't need asking twice as he made ground into the area before leaving Cox with no chance with a thundering shot that screamed into the far corner.*

Apr 1, 1989: Mansfield 3 Wolves 1

WOLVES: Stowell, Bellamy, Robertson, Streete, Steele (Venus 46), Vaughan, Thompson, Robinson (Downing 79), Bull, Mutch, Dennison.
Goal: Bull (30).
Att: 9,205.

GOAL-COUNT

114 - *Steele's centre from the right was too deep but Vaughan showed excellent composure to return a short cross which saw Bull send a floating header over Parks from eight yards.*

Apr 8, 1989: Wolves 2 Brentford 0

WOLVES: Stowell, Thompson, Venus, Streete, Robertson, Vaughan, Steele, Downing (Robinson 75), Bull, Mutch, (Chard 86), Dennison.
Goals: Streete (25), Bull (55).
Att: 14,196.

Turner, disappointed earlier in the day when the club's long-time council-owned Castlecroft training ground was handed over by the local authority for rugby use, admitted his side hadn't played well - and they toiled again three days later on the blackest afternoon in British sporting history.

Any satisfaction Wolves might have felt at emerging from their trip to bottom-of-the-table Aldershot with three points was immediately shattered when they learned of the death of 94 Liverpool fans at the FA Cup semi-final against Nottingham Forest at Hillsborough. The Sherpa Van return against Torquay three days later was the first major match to be played in England after the disaster and, in front of a disbelieving 22,532 crowd who generated club record gate receipts of £91,137, Wolves found themselves trailing 2-0 before half-time.

Dean Edwards, discarded by Turner both at Shrewsbury and Wolves, added another goal to his first-leg effort and left the manager with that feeling that "someone has grabbed hold of your stomach and squeezed it over and over again." A 3-2 aggregate defeat against the Fourth Division also-rans was rounded off by a couple of Bull misses and the stark realisation that a glorious day-out at Wembley had been snatched away.

In his diary of the season, "The Only Way Is Up," Turner described it as his worst day since he had been

GOAL-COUNT

115 - Substitute Gooding found Bull with a short pass following Streete's long free-kick and he galloped into a precious yard or two of space before driving a characteristic low right-foot shot into the far corner from 15 yards.

116 - Dennison provided a headed through ball, Mutch wrong-footed Torquay's defence and Bull stormed clear to hammer an unstoppable shot past the advancing Kenny Veysey.

Apr 12, 1989: Torquay 1 Wolves 2, Sherpa Van Trophy, area final first leg.

WOLVES: Hansbury, Thompson, Venus, Streete, Robertson, Vaughan, Chard (Gooding 81), Downing, Bull, Mutch, Dennison. Sub: Robinson.
Goals: Bull (86, 89).
Att: 4,612.

GOAL-COUNT

117 - Gooding caught Aldershot's defence square with a through ball from just inside the home half and Bull got a yard or two ahead of his markers to rifle a low left-foot shot under the advancing Tony Lange from just inside the area.

Apr 15, 1989: Aldershot 1 Wolves 2

WOLVES: Stowell, Thompson, Venus, Clarke, Robertson, Vaughan (Robinson 79), Gooding, Downing, Bull, Mutch, Dennison (Chard 79).
Goals: Bull (39), Dennison (68).
Att: 5,465.

Whoosh ... blasting home the first of the two goals that saw off Bristol City on Bank Holiday Monday - and that proved enough to secure promotion again.

sacked by Aston Villa, and the gloom was still hanging heavy as Swansea escaped from Molineux with a draw four days later.

But, after the on-loan Stowell had been recalled to Everton because of an injury scare over Neville Southall, Wolves found a ray of sunshine in the East. East Anglia to be precise. Bull had been called up for his second England under-21 game and used the return against Albania at Ipswich to plunder his first international goal - a 47th minute turn and shot that thrilled the 500 Wolves supporters in a 6,073 crowd.

Turner wasn't present at Portman Road - he was spying on forthcoming opponents on a night on which slip-ups by Sheffield United and Port Vale left Wolves within a few points of the title. But Bull's qualities were no secret any more and Venables, George Graham, John Lyall, Graham Taylor, Dave Stringer and Rangers' Phil Boersma were among the vast array of talent-spotters at the international.

Garry Pendrey resigned as manager of relegated Birmingham two days later before Wolves rounded off their April programme with the goalless draw at Huddersfield that left promotion tantalisingly out of reach as they took on Bristol City on May Day afternoon.

GOAL-COUNT

118 - *As Mutch flicked on Gooding's through ball, there was hardly a hint of a chance until Bull gathered momentum brilliantly to shrug off Rob Newman and beat Waugh with a low right-foot shot that scorched into the far corner from just inside the area.*

119 - *Mutch lifted a short pass into the path of Bull, who brought it under control with a superb first touch and drilled home a close-range shot.*

May 1, 1989: Wolves 2 Bristol City 0

WOLVES: Hansbury, Bellamy, Thompson, Streete, Robertson, Vaughan, Gooding, Downing, Bull, Mutch, Dennison. Subs: Chard, Robinson.
Goals: Bull (36, 88).
Att: 17,351.

Bull duly lifted a subdued Bank Holiday crowd with two more crackers, the second of them making him the first man since Middlesbrough's George Camsell between 1926 and 1928 to total 100 goals in the space of two seasons. It was a phenomenal achievement that left Bull two short of a second consecutive half-century and he beamed: "It has been another great season. I hope I can pass last season's 52 but it means doing better than one goal a game."

Despite all the satisfaction that rightfully unfolded over the next few weeks, there was a feeling of anti-climax as Wolves finally clinched promotion. Four and half hours after the completion of the victory over Bristol, rivals Port Vale suffered the surprise home defeat against

Northampton that ensured Wolves were going up again.

Turner was actually in his car on the way out of Vale Park with his loyal chief scout Ron Jukes when he heard confirmation of the club's latest rise. He immediately called secretary Keith Pearson and physio Paul Darby for a celebratory drink on the way home and said later: "We have led the table for six months and that has brought extra tension. There's a big difference between the Third Division and Second Division but this is no time to look too far ahead. Let's enjoy the rest of this season and then look to the future."

These were dizzy days for the Molineux faithful and, after Bull had become the first Third Division player ever to figure in the voting for the Footballer of the Year award (the prize going to Liverpool's Steve Nicol), he was joined by team-mate Mutch in the squad named for the end-of-season England B tour to Switzerland, Iceland and Norway.

> ## GOAL-COUNT
>
> ***120*** - *Dennison picked out Bellamy at the near post, the defender nodded on and Bull stormed in at the far post to head home powerfully.*
>
> *May 6, 1989: Wolves 3 Northampton 2*
>
> *WOLVES: Kendall, Bellamy, Thompson, Streete, Robertson, Vaughan (Robinson 75), Gooding (Chard 82), Downing, Bull, Mutch, Dennison.*
> *Goals: Bull (22), Thompson (45, pen), Mutch (53).*
> *Att: 15,259.*

The joint call-ups were celebrated with a goal apiece in the following day's exciting home win over Northampton - Wolves' 4,000th Football League game - but title rivals Sheffield United's win over Swansea meant the championship champagne had to stay on ice for another three days.

That was when Sheffield visited a sell-out Molineux bursting at the seams with 24,321 inside - the club's highest gate for six years. Wolves needed a point for the title, the Blades a point for promotion and Bull a goal for his 50. To everyone's massive enjoyment, all three targets were reached.

> ## GOAL-COUNT
>
> ***121*** - *Vaughan sent Mutch away for a measured left-wing cross which sailed over the keeper and left Bull to head home his 50th goal of the season.*
>
> *May 9, 1989: Wolves 2 Sheffield Utd 2*
>
> *WOLVES: Kendall, Bellamy, Thompson, Streete, Robertson, Vaughan, Gooding, Downing, Bull, Mutch, Dennison. Subs: Chard, Robinson.*
> *Goals: Bull (42), Dennison (58).*
> *Att: 24,321.*

Bull, who had received another international call in the meantime - for the under-21 game against Poland in early June - was bristling with happiness

as he savoured a night prevented from falling flat by a tremendous free-kick equaliser by now-established Northern Ireland international Robbie Dennison.

"When we arrived in the Third Division, we expected it to be tougher than the Fourth Division," he said. "And it was. But only for a few weeks. I can't believe what has happened to me. I know I scored 52 goals last season but I never thought I would seriously challenge that total again. For me to get my 50 and to see the fans celebrating again was a fabulous feeling. It seems at the moment the season is never going to end - and I don't really want it to."

Mutch was more muted during the celebrations, drawing the comparison between a local-boy-made-good like Bull and an exiled Scouser like himself. He even expressed disappointment at not having a new contract offered to him during a season which was to bring him 23 goals to go with the 23 he had scored in 1987-88. But, while he planned to sit back and consider any offers that may come along in competition to the summer-time carrot Wolves would dangle before him, Bull's fantastic rise was set to scale new heights.

Bobby Robson, having compared him to Gerd Muller earlier in the season, announced his plans both to go on the B tour and to draft Bull into his senior side if necessary for the following Rous Cup matches. He even compared him with Lineker by saying: "It's so refreshing to see a player so direct and uncomplicated.

"What has surprised us most is that, as well as scoring goals and being strong, he can also lay the ball off well, shield it and combine well with other players. His first touch is surprisingly good. He likes the ball where it hurts - in front of him. Many players these days prefer to play with their back to goal but he wants the ball, like Lineker, where he is likely to score. He is on the B team tour on merit and, make no mistake, I fully intend to play him."

Wolves, whose players were hailed by Turner as "the best group I have worked with in 20 years for attitude and willingness," still had a little unfinished business in the shape of away games against Preston and Wigan. For Bull and Mutch, the trip to the Deepdale plastic was the swansong for the season and Mutch scored twice in a thrilling 3-3 draw before both linked up with the England B squad while their club colleagues were going on another open-top bus tour round Wolverhampton the following day.

The Midlands Soccer Writers Player of the Year trophy, previously held by the likes of Trevor Francis, Cyrille Regis, John Aldridge, Nigel Clough and Lineker, was awarded to Bull in his absence as Wolves, the first club to win the Fourth and Third Division titles in consecutive years, also savoured smashing their points-in-a-season record for the second year running.

69

The curtain came down on the domestic season at Wigan with a third successive draw but there were worrying noises from abroad as Mutch - now clutching and considering Wolves' new contract offer - was carried off with an ankle injury in the Paul Gascoigne-inspired B win in Switzerland that constituted the striker's international debut.

Thankfully, it wasn't serious and he returned as substitute in the freezing temperatures of Reykjavik three days later in a game against the full Icelandic side. Bull came up with the goods yet again by shrugging off a defender and firing home one of the goals in England's 2-0 win and Turner, having been named Third Division Manager of the Year, was glowing with pride.

He and his non-international players were in Majorca celebrating their success when news filtered through of another Bully strike, this time in Stavanger against Norway B. And it was the most surprising goal of the striker's season as it came from a second-half penalty. Bull had shied away from spot-kick duties at club level ever since scoring in a Full Members Cup shoot-out for Albion against Chelsea, and might have had 57 goals for Wolves in 1988-89 had he taken, and scored, all their penalties during the campaign.

Nevertheless, he had carried his club form on to the international stage with three goals in five appearances and drew another round of compliments from coach Dave Sexton. "Bull went on for Paul Stewart at half-time and revitalised us," he said. "He has had a very good tour and I am sure he would cope more than adequately in the senior side. Without hesitation, I would recommend him. He would not let anyone down. He is so enthusiastic and would be a good weapon at full international level. It's just a question of Bobby Robson deciding who he needs and when."

Bull, narrowly beaten by John Fashanu for a late call-up for the visit of Chile to Wembley, had actually scored 53 goals during the season - one more than 12 months earlier, albeit with the help of five England games. And the inevitable crowning glory of his magnificent two seasons' work was only a phone call away. Then it came.

Two days before the most famous international game of them all, Steve Bull - the kid off a council estate in Tipton who had once been told he would never play professional football because of a knee condition - was summoned to the full England squad. Further withdrawals on top of the glut caused by the Liverpool v Arsenal title cliffhanger at Anfield opened the door and Bull was off to Glasgow for his possible senior debut against Scotland at Hampden Park.

He was to be on the bench for the May 27 Rous Cup match but manager Robson said: "If circumstances make it necessary for me to use him, I will

70

Above: Thumbs-up ... Bully in the driving seat after hearing of his first call-up
to the senior England squad. Below: Joyous celebrations back at Molineux
as he shares the delight of the moment with manager Graham Turner
after Wolves had become the first club ever to win the titles of all
four divisions of the Football League.

have no hesitation in sending him on. I shall not worry about the fact that he has hardly played outside the Third Division."

Somehow, fate suggested Bull would make his grand entry in the only manner he knows. And he did. Going on in the white No 16 shirt as a 31st minute substitute after Fashanu had been injured in a tussle with Paul McStay, he quickly made himself at home in a side leading through Chris Waddle's 20th minute header.

He teed up half-chances that were squandered by Tony Cottee and Trevor Steven then thundered a shot of his own narrowly wide of Jim Leighton's post. But he got his sights exactly right ten minutes from the end. Challenging with Dave McPherson for Gary Stevens' hanging cross from the right, he received a fortunate bounce off his own shoulder before ripping a low right-foot shot into the corner from some 15 yards.

"I can't begin to describe how I felt just then," he told author Rob Bishop in his 1990 biography "Bully," adding: "I didn't know which way to turn to celebrate, so I just dropped to my knees. I could have cried." That's just what mother Joan did back in the Black Country while girlfriend and wife-to-be Julie, watching on TV in her bedroom at home near Cannock, had the same emotions. "The tears came to my eyes," she said. "I couldn't wait to see him when we picked him up from Heathrow Airport that night. I was so proud of him."

Turner, whiling away the last few hours of Wolves' Majorcan trip, caught up with the news in a phone conversation from Palma Airport with his youngest son Andrew. The match had been videod from the moment Bull had entered the arena, and the proud manager watched the recording with his wife Ann over and over again when he returned home late that night. "I had a feeling of great pride that Steve was a member of the Wolves team, and that he had come on in leaps and bounds since he had joined us," Turner said.

Bull was typically down-to-earth as he summed up: "I was a little nervous to start with but I quickly settled into my normal game and getting a goal for England was a tremendous feeling." His reward was to immediately be drafted into the England squad for the following Saturday's World Cup qualifier against Poland at Wembley, having already been named for the under-21 international between the same two countries at Plymouth the previous night. Then, there was the possibility of a midweek trip with the seniors to Copenhagen.

"His schedule is beginning to worry me now," Turner added, conscious that the player's season was dragging on towards the second week of June. "He has been on such a high for a long while and played so many matches that he really needs a rest. After those two England games, that's it - a complete break for five weeks."

Wolves fans had had to travel far and wide to see their favourite in his national colours, the game at Ipswich being Bull's closest port of call so far with his country. Only a handful made themselves known with their gold tops in the 63,282 crowd at Hampden - the biggest gate the player had appeared in front of to date - but an astonishing 500 or more Wolves supporters turned Plymouth's Home Park ground into a Molineux-by-the-Sea on the night Bull and Mutch played in a 2-1 home win over the young Poles.

Neither scored but Bull had become something of a lucky omen, all seven of his international appearances resulting in victories. And he was on the sidelines, albeit firmly in the shadows of the returning Lineker, Barnes, Beardsley and Smith, when the senior game emphatically went England's way the following afternoon. Bull, probably still blissfully unaware he was the first Wolves player to score in a senior England game since Ron Flowers in 1962 and only the third Molineux man after Johnny Hancocks and Dennis Wilshaw to score on his full England debut, was struggling to take it all in.

"Everything is happening a bit quickly at the moment and I must admit I'm starting to feel a bit tired," he said. "But I'm quite happy to play anywhere while the chance is there. How can you not be excited about playing for your country? I keep watching the video recording of the Scotland game and feel like crying when my shot goes in."

Bull's very last game of an exhausting, exhilerating, explosive season was a 20-minute run-out as substitute for Beardsley away to the Danes. He didn't score, nor really threaten to, but the game provided further evidence that the starlet first discovered on a parks pitch by Sid Day had arrived on the big stage.

Turner was occasionally tortured by thoughts of how his star man's head might be turned by mingling with the Gascoignes, the Shiltons, the Walkers and the Robsons - players who might just try to alert him of the need for seeking a move to the top flight and open his eyes with talk of the riches on offer up there. But the manager need not have worried.

Bull, whose season had started ten months earlier on a miserable Saturday morning at Bury in front of 4,314 spectators, ended it by underlining that he was, indeed, a one-off. "Playing for England doesn't change anything," he said. "I am happy to commit myself to Wolves for the next four years. This is my home county and my home crowd. They love me and I love them. If I can keep scoring goals and getting them up, it will be tremendous."

BULLY'S 1988-89 STATISTICS:
Played 55 (45 League, 2 Littlewoods Cup, 1 FA Cup, 7 Sherpa Van Trophy).
Goals 50 (37 League, 2 Littlewoods Cup, 11 Sherpa Van Trophy).

CUMULATIVE WOLVES CAREER:
Played 150 (119 League, 6 League Cup, 18 Freight Rover/Sherpa Van Trophy, 3 FA Cup, 4 play-off).
Goals 121 (86 League, 26 Freight Rover/Sherpa Van Trophy, 5 League Cup, 3 FA Cup, 1 play-off).

Steve Bull, Wolverhampton Wanderers and England.

SECOND COMING

1989-90

The world was Steve Bull's oyster when he finally departed in early June for his close-season break. He could have afforded to travel anywhere on the globe for a summer holiday and could probably have had his pick of a few of Europe's better-known clubs when he returned.

Instead, he and girlfriend Julie Dace chose a fortnight in a caravan in Great Yarmouth to recharge the batteries before he came home to further commit himself to his beloved Wolverhampton Wanderers.

Amid the super-striker's flurry of no fewer than eight international appearances at various levels at the end of 1988-89, Graham Turner had expressed fears of the burn-out factor and insisted Bull - now conservatively rated at around £1.5m - should put up his devastating feet.

But the reality was somewhat different. The player had little truck with unwinding and, a few days into his break, he was growing bored. "It's amazing how even a week off can make you feel such a lot better," he said after the club had reported for pre-season training on July 11. "I can't wait to get cracking again."

The same applied to Andy Mutch. Despite considerable interest from other clubs and much concern among Wolves fans, the ex-Southport marksman signed a new two-year contract at Molineux in early July and said: "I am sure we can be challenging for promotion again. But I hope people don't assume we can carry on scoring goals at the same rate. It's going to be tougher from now on."

Wolves, having freed Jackie Gallagher from the side who won the Third Division, prepared for life in the Second by splashing out £150,000 on keeper Tony Lange - one of the men who had defied them as an Aldershot player some two and a bit years earlier. They invested the same amount on Southend central defender Shane Westley and nearly as much again to recruit strikers John Paskin (£75,000) from Albion and Paul McLoughlin (£45,000) from Hereford.

For the second successive summer, Turner was in dispute with the club over a contract, his pride bruised by the fact there had been no move to tie him up on a long-term deal after back-to-back title triumphs. Only 12 months

75

remained on his contract but, before a five-day pre-season trip with his players to Anglesey, he was told by owner Tony Gallagher not to worry. "If you want a ten-year contract, you can have one," said Gallagher. The little-seen building boss was a rugby fan rather than a watcher of football, but he said: "We are aware Graham is highly respected in the game but we also think he is like Steve Bull - his heart is in Wolverhampton. He's a dedicated man and he's a winner."

Bull, after signing another new contract, further protected his interests by forming a company to handle his financial affairs and off-field promotion work. Coach Barry Powell and physio Paul Darby were entrusted as shareholders while the player himself became chairman of Steve Bull Limited. One of the trio's first decisions was to complain when a local pub named a beer after him - something they felt was not in keeping with a star sportsman.

Bull picked up where he left off with a brace in a warm-up game at Millwall, one of them coming from his first penalty for the club. He scored two more in a nostalgic Molineux reunion with Moscow Dynamo and sounded the ominous warning to future opponents: "I feel sharper than I've ever felt at the start of a season."

With Bull and Mutch now challenged by Paskin and McLoughlin, Wolves seemed stronger in the striking department than they had been for years - and what a shame that turned out to be! A young hopeful by the name of Stan Collymore had arrived at Molineux on YTS terms following a terminated stint at Walsall and showed his potential with two goals in a Bass Charity Vase defeat against Notts County at Burton.

Turner said of the unknown forward: "He might have a lot to offer us. He certainly knows how to put the ball away." Sadly, the manager was later to explain how on-field promise was not matched by off-field discipline and Collymore was released within a few months, non-League neighbours Stafford Rangers picking him up for nothing. Turner, who was rightly praised for many years following Bull's cut-price arrival in 1986, clearly undid some of his good work the day he decided it was not worth tolerating the weaknesses of a striker destined to be rated an £8.5m superstar.

On the eve of Wolves' first season in the higher divisions for four years, Turner rocked the boat by publicly describing as unsatisfactory the offer of a one-year contract extension. His rejection came at the time he was launching his promotion diary from the previous campaign and several journalists questioned whether the title should be changed from "The Only Way Is Up" to "The Only Way Is Out."

The matter was happily resolved a few days later but not before Wolves' season had begun disconcertingly with a 4-2 defeat at Middlesbrough. An odd-goal midweek win at home to Lincoln left Turner's side with a shaky foothold in the Littlewoods Cup and, although Bull opened his account four days later to earn Wolves their first point, visiting Bradford exposed more shortcomings in a side Turner admitted were struggling to cope.

An awkward return at Lincoln was safely negotiated with stunning goals by Bull and Robbie Dennison and the season was still in its infancy when the striker received the first call from his country - for an under-21 trip to Sweden. Despite the faltering start, Bull believed it was business as usual for the club and insisted: "We're traditionally slow starters but we have at least got out of the starting gate."

A Sunday beating at Swindon hinted at a darker picture, though, and Westley's sending-off added to the gloom as Wolves found themselves bottom of the table after three League matches. Bull's mixed fortunes to date were summed up when, for the first time in eight games for England, he was on the receiving end with a 1-0 defeat in Uppsala against the emerging Swedes.

Back on home soil, Lange's late penalty save from Derek Statham earned Wolves a turgid goalless home draw with Stoke that lifted them one place. But they were back in the wooden spoon position after a nightmare mauling by Brighton under the Molineux lights in a game in which Bull's first-half goal was small beer against the four rammed in by the visitors.

The match was the 136th and last of skipper Alistair Robertson's Wolves career, and the concern at a run of eight League games without a win - the

> ## GOAL-COUNT
>
> **122** - *Dennison took the free-kick quickly and Bull gained a yard to plant a sideways header wide of Tomlinson.*
>
> *Aug 26, 1989: Wolves 1 Bradford 1*
>
> *WOLVES: Lange, Thompson, Venus, Robertson, Westley, Vaughan, Dennison, Gooding, Bull, Mutch, Downing (Chard 28). Sub: McLoughlin.*
> *Goal: Bull (69).*
> *Att: 13,784.*

> ## GOAL-COUNT
>
> **123** - *Bull was poorly placed with a flat angle and a cluster of bodies in front of him but, in a blur of power and timing, the ball flashed past Andy Gorton from a left foot that is becoming as dangerous as the right.*
>
> *Aug 30, 1989: Lincoln 0 Wolves 2, Littlewoods Cup, first round second leg.*
>
> *WOLVES: Lange, Thompson, Venus, Robertson, Westley, Vaughan, Chard, Gooding, Bull, Mutch, Dennison. Subs: Bellamy, Paskin.*
> *Goals: Bull (17), Dennison (56).*
> *Att: 6,733.*

club's worst for five seasons - brought drastic action. "We're not kidding ourselves," Turner admitted. "We're obviously under pressure." And he promptly ordered all his first-team players to report for reserve team duty the following night before he made four changes for the weekend trip to Ipswich.

Amazingly, one of them resulted in Bull being left behind. Not on merit but because, for the first time in nearly three phenomenal years, he was unfit. After scoring 124 goals in a 157-game stretch broken only by suspension, ineligibility and an England call, a virus had floored the mercurial marksman and left Wolves as lambs to the slaughter. But, with Paskin and Tom Bennett in the starting line-up for the first time, they responded superbly to record a 3-1 win that proved to be the turning point of their campaign.

They had Bull back for Turner's first competitive return to Villa, where they narrowly and thrillingly lost the first leg of their Littlewoods Cup tie against the Graham Taylor side destined to finish runners-up in the championship race. Then they made it two League wins in a row with substitute Paskin's last-minute winner at home to Plymouth.

Wolves were on the move at last and Bull sensed he was in for a good night when he dropped the jackpot on the one-armed bandit at the team's hotel before the game at Barnsley. On the field, he duly delivered a brace that earned his side an entertaining draw but he feared the match might have a very serious down-side. He temporarily thought he had broken his leg in a collision with Malcolm Shotton but recovered to be able to complete the 90 minutes and give his verdict on the season to date.

GOAL-COUNT

124 - Bull reacted sharply to scramble in Shane Westley's knockdown on the half-hour.

Sept 12, 1989: Wolves 2 Brighton 4

WOLVES: Lange, Bellamy, Venus, Robertson, Westley, Vaughan, Thompson, Gooding (Paskin 79), Mutch, Dennison (McLoughlin 83).
Goals: Bull (30), Mutch (55).
Att: 12,338.

GOAL-COUNT

125 - Dennison had the satisfaction of providing the cross, John Paskin and Vaughan both challenged strongly and Bull struck with a left-foot shot from near the penalty spot.

126 - Shotton mis-headed Streete's long free-kick and left Bull clear to rifle home a characteristic low drive.

Sep 26, 1989: Barnsley 2 Wolves 2

WOLVES: Kendall, Bellamy, Venus, Streete, Clarke, Vaughan, Bennett, Gooding, Bull, Paskin, Dennison. Subs: Downing, McLoughlin.
Goals: Bull (38, 53).
Att: 10,161.

Power, concentration and determination combine to send another shot roaring

His tally of five goals in 11 outings was now respectable but he admitted: "It has been a terrible start as far as I'm concerned. I have not felt right and my pace is not there yet. For some reason, it's taking me ten yards to get going on a run. I can only put it down to the virus that floored me a couple of weeks ago but it's slowly coming back. In another two or three weeks, I'm sure I will be 100 per cent."

Portsmouth quickly saw that prediction come true as the England international crashed in two late beauties in a 5-0 annihilation in the Molineux sunshine. The win set Wolves up nicely for the return against Villa on Turner's third Molineux anniversary. But they couldn't quite do enough in a tie which brought Bull his bravest goal for the club so far.

He was poleaxed and knocked out in a collison with Nigel Spink and Paul McGrath while heading Wolves' equaliser, becoming so disorientated that he asked Paskin after treatment for both the score and the side's scorer!

Such was the concern over the striker following the initial fears that he might have swallowed his tongue, that he had to be woken every two hours in his bed at home that night for checks. Thankfully, he was all right but, having been doubtful with a hamstring strain for a tie that brought Wolves record gate receipts of £108,000, Bull was suddenly running into fitness problems wherever he turned, and had to be cleared by the club doctor before lining up in the following Saturday's

---

GOAL-COUNT

127 - *Bull ran on to a fine through pass from Bennett and, as Knight came out, let fly with a fierce drive which gave the keeper no chance.*

128 - *There was no stopping Bull and he added to Pompey's misery with another typical near-post shot from Downing's fine pass.*

Sep 30, 1989: Wolves 5 Portsmouth 0

WOLVES: Kendall, Bellamy, Venus, Westley, Clarke (Chard 71), Vaughan, Bennett, Gooding (Downing 82), Bull, Paskin, Dennison.
Goals: Dennison (51, 68), Venus (63), Bull (78, 86).
Att: 13,677.

GOAL-COUNT

129 - *Bull was poleaxed by keeper Nigel Spink when, with remarkable agility and bravery, he headed home Vaughan's left-wing cross a split second before the most sickening collision.*

Oct 4, 1989: Wolves 1 Villa 1, Littlewoods Cup, second round second leg.

WOLVES: Kendall, Bellamy, Venus, Streete (Downing 74), Westley, Vaughan, Bennett (Chard 72), Gooding, Bull, Paskin, Dennison.
Goal: Bull (76).
Att: 22,754.

80

undeserved home defeat against leaders Sheffield United.

Rangers manager Graeme Souness was at Molineux for both games and Bull - assured by Bobby Robson he would be in the senior England side again before the end of the season - returned to the international limelight with two goals, one a header and the other a shot, in the under-21s' win over Poland in Jastrzebie Zdruj.

England's seniors ensured their World Cup qualification the following night and, at the start of the countdown to Italia 90, Turner had no grumbles about the treatment being given to his star asset from those at Lancaster Gate. "It was far better for him to play for the under-21s and score a couple of goals than sit out the World Cup qualifier on the bench," the manager said. "I have no doubts he can be successful on the supreme stage. I think Bully can get to Italy."

Bull, who shared a room in Poland with his old Albion team-mate David Burrows, rated his first two-goal international performance his best so far for England. But he was setting his sights with typical modesty on the finals looming some eight months away. "It would be the experience of a lifetime to be involved in something like the World Cup, even if it was just as a

> ## *GOAL-COUNT*
>
> *130* - *For virtually the first time, Bull escaped the shackles of Chris Whyte, chested down Mutch's far-post cross and finished characteristically with a shot that fizzed low into Albion's net.*
>
> *Oct 15, 1989: Albion 1 Wolves 2*
>
> *WOLVES: Kendall, Bellamy, Venus, Streete, Westley, Vaughan (Downing 53), Thompson, Gooding, Bull, Mutch, Dennison. Sub: Paskin.*
> *Goals: Dennison (45), Bull (90).*
> *Att: 21,316.*

member of the squad," he said. "And, to be honest, that's as much as I can hope for. I can't see me being anything other than a second-choice striker."

Bull flew back home for the game Wolves supporters had been relishing ever since the fixtures had been drawn up; the first meeting with Albion for five and a half years. And he shared their enthusiasm as he announced: "This is a special match for me. I have been waiting for this game for a long time because I still have a high regard for Albion. I would love to go back there and score in a Wolves victory. That would be extra special."

Once more, the man with the Midas touch delivered. A minute from time and nine minutes after the outstanding Mark Kendall had saved Bernard McNally's penalty to keep the score at 1-1, Bull sent the gold and black hordes at the Smethwick End of The Hawthorns into raptures by despatching the winner. It was a goal to put player and fans alike in dreamland but he confessed afterwards: "I was rubbish. I was tired after coming home from

Poland and just didn't feel like running. It's nice to come back here and score the winner in the last minute and I'm just glad we've won a derby after losing to Villa."

Despite the transfer-listing of the out-of-favour Lange, Phil Chard and Tim Steele, Wolves were in the top half of the table and remained on a high as goals by the old firm of Bull and Mutch saw off visiting Port Vale to give Turner his 100th win as the club's manager. The strikers' 1989-90 totals stood at ten and six respectively and Bull proclaimed: "We're on our way. The team are really clicking into gear now and I'm convinced we have what it takes to make a real bid for promotion this season. Who's to say we won't follow the pattern of previous seasons and go on to make a success of things after a slow start?"

> ## GOAL-COUNT
>
> *131* - *Bull produced a powerful left-foot finish after Westley's crunching midfield challenge had released Dennison for a delightful defence-splitting pass.*
>
> *Oct 17, 1989: Wolves 2 Port Vale 0*
>
> *WOLVES: Kendall, Bennett, Venus, Chard, Westley, Vaughan, Thompson, Downing, Bull, Mutch, Dennison. Subs: Paskin, McLoughlin.*
> *Goals: Mutch (2), Bull (34).*
> *Att: 18,123.*

Bull's international ambitions received another endorsement from Dave Sexton as Alan Smith, Nigel Clough, Mark Hateley, Mike Newell and Kerry Dixon emerged as his main rivals to partner Gary Lineker and Peter Beardsley. But, after he and Mutch were shut out in a grim 1-0 defeat at Leeds, it took a twice-taken Thompson penalty to take a point off Oldham at Molineux.

Turner, who had expressed concern at being unable to compete in the transfer market with Leeds, West Ham and Newcastle, splashed out his biggest Wolves fee so far when he recruited midfielder Paul Cook from Norwich for £250,000 at the end of October. Chard rejoined Northampton for £50,000 at the same time and there was an upbeat feeling as the club and a huge army of fans headed off for a midweek date at Leicester. But it turned into a deeply unhappy night for Bull.

Bobby Robson had already made it known he would be at Filbert Street to check on the striker and had no choice other than to enter a rare black mark against him for the third sending-off of his Molineux career. Reacting angrily to a professional foul by Steve Walsh just before the interval, Bull shoved the defender in the face and was ordered off by Bishops Stortford referee Graham Pooley.

The sickening despair suffered by Bull, who sat alone in the visitors' dressing-room throughout the rest of the 0-0 draw, was intensified the

Don't look now ... old adversaries Steve Walsh and Steve Bull renew acquaintances.

following day, Robson announcing he was to have recalled the Black Country's favourite son to his senior side for the Wembley clash with Italy in mid-November. Now, Bull would be suspended and available only for the previous evening's B international between the same countries.

"I know I've blown it," said the distraught central figure of a feud that was to be repeated when he and Walsh clashed again at Molineux. "I've just got to knuckle down now and see if I can earn another call-up against Yugoslavia in December. I once made a promise to myself that I would never get sent off again but there's only so much provocation I can take before something has to give. I'm sick and bitterly disappointed about my dismissal. It was purely frustration that led me to push Walsh away. But I promise you all one thing: It won't happen again."

Robson, who had spoken to Turner before the match, offered some words of consolation to Bull personally afterwards and then said publicly: "In the long term, this incident won't affect his chances, as long as he learns to control himself. But he has got to watch it. Being sent off for the third time doesn't look too good on your record. We think a lot of him and, at under-21 and B team level, he has already shown he can cope with provocation. That's why I was surprised he reacted like that."

An unhappy week ended happily for Bull with a Molineux winner against fifth-placed West Ham before owner Tony Gallagher became the latest figure to underline the player's value to Wolves. "We have already turned down approaches of more than £2m for

> ## GOAL-COUNT
>
> *132* - Bull was played through by a superb touch from Mutch and he outpaced Strodder before beating Parkes at last with a mighty right-foot drive which the keeper could only palm into the net.
>
> Nov 4, 1989: Wolves 1 West Ham 0
>
> WOLVES: Kendall, Bennett, Venus, Bellamy, Westley, Downing, Thompson, Cook, Bull, Mutch, Dennison. Subs: Paskin, Vaughan.
> Goal: Bull (66).
> Att: 22,231.

Bull," he revealed. "He's worth at least twice as much to the club's future." And, emphasising he was aware of the public feeling, he added: "I think I would have an entire town after me if I sold him."

After figuring in a dismal Zenith Data Systems Cup exit at Sheffield United and a League draw at Sunderland, Bull signed off before suspension with his 11th international appearance. Once more, the call-up took him a long way from home but Wolves fans, who had already launched a "Follow Bully to Italy" fund in the countdown to the World Cup finals, numbered around 200 as he impressed but failed to score in a 1-1 draw against Italy B at Brighton.

For the first time, Turner watched him in action for his country and then ordered him in for extra training during his suspension to compensate for what the player called the most boring spell of his career. During his ban, Bull abandoned a Dougan-like plan to watch the home defeat against Blackburn from the South Bank terraces, conservatively opting instead for the disused Waterloo Road terraces. Then he stayed at home as Wolves' dismal 3-1 defeat at Watford left them in mid-table.

The absence of midweek matches at this time meant Bull's three-match ban actually spanned 25 days - a spell incorporating his own third Molineux anniversary. His first three years had yielded an astonishing 132 Wolves goals from 171 appearances and he received another major fillip when he was named in the senior England squad for the pre-Christmas friendly against Yugoslavia - a match that offered him the mouth-watering possibility of playing in a Wembley international for the first time.

After Middlesbrough had been beaten 2-0 at Molineux in the last game of his suspension, Bull returned with two goals in a testimonial game for full-back Archie Richards at Kidderminster, then hit three in a leisurely kick-about against Worcestershire's cricketers in a match in aid of leukaemia sufferers.

Later in the same week, he donned the meet-the-people hat he wore with increasing assurance, first by signing around 2,500 autographs at Quaser sessions and then bringing the fans out in their masses again for the launch of his biography "Bully."

But it was to League action that he was looking most longingly and, by big coincidence, his joyously acclaimed comeback unfolded at the ground where he had last been seen in competitive action - Brighton. He didn't score and it took a free-kick special from Dennison to rescue a point against one of Wolves' bogey clubs, but it seemed fitting that the World Cup draw was made on the same afternoon, pitching England into the same group as Egypt, Holland and the Republic of Ireland.

And Bull was given another indication that Italia 90 was by no means an impossible dream as Robson confirmed early in the week that the Wolves mega-hero would be in the starting line-up to face the Slavs. "We said we wanted to have another look at Bull but our priority at the start of the season was to qualify for the World Cup," the manager said. "Now we have done that, I want to look at some players."

News of the player's selection for his first senior start prompted another exodus of Wolves followers in his slipstream. But Turner, the subject of interest from Manchester City, expressed a note of slight pessimism by admitting the game might be coming at a difficult time for a player who had been suspended and who had also been suffering from another bout of flu.

Even so, the proud manager said: "Nothing amazes me about Steve Bull. He has an incredible record over the last two years and I think he could form a partnership with most front men. A lot of Lineker's goals come from close range but Steve doesn't score many like that. He is very good at taking the ball and holding players off."

Bull already had double the number of full caps won by another legendary Wolves centre-forward, John Richards, and the 1970s goal machine confirmed he was a member of the appreciation society by saying on match-day: "My heart is with Steve Bull tonight.

"If England can provide him with the same sort of service they have given Gary Lineker, then I think he might be an even better striker. There's an awful lot of ignorance about Steve outside this area, especially with the London-based Press. They dismiss him as raw but he's aggressive and fast and has superb positional sense. He has such a fantastic record that people are expecting miracles from him. But he has the knack of coming up trumps every time a test like this comes along."

Much to his disappointment, Bull's name was absent from the score-sheet. But he played throughout England's 2-1 win - their 100th at Wembley - and produced a performance he believed had let no-one down. "It will remain one of the proudest nights of my life," he said afterwards. "When I looked around and saw the likes of Peter Shilton, Terry Butcher, Gary Lineker and Bryan Robson, it was difficult to take in that I was on the same pitch.

"But I thoroughly enjoyed the experience. That's really what it was - an experience to learn from and treasure forever. I don't think I let myself down and, while it would have been smashing to have topped it off with a goal, perhaps that was asking too much. To line up and listen to the national anthem brings a tear to your eye. That's the only time a few nerves got to me."

His performance received mixed reviews nationally, although his claims were promoted in a big way by team-mate Chris Waddle and by one of the Class of 66, Geoff Hurst. "Bull was indirectly or directly responsible for both Bryan Robson's goals," Hurst said. "It has been one hell of a time for him but he is definitely worth another crack."

Bull, as usual, was touched by the support he received from Wolves fans away from the homely club environment of Molineux, and added: "The best way to thank those fans is to turn it on for Wolves."

His wishes didn't come true immediately for he missed out again in a 2-2

86

draw at Oxford that was secured by goals from Mark Venus and Dennison. The club went into Christmas on the fringes of the top ten and with their leading scorer without a goal in six matches for club and country.

And, after Wolves had been named BBC Midlands' Team of the Year, his return to the score-sheet was no happy event as his side slipped to a surprise Boxing Day defeat at home to Hull. Keith Downing, lining up in a midfield who had now lost the popular Mick Gooding - sold to Reading for £65,000 - scored Wolves' 6,000th League goal as Bournemouth were safely despatched at Molineux four days later, and the 1980s ended with the club tenth in the table, one place above Albion but 15 points behind second-placed Sheffield United.

Wolves needed to do something spectacular if they were to achieve automatic promotion for the third year running and the new decade was rung in on exactly the right note. A trip to Newcastle wasn't exactly a dream January 1 fixture but the club's fans turned it into a memorable occasion thanks to the magnificent, selfless efforts of Albert and Muriel Bates.

The man-and-wife duo at the head of the Official Wolves Supporters Club even offered their Penn house as collateral as they committed themselves to tens of thousands of pounds to charter six

GOAL-COUNT

133 - *Bull cracked in his first goal for seven and a half weeks - a powerful close-range shot after brilliant work on the left by Dennison and Venus.*

Dec 26, 1989: Wolves 1 Hull 2

WOLVES: Kendall, Vaughan (Downing 62), Venus, Bellamy, Westley, Streete, Thompson (Paskin 74), Cook, Bull, Mutch, Dennison. Goal: Bull (20). Att: 19,524.

GOAL-COUNT

134 - *Bull crashed home a near-post shot after a terrible mistake by Bjorn Kristensen and a fine cross by Paul Cook.*

135 - *Bull waltzed round former Wolves keeper John Burridge from Downing's through ball.....*

136 - *.....then he headed home at the far post after Dennison's corner had been helped on.*

137 - *Bull had the supporters' heads in the clouds again when Dennison put him clear to go round Burridge and score left-footed for a repeat of his second goal.*

Jan 1, 1990: Newcastle 1 Wolves 4

WOLVES: Kendall, Bennett, Venus, Bellamy, Downing (Jones 85), Streete, Paskin, Cook, Bull, Mutch, Dennison (McLoughlin 81). Goals: Bull (50, 56, 59, 76). Att: 22,054.

planes out of Birmingham en route for the North East. With the Hatherton Wolves filling another plane and director David Gallagher flying separately with members of his family, an incredible 882 fans got airborne that day in an eight-strong squadron that wrote some national headlines.

Wolves' players, who had travelled more routinely by coach the previous day, knew they had to produce something special to reward the flying fans - and one man, in particular, showed once more that the sky was the limit. Steve Bull had been a bystander as keeper Kendall beat out Mick Quinn's early penalty, then he wreaked havoc in front of a disbelieving Bank Holiday afternoon crowd.

He unleashed a tremendous hat-trick in ten minutes at the start of the second half and made it four after promotion rivals Newcastle had pulled one back. It was finishing out of the very top drawer, arguably the most golden of the many, many golden displays the player had unveiled in the famous gold shirt.

Monarch Airlines had never witnessed anything like the celebrations that followed at 33,000 feet on the way home but it wasn't just Wolves fans who had their heads in the clouds that day. Veteran North East correspondent Doug Weatherall wrote in the Daily Mail the next morning: "Bull's finishing was magnificent. The likes of Newcastle goal-scoring legends Jackie Milburn and Malcolm Macdonald would have been proud of strikes like them. Not since Jimmy Greaves scored four of six Chelsea goals at St James's Park 28 years ago has a visiting player been given such an end-of-match ovation by Geordie fans."

It was Wolves' first win on Tyneside for more than 30 years and equalled the biggest victory they had managed anywhere on their travels for a decade. On a personal theme, it was the first time Bull had repeated, in an away match, the four-goal feats he had managed at home to Preston and Port Vale, and it was his first hat-trick for nine months.

Turner described his No 9 as "red-hot again" while the player himself was happy to have quietened the doubters. "People said I had dried up but this might make them think again," he said. "It was an unbelievable way to start the year. I always think of the fans and it's great to give them something to cheer after they turned out in such numbers so far away from home."

The game took Bull's tally to 16 for the season but there was to be no happy follow-up. Although the total clicked on to 17 at home to Ron Atkinson's Sheffield Wednesday five days later as Wolves led with 15 minutes to go, the club's miserable FA Cup record continued with another third-round knockout. For Bull, defeat was even more disappointing as his first taste of penalty-taking in a competitive game for the side resulted in a poor kick being saved by Chris Turner.

It was a depressingly familiar story but Bull's spirits were lifted in midweek when he and David Platt were named for an England get-together at Lilleshall in a 30-man squad from whom the World Cup party were likely to be selected. He was once more the only player chosen from outside the top flight and he underlined why as he rifled in a late equaliser at Bradford City to make it six goals in three matches. It was the second time he had levelled the scores in draws against the West Yorkshire club in 1989-90.

Injuries and suspension had already separated Bull and Mutch seven times on the team-sheet during the season and, when the willing No 10 limped off early in the following Saturday's match at home to Swindon, a threat to their partnership emerged. Paul McLoughlin, the stand-by striker who was yet to start a first-team game for the club, went on as sub and scored the two late goals that turned a probable defeat into a 2-1 victory against the division's third-placed team.

There was considerable speculation in the fortnight's break that followed that the amiable West Countryman might dislodge the most famous strike duo outside the top flight. But Turner stayed loyal with the fit-again Mutch for the visit to storm-hit Plymouth - and he duly obliged with the only goal of the game, Wolves' 50th of the season.

It was Wolves' third away win of the campaign and, on the day Graham Taylor was named Manager of the Month for a record third time in a season, it was enough for Turner to sound a hopeful note as he saw his side sitting

GOAL-COUNT

138 - *Worthington was penalised for hand-ball midway inside Wednesday's half and Bull made a terrific run to meet Dennison's free-kick and guide a delightful header low to Turner's right from close range.*

Jan 6, 1990: Wolves 1 Sheffield Wednesday 2, FA Cup, third round.

WOLVES: Kendall, Bennett, Venus, Bellamy, Downing, Streete, Paskin (Jones 20), Cook, Bull, Mutch, Dennison. Sub: McLoughlin.
Goal: Bull (70).
Att: 23,800.

GOAL-COUNT

139 - *Bull chested down Bennett's right-wing centre and found a yard of space to drive low past Tomlinson from close range.*

Jan 13, 1990: Bradford 1 Wolves 1

WOLVES: Kendall, Bennett, Venus, Bellamy, Downing, Streete, Jones, Cook (McLoughlin 82), Bull, Mutch, Dennison. Sub: Thompson.
Goal: Bull (86).
Att: 10,680.

in sixth place. "I have always felt we should be optimistic about the Second Division and I have seen nothing to make me change my mind," he said. "It's going to be very difficult catching Leeds and Sheffield United but we have to be very pleased with the way things are going."

The promotion fires were burning even more brightly when Ipswich were unluckily edged out at Molineux to become Wolves' fifth victims in six League games. Bull, who was flattered to hear that councillors in Tipton were trying to name a street after him, scored one of the goals as the side came from behind to win for the second successive home match. And he summed up: "For the first time this season, we have really felt we belong in the promotion race. There's still a long way to go but we are one of the sides to beat at the moment and I fancy our chances against any team."

> ## GOAL-COUNT
>
> **140** - *Cook swung over a firmly-struck corner to the far post, where Bull came roaring in to plant a powerful header past Forrest.*
>
> *Feb 10, 1990: Wolves 2 Ipswich 1*
>
> *WOLVES: Kendall, Bennett, Venus, Westley, Downing, Streete, Jones, Cook, Bull, Mutch, Dennison. Subs: Thompson, McLoughlin.*
> *Goals: Bull (40), Linigham (og, 46).*
> *Att: 18,781.*

The climb to fifth place left Wolves within one win of making this their best start to a calendar year since the war and interest was so high that around 7,000 tickets were quickly snapped up for the following Saturday's trip to bottom-of-the-table Stoke - Turner's 200th as the club's manager.

The previous 199 had included 107 wins and only 47 defeats but this was to be no happy occasion as Wolves slumped to a deserved 2-0 defeat on Bull's first competitive visit to the Victoria Ground. It was the first time the side had failed to score since November 7.

Nevertheless, Wolves' progress towards the play-offs, and the continued heroics of their now famous leading scorer, was starting to cause some embarrassment with the game's ruling bodies. The international date of April 24 was to come only 24 hours after Wolves had a League game scheduled at Bournemouth, and involvement in the play-offs would result in Bull being delayed from joining England's World Cup preparations, if indeed he were to be selected. Clearly, the FA had not seriously expected a player from outside the top flight to go to the greatest football show on earth.

There was talk of Bull being flown solo to England's training camp if necessary but the player himself remained typically pragmatic. "There's no point me worrying," he said. "It would be great to go to Italy, even if it

Trying to impress ... battling with Watford's defenders on the day Bobby Robson visited Molineux to check on him.

comes at the end of a long hard season.

"If I am needed for the World Cup, I wouldn't be able to get on the plane quick enough. But, if Wolves are in with a chance of the First Division, I will be going flat out for that as well. How can we fail to be excited at the thought of going up for the third year running? If things go my way, it could be early July before I get my feet up and think about a holiday away from it all. But you have to make the most of your opportunities in what is a relatively short career."

So highly did Wolves regard their most valuable asset that they insured him for a staggering £2m, taking out a policy to cover the unthinkable. Officially, it meant he was rated by the club at something like 30 times the £64,000 they bought him for from Albion. Bull previously came under Molineux's standard sports insurance scheme but that would have rendered his employers to collect only around £50,000 in the event of him having to retire through injury.

The club's owners said it was a specific one-off policy, adding: "It's just sensible business practice. The premiums are substantial but, were the club ever to lose Steve Bull - heaven forbid - our loss would be virtually incalculable."

The Stoke game proved to be Floyd Streete's last for the club, his place in the back-four going to Gary Bellamy on the following Saturday afternoon. That was the day Bobby Robson dropped in at Molineux for the first time in several years and the subject of his attention didn't disappoint, scoring the equaliser in the wasteful home draw with Watford.

The national manager, who had watched the game from an executive box in the company of Jack Harris

> ## GOAL-COUNT
>
> *141* - *McLoughlin did well to go round Drysdale on the right and his fine cross was powerfully headed home from six yards by the in-rushing Bull.*
>
> *Feb 24, 1990: Wolves 1 Watford 1*
>
> **WOLVES: Kendall, Bennett, Venus, Westley, Downing, Bellamy, Steele, Cook, Bull, McLoughlin, Dennison. Subs: Bennett, Jones.**
> **Goal: Bull (13).**
> **Att: 16,187.**

and Billy Wright, said of Bull's performance: "He took his goal well and his second goal well, although that was offside. He didn't get a lot of good service but the idea was to see him where he is popular and where he might do well."

Bull, who had been forewarned by physio Paul Darby about Robson's presence, was satisfied with his showing. "Even apart from my goal, I was pleased with my contribution," he said. "My touch was good and, as well as

93

having the ball in the net twice, I felt I achieved something in the approach work."

The goal took Bull's tally for the season to 20 with February not yet out and meant three of his last four entries on the score-sheet had come from headers. But there was anger at Molineux over stories about his strike-partner.

Newspaper stories suggested Villa were interested in signing the ten-goal Mutch for £800,000 but Turner retorted sharply: "It is three and a half years since I left Villa and I have never said a word about any individual there. If they want to do business with Wolves or any other club, there is an accepted way and that's manager to manager or chairman to chairman. Stories like this can have an unsettling effect on players."

The manager issued an attacking cry as Wolves went into March - and his players answered his call in style with a 3-2 win at Blackburn brought about by Downing's second-half winner. The game brought another brace for McLoughlin and it was strange that the player, having twice scored two in a match, was destined not to hit the target for the club again.

Wolves were still sixth and climbed two more places with an impressive midweek victory at Portsmouth marked by a Bull goal in a contribution he described as "a bit of a nightmare." If the striker really felt downcast at his efforts, though, he was lifted later in the week when he was named in a 20-man England squad for the home game against Brazil at the end of the month.

> ## GOAL-COUNT
>
> *142 - Bull ended a goal famine that had lasted all of ten days when he lashed home right-footed after Martin Kuhl's atrocious back-pass.*
>
> *Mar 6, 1990: Portsmouth 1 Wolves 3*
>
> *WOLVES: Kendall, Thompson, Venus, Westley, Downing, Bellamy, Steele, Cook, Bull, McLoughlin, Dennison. Subs: Bennett, Jones.*
> *Goals: Bellamy (36), Fillery (og, 77), Bull (90).*
> *Att: 12,284.*

It gave Bull a chance of his second international appearance at Wembley but he said: "I must admit it came as a surprise when I learned I would be facing the Brazilians at Wembley rather than playing for England B in Eire the night before. The Brazil game is the one everyone seemed to think would be the time for Bobby Robson to put out his strongest possible side. I feared that would mean no place for me but, now I'm in, how else can I look on it but as a big boost to my chances of going to the World Cup?"

Stories were rife of how England players would reportedly pick up £75,000 each if they lifted the cup, and Bull added: "For someone like me, who was picking up £27 a week for glueing bits of beds together a few years ago, that's some living! But the money is something to leave other people to worry about. In fact, I don't see a lot of the money I earn now. It's just put away for the day when I can no longer play."

Bull was back on target in a dismal Molineux draw against a Barnsley side who equalised after being reduced to ten men, then an off-field development to gladden supporters' hearts unfolded in the following week. Sir Jack Hayward, a hugely popular Wolverhampton-born industrialist now earning his fortune in the Bahamas, revealed he was ready to buy the club to prevent any chance of it once more passing into Bhatti-like hands.

Sir Jack's son, Jonathan, a Northumberland-based dairy farmer, had been watching Wolves around the country for several months and even stayed at the team's overnight hotel before they suffered their now usual beating at Sheffield United - a 3-0 defeat that came in Bull's 150th League appearance for the club.

Hayward Jnr, a former Sussex second-team cricketer, had developed a deep liking for the Molineux scene and said: "Since I have been watching Wolves, it has been one long fairy story. From virtually nowhere, the club have been turned round and now we have an exciting team to watch."

Sir Jack was in Britain in mid-March to pursue his dream purchase, facing the club's travelling media men for the first time after another unhappy away-day - this time as Port Vale recorded their first League win over Wolves since 1926 - and saying of a London meeting with Tony Gallagher: "There's a willing buyer, a willing seller and I shall return in a couple of weeks in the hope of seeing it through."

One of the first moves Sir Jack had in mind, if successful, was to invite the legendary Billy Wright - veteran of some 541 League and cup games for Wolves - to become a director. "If I buy the club, I will ask Billy to join the board," he promised. "He is the greatest player Wolves have ever had."

Amazingly, chairman Jack Harris, unless accompanied by club secretary Keith Pearson, Wright or the Haywards, was often on his own at Wolves matches, with the only other director in attendance, David Gallagher, tending

> ## *GOAL-COUNT*
>
> *143* - *Cook swung over another superb dead-ball from near the corner flag and Bull got the vital touch with his head as the ball flashed low into the net.*
>
> *Mar 10, 1990: Wolves 1 Barnsley 1*
>
> *WOLVES: Kendall, Thompson, Venus, Westley, Jones, Bellamy, Steele (Mutch 22), Cook, Bull, McLoughlin, Dennison. Sub: Bennett.*
> *Goal: Bull (60).*
> *Att: 15,995.*

On the ball ... a powerful run during Wolves' late-season win
over a Leeds side heading for the top flight.

96

not to travel with the team. It was a peculiar state of affairs but one that was soon to be redressed.

In between their sound hidings at Bramall Lane and Vale Park, the first of them the equal heaviest of Turner's reign, Wolves kept their challenge alive with another ecstatically acclaimed triumph over Albion. This time it was at Molineux but the plot was just the same, Turner's side coming from behind to pinch the points 2-1 thanks to a late Bull winner.

"If I had ordered someone to write a script for tonight, it couldn't have gone much better," smiled Bull amid the warm after-glow of yet another precious match-winner. "Mind you, I should have had a hat-trick and, in the first half, I was terrible. But one thing I always make sure I do is believe in myself and keep pegging away - and it paid off."

Bull was confronted on his way out of Molineux by Albion chairman Sid Lucas, who greeted him with the words: "You did us again, you beggar." And the striker still had that date with the Brazilians to look forward to.

During the late-March get-together, Bull shared a room with Platt but he didn't have the chance to link up with the Villa star on the pitch, remaining on the Wembley sidelines as an unused substitute. He did, however, have the dubious pleasure of sitting next to Paul Gascoigne on the bench as a Lineker goal secured victory!

"It's very nice to be part of the international scene and nicer still to be thought of as a possible for Italy," said the Wolves striker. "But actually forcing my way into Bobby Robson's first-choice side is going to be a different matter. At the moment, Gary Lineker and Peter Beardsley are England's best strikers and my job is to prove I am worthy of replacing one of them or at least being ready to step up if they are left out for any reason."

Bull, like Wolves' side as a whole, had hit an inconsistent patch and, even in a 1-0 home win over champions-elect Leeds, the promotion impetus appeared to be running low. Indiscipline from several players on the field, and the resulting rash of suspensions, had become another worry over recent weeks and Mutch was sent off for violent conduct in the brought-forward clash at Bournemouth. The referee was the same Graham Pooley as had

> ## GOAL-COUNT
>
> **144** - *After Mutch had fed the ball forward following Kendall's long kick, Bull faced a head-to-head with Stuart Naylor for the third time and, on this occasion, he speared a powerful right-foot shot low into the far corner.*
>
> *Mar 20, 1990: Wolves 2 Albion 1*
>
> *WOLVES: Kendall, Bennett, Thompson, Venus, Westley, Bellamy, Steele, Cook, Bull, Mutch, Dennison. Subs: McLoughlin, Jones.*
> *Goals: Cook (43), Bull (77).*
> *Att: 24,475.*

ordered Bull to an early bath at Leicester five months earlier but there were no complaints whatsoever this time, especially after skipper Bellamy's late header had earned the ten men a deserved point.

The rampaging Bull, duly selected in the PFA Second Division select side by his fellow players, was right out of luck at Dean Court and admitted: "Whereas I scored two and missed one last season, I am now missing two and scoring one. You are bound to get in a rut at some stage in a long season." But it was all to come spectacularly right when he went into the re-match against Leicester.

Pre-match requests for interviews on the reunion with Steve Walsh were waved aside but Bull had an answer up his sleeve for match-night. He rattled in his first Molineux hat-trick for over a year in a magnificent 5-0 victory, his second goal leapfrogging him over Peter Broadbent (145) and making him the fifth highest scorer in Wolves' all-time history behind John Richards (194), Billy Hartill (170), Johnny Hancocks (168) and Jimmy Murray (166). The hat-trick goal was Bull's 150th for Wolves and Albion but he said afterwards: "Don't ask me what has suddenly changed. I'm not doing anything different but I feel sharper than I've felt all season."

The player's 1989-90 tally now stood at 26 - one more than his summer-time target - so he promptly revised the figure to 30, with a minimum of six matches to be played. Of his skirmish with Walsh, he said simply: "I'm happy I had the last word in the way that really matters - scoring goals."

Bull's inevitable reward was a place in the England squad for the forthcoming international at home to Czechoslovakia and there was another boost for Wolves almost immediately when Colin Taylor, destined to finish the season with more than 50 goals in the reserve and youth sides, was named in the England youth squad for the first time.

GOAL-COUNT

145 - *The ball broke to Bull 20 yards out and he did the rest with a rasping low right-foot drive.*

146 - *Vaughan's brilliant work was carried on by Mutch for Bull to hook in the goal of the night from ten yards.*

147 - *Dennison received Thompson's quick throw, unselfishly ignored the chance to complete his first Wolves hat-trick and squared instead for Bull to round off a trio of right-foot shots.*

Apr 10, 1990: Wolves 5 Leicester 0

WOLVES: Kendall, Bennett, Thompson, Westley, Downing (Jones 27), Bellamy, Steele, Vaughan, Bull, Mutch, Dennison. Sub: McLoughlin.
Goals: Bull (7, 65, 70), Dennison (17, 49). Att: 18,175.

98

But there was to be no happy follow-up for the club and, for the second successive year, Easter proved a miserable time. Wolves lost both at home to Newcastle and away to struggling Hull without scoring and the promotion dream was in danger of collapse.

But Bull breathed new life into their hopes by responding with what he called his best goal of the season in the home win over Oxford.

On the same day, the striker had a vote of confidence from Manchester United manager Alex Ferguson, who wrote in a syndicated newspaper column: "Outside the option of playing John Barnes, I feel that Bull is the next best bet. Bull has credibility problems as an international-class striker because he has scored all his goals outside the First Division and is at his best when running on to balls hit into the space behind defenders - an aspect of his game which many feel would be rendered ineffective against teams using man-marking and a sweeper.

> ## GOAL-COUNT
>
> *148* - Bull was once more Foster's tormentor, taking a couple of strides inside before beating Judge with a phenomenal right-foot shot into the top far corner from 15 yards.
>
> Apr 21, 1990: Wolves 2 Oxford 0
>
> WOLVES: Kendall, Bennett, Thompson, Venus, Vaughan, Bellamy, Steele, Downing, Bull, McLoughlin (Paskin 80), Dennison. Sub: Jones.
> Goals: Downing (40), Bull (65).
> Att: 13,556.

"However, I feel Bull, although not the best of players in terms of his ball skills, would cause any team trouble with his remarkable strength and aggresion. Moreover, he is a natural goalscorer. Even at international level, you don't need to be a great footballer to be a great goalscorer. West Germany's Gerd Muller was a perfect example."

Bull, having figured in the making of England's World Cup record, went into action against the Czechs under pressure from Arsenal's Alan Smith, who had scored twice in a B international the previous night. The response was magnificent. Never one to shirk a challenge, Bull scored twice on a Wembley occasion on which he would have received much more national credit had a certain Mr Gascoigne not had one of his best matches for the side.

The Tottenham midfielder hit the tremendous long pass from which Bull rocketed a fizzing right-foot shot past visiting keeper Ludek Miklosko in the 18th minute and then crossed from the right for the Wolves striker to thunder a header into the roof of the net early in the second half.

It was high-quality finishing that left Bull sighing: "What a great day! I was delighted to get on the score-sheet again. It was my proudest 90 minutes

Bouncing the Czechs ... Bully on the rampage during his two-goal starring role at Wembley in April, 1990.

yet in an England shirt. I always thought the thrill of scoring on my senior debut against Scotland would take some beating but to score twice in a full international has to overshadow anything else I have done in my England career. I still don't know where it leaves me in the countdown to the summer but it obviously hasn't done me any harm."

Robson praised Bull's efforts enormously by saying: "He took his goals expertly and is a very eager, brave and willing player. His first goal was a shot of high merit. If Van Basten, Maradona or Gullit had hit one like that, you would have said it was great finishing. What he does not do as well is lead the attack like Paul Mariner or Trevor Francis. He likes the ball knocked over the defence rather than to have to knock it back to supporting players."

It was only when Bull arrived home and picked up the following evening's paper that he realised problems still lay ahead. Robson had devoted a chunk of his morning-after Press conference to expressing fears about the striker linking up with the World Cup squad if he was involved in the play-offs.

Contrary to the FA's earlier noises, the manager said: "It's a real threat to Bull's chances of going to Italy. It's a very bad state of affairs for him and us. It's nothing I can really talk to Graham Turner about. Getting to the First Division is very important for Wolves and there's not really anything anyone can do."

Bull was in danger of becoming a victim of his own success, faced by the dilemma: "Score enough goals to get Wolves into the play-offs and you might play yourself out of the World Cup." But, if the issue was troubling him, it didn't show. "It's something beyond my control, so there's no point worrying about it," he said. "I have done my job. It's Bobby Robson's job now to decide whether or not to pick me.

"Of course I would like to go to the World Cup. Which footballer wouldn't? I also realise it might be my only chance to play in one because there's no guarantee I won't be injured or past it in '94. But Wolves come first. Trying to get them to the First Division is the big thing and always will be. Playing big matches for England is a bonus."

The national manager's comments may have been water off a Bull's back but they infuriated Turner, who saw them as needless scare-mongering. "Steve did well enough to convince the doubters he was worthy of a place in the squad," he said. "I am equally convinced that, if that's Bobby Robson's opinion as well, he will take him to Italy regardless of any complications caused by the play-offs. The comments attributed to him were untimely and insensitive. From the club's point of view, two days before what is a crucial match, we want everybody performing to their best. This couldn't have come at a worse time. I would have thought that, if any comments were needed on the play-offs, they could have waited a week."

Sadly for Wolves, as soon as the issue surfaced as a major problem, it disappeared for all the wrong reasons. A 1-0 home defeat against rivals Sunderland left them out of the running barring a freak combination of results elsewhere, and even the ever-optimistic Bull conceded: "The dream is over. We have to accept that, while other teams have come on strong over these final hurdles, we have fallen away."

Maximum points from the daunting last two games away to Oldham and West Ham were only the start of Wolves' requirements and the final nail came in the unlikely setting of a Thursday night out at Boundary Park. A point from an enterprising 1-1 draw, secured by substitute Steele's late equaliser, was not enough and Wolves, for only the second time in nine years, ended a season neither promoted nor relegated.

Or at least they wished it had ended there, for a trip to an emotional Upton Park less than 48 hours later was a game they could well have done without. Wolves looked drained in the East London sunshine, nobody more so than Bull, who did himself no favours with a jaded display in front of the watching Robson in his side's heaviest defeat under Turner.

The England manager clearly wasn't flavour of the month with the occupants of the packed visitors' enclosure and received some verbal abuse from fans who produced a full-throated chorus of "Stevie Bull must go to Italy" before setting off for home. West Ham's 4-0 romp was a swansong for the retiring Liam Brady, the game also proving a farewell for Wolves keeper Kendall, who was freed shortly afterwards along with countryman Nigel Vaughan and the two defensive rocks from the old lower-division days, Streete and Robertson. Shortly afterwards, the luckless Robert Kelly retired with his long-term back injury.

In the aftermath of the failed promotion attempt - Wolves finished an unflattering tenth after standing higher in the table for much of the campaign - the club were duly taken over by the Haywards and further boosted by a lucrative sponsorship deal with tyre giants Goodyear. But the season was far from over for Bull.

BULLY'S 1989-90 STATISTICS:
Played 48 (42 League, 4 Littlewoods Cup, 1 Zenith Data Systems Cup, 1 FA Cup).
Goals 27 (24 League, 2 Littlewoods Cup, 1 FA Cup).

CUMULATIVE WOLVES CAREER:
Played 198 (161 League, 10 League Cup, 18 Freight Rover/Sherpa Van Trophy, 4 FA Cup, 1 Zenith Data Systems Cup, 4 play-off).
Goals 148 (110 League, 26 Freight Rover/Sherpa Van Trophy, 7 League Cup, 4 FA Cup, 1 play-off).

TAKING ON THE WORLD

SUMMER 1990

As he was watched first by Dave Sexton at Oldham and then by Bobby Robson at West Ham, Steve Bull was on the brink of receiving an invite on to world football's ultimate stage.

The World Cup finals were just round the corner and he had already been named for the May 15 home friendly against Denmark. But, before putting himself once more in the gaze of the big-money talent-spotters, he had a familiar message for his admirers back home in the Midlands.

"If you read any rubbish about Steve Bull being dissatisfied with another year in the Second Division, ignore it," he said. "I am as committed as ever to the club and more than happy to stick around and hopefully score the goals that can help us make the final jump into the big time."

Bull, who had another two years on his contract, added: "I'm not interested in going anywhere. People have told me that the Second Division can harm my prospects with England but it hasn't so far, has it?"

Disappointingly, Bull was left out of the starting line-up in favour of John Barnes for the Denmark game. But, at the end of a day marked by Kenny Hibbitt's appointment as Walsall manager, the striker went on in place of Lineker for the last 20 minutes of England's odd-goal win.

And there was a lovely ring to the timing when Bull finally received the magical World Cup call. Billy Wright, the proud holder of 105 caps for his country, had been appointed a Molineux director shortly before on the same day that Sir Jack Hayward had written a £2.1m cheque to assume ownership and promise every possible effort at making Wolves "the leading club in Great Britain that they once were."

As Sir Jack scotched fears of a move to a new ground and pledged instead to create a Molineux for supporters to be truly proud of, Bull was looking ahead to a summer in the sun. "I shall head for Italy ready to work hard and grab an opportunity if it comes my way," he said.

"I am not going for a sun-tan and to sit back and let the others get on with it. I know I am going as back-up to the likes of Gary Lineker and John Barnes. But I have played with Gary a couple of times now and I feel comfortable alongside him. I know I can do the job and so does the manager or he would not have picked me. I won't wish an injury on any player but I shall be twitching on the bench through the tournament, bursting to get on."

Bull praised Turner for helping him graduate to world football's showpiece event and also offered a public thank-you to Nobby Stiles, one of the famous Class of 66. "It was Nobby who got me sorted out at the start," he said. "I have got so much to thank him for. When I went to Albion, I was rough, raw and ready. I just used to run round like a mad-man. It was Nobby who showed me the ropes, calmed me down a bit and taught me what professional football was all about. I will never forget what he did for me."

Another substitute's outing came Bull's way in the 2-1 Wembley defeat against Uruguay, this time a 16-minute stint in place of Lineker. And, as the squad - minus David Rocastle, Alan Smith and Dave Beasant from the party assembled at the end of the League season - jetted to the Continent, Graham Taylor was already emerging as a hot favourite for the manager's job when Robson retired in mid-summer. The Villa manager, having led his club to runners-up spot behind Liverpool in the championship race, was to spend the month in Italy as well, working both as a spy for Robson and as a summariser for TV.

There was a stop-off en route for Sardinia for the players, though, and a final warm-up international in Tunisia. It was another unconvincing England performance and they were lurching towards an embarrassing 1-0 defeat when salvation came from an increasingly familiar source. Gascoigne applied just enough weight to reach Barnes with a pass out to the left in the dying seconds and the winger's cross was despatched into the Africans' net at the near post by the head of the stooping Bull.

It was another kick in the teeth for the faction who argued the Wolves hero lacked the refinement necessary for the ultimate stage. What they certainly couldn't dispute, however, was his sheer volume of goals.

He had now scored roughly once for every hour he had spent on the field in international football and said boldly: "My confidence is sky-high. It has never been better. I just want to get out there and play all the time. If the manager picks me, I will score. It's a great feeling. If they tell me to get out there with ten minutes to go, I will give it all I've got."

Turner, whose own future had been secured by the Haywards with a five-year contract set to run to the summer of 1995, was a proud man as he surveyed the big build-up from home. "A look at Bully's scoring record for England sides shows he is getting an international record almost as phenomenal as for us," he said.

No sooner had the players arrived in the searing heat of their Sardinia training camp than Bull was up to his old tricks, scoring twice in a 6-0 warm-up win over Cagliari. It instantly endeared him to the watching hordes of England fans and provided another boost to his hopes of figuring in the starting line-up when it was all to start for real against Jack Charlton's renowned Republic of Ireland battlers on June 11.

Two more Bully goals rained in during a practice match against a Sardinia Select X1 and, as Genoa's name was mentioned as the latest in a long line of clubs interested in snapping him up, another hands-off warning was sounded from England. Jonathan Hayward had spent only a month or so in the vice-chairman's seat at Molineux but he told the hovering vultures: "They are wasting their time. It doesn't matter how many millions we are offered for Steve, we do not need their money and there's absolutely no point in anybody even getting in contact with us. We consider him the best striker in the country."

Bull's popularity among expectant Wolves fans had never been higher and, when Express & Star assistant sports editor Martin Swain arrived on the island for duty, it was with aching arms, courtesy of carrying a sackful of some 750 good-luck messages from readers for the Molineux favourite. A further 250 had been sent direct by post.

If the striker needed any extra incentive, it had been supplied by what he called "the best fans in the business." He described the tribute, which turned the heads of other players and journalists in attendance, as fantastic, and told the faraway well-wishers: "No matter what happens over the next few weeks, you have all made this an experience I shall treasure for the rest of my life. I have never felt better, fitter and stronger."

The early signs were that Bull would have to start the tournament on the subs' bench in the shadow of Lineker and Beardsley. But a TV poll featuring 25,000 callers brought him 64 per cent of the vote as Lineker's strike-partner. And excitement in Wolverhampton was so high that the town's speedway team had their fixture postponed on the night of the Irish match, so fans could follow the local football hero's fortunes instead.

Former Wolves record signing Andy Gray did not share, though, in the clamour that was soon to prompt Jimmy Greaves to appear in a TV studio bearing the message "Let the Bull loose" on the front of his shirt. Two hundred of the garments were subsequently rushed into the Molineux club shop but the ex-Scottish World Cup striker argued: "Bully is Robson's secret weapon. He is right to stick with Beardsley because the Irish defenders will have a more difficult time coping with his sort of trickery than Bull. But Bull is breathing down his neck."

Bryan Robson described the Wolves No 9 as "red-hot" but, when the curtain went up, the first night was to end in utter disappointment. Although

A goal-den moment for England in World Cup year.

England struggled pitifully against the side who had beaten them in the 1988 European Championships in Stuttgart, Bull was kept on the bench until replacing goalscorer Lineker six minutes from the end of a feeble 1-1 draw. Even when the ineffective Beardsley had gone off after 70 minutes, midfielder Steve McMahon had won the nod to take his place. The clamour for Bull's inclusion merely increased from that night.

Two days later, the doors of the England training camp were opened for the benefit of fans, and there were chants of "Bully, Bully" in the warm air from admirers who also converged on him in big numbers in search of autographs and pictures. "I haven't met one fan out here who doesn't think Bull should play," said supporter Paul Abbotts, from Willenhall. "It doesn't matter who you talk to - Scousers, Geordies, Manchester United fans or Cockneys - they can't understand why he is not in the side."

The impatient Bull was left to hope in the build-up to the second game that his scoring record would speak for itself. Before the clash with Holland, he argued he could strike up a successful partnership with Lineker on the basis that, whatever chances one might miss, the other would score from.

When selection time came round, Beardsley was duly axed but it was only substitute duty again for the crew-cut striker itching for his place. Manager Robson opted instead for the sweeper system he had previously neglected and Bull had to be content with another outing off the bench - this time 32 minutes as replacement for Chris Waddle. Despite the goalless stalemate, it was a bright England display that would have been brighter still if the eager Bull had not flashed a header wide with his first touch.

The general concensus was that the Wolves man, who was to spend the next day downing a beer or two with team-mates Lineker, Gascoigne and Barnes on a millionaire's yacht, had not let himself down. But Robson said of his miss: "It was a good chance and, although he had just gone on, I'm afraid you have to deal with that at this level."

Wolves were busy snapping up Derby centre-half Rob Hindmarch for £350,000 as Bull, in the countdown to the clash with the little-known Egyptians, was at last put on stand-by to end a worrying England run of only four goals in five matches. Lineker, scorer of seven of the country's last eight World Cup goals, was a doubt with a toe injury but recovered to take his place alongside the undisputed people's champion.

Yet, after all the excitement of Bull's appearance in the starting line-up, it was defender Mark Wright who headed the only goal in a stuttering England victory that ensured progress to the last 16. Another mish-mash of a performance - summed up by the ineffectiveness of wingers Waddle and Barnes - left the two strikers isolated, and Bull cut a dejected figure as he

108

was replaced by Beardsley in the dying minutes.

"We're through but I can't say I enjoyed myself," he said. "To think I have played in an England team who have qualified for the last 16 is fantastic. But I wish I could have played a bigger role. I never got the service I thrive on at Wolves, apart from one half-chance at the near post in the second half."

The result of Bull's disappointing last night in Cagliari was a quietening in the call for Robson to pick him, and he was back on the bench - albeit off it again in place of Barnes after 74 minutes - as the country's campaign really started to take off on the evening they beat Belgium in Bologna. For the watching millions at home, it may have looked as though Bull had produced the decisive swing of the right foot that despatched a memorable volley into the net in the last minute of extra-time. But the honour had, in fact, gone to his room-mate David Platt.

Bull, having played a lively part in the tense win, was upbeat afterwards and predicted: "We can go all the way to the final. We have reached the quarter-final without getting out of third gear." Perhaps the good-luck message Turner had rung through to him before the game - the manager was by now in Italy with his backroom colleagues Garry Pendrey, Barry Powell and Paul Darby - had done the trick.

Although heartily sick of the sight of pasta and longing for a good plate of fish and chips, Bull was in better spirits as the squad's criss-crossing of Italy continued with a flight to Naples in readiness for the last-eight meeting with the emerging threat of Cameroon. Again, there was to be no place for the lower-divisions' only representative in Robson's party but he was cheered to see Platt's goal and Lineker's brace of penalties turn round a difficult tie in England's favour.

The side, preparing for the arrival of wives and girlfriends, still weren't playing particularly well but had carried the flag into the semi-final for the first time since 1966. Platt had done so much to bring their challenge alive and a certain Paul Gascoigne was achieving great things along with Lineker.

Bull had inadvertently retreated into the shadows and knew full well where he would be for the game against West Germany in Turin; somewhere where he was likely to suffer a few more splinters! Sure enough, he was a sub - an unused one at that - as the full drama of a balmy July night unfolded before him. England trailed to a wickedly deflected goal, equalised with a peach from Lineker and then had Gascoigne reduced to tears by the booking that would rule him out of the final if England got there. They didn't. Waddle and Stuart Pearce failed in the heart-stopping tension of the penalty shoot-out and the Germans were on their way to taking the biggest prize in football from the spoiling Argentinians.

Home-time couldn't come quickly enough for Bull but, before he and his colleagues flew into Luton to a heroes' reception, there was the third-place play-off with the hosts in Bari. Five changes were made - including the resting of the spot-kick casualties - but there was no promotion for Bull, whose World Cup ended with another 90-minute stint on the bench. England gallantly lost 2-1 and, for one man, the road to Cannock stretched out invitingly.

From what became known as the heartbreak hotel, he reflected afterwards: "I came out here looking forward to scoring in the World Cup. That would have been something to remember as long as I live. But it hasn't worked out that way. I don't mind admitting that, when we step on the plane heading for Luton tomorrow morning, I shall be a happy man."

Wolves, having signed keeper Mike Stowell from Everton in the latter stages of Bull's Italian Job, completed another important piece of business shortly after his return. A 15-minute meeting was all it took for the striker - now rated in the multi-million pound bracket - to further commit himself to the Molineux revival. He was already under contract for two more years but added another two to the deal before leaving with Julie for a Cyprus holiday.

Bull was reported to be on around £2,000 a week at the club - a king's ransom by comparison with a few years earlier and by far the highest wage ever paid to a Wolves player. But chairman Jack Harris said: "If we can't pay him something like what he could get at Arsenal, Manchester United or Spurs, it would not be fair to keep him." Fortunately, Bull didn't want Highbury, Old Trafford or White Hart Lane. Or Genoa. No matter who might have tapped him up at Italia 90, Wolves were still everything to him.

Back from Italy with two goals against Oldham, this one his 150th for the club.

110

ONLY ANOTHER 27!

1990-91

As Graham Taylor was duly appointed England manager in succession to the departing Bobby Robson, Wolves players - new and old - were made to wait for their reunion with Steve Bull. After his lengthy summer exertions, he was given a month off to recuperate and it was August 1 when he reported back for training.

In the meantime, popular Brian Roberts had arrived in addition to big-money buys Hindmarch and Stowell, and Turner had carried out something of a clear-out in the wake of a promising 1989-90 season at the club. But Bull was staying put.

"Why should I want to leave?" he repeated. "I might be able to earn more elsewhere and pick up a big signing-on fee. But this is where my house is, where my family are and where I am among friends. All that is worth First Division wages to me. I suppose this would have been the time to move on if I had wanted to but I have always said I wanted to stay at Wolves."

Bull must have thought he was back in Italy on the Friday night Arsenal visited Molineux for Wolves' first friendly after returning from a training camp in Anglesey. Not just because of the sweltering weather but because he was named as sub! A toe injury prompted Turner to ease him back gently and he was again on the bench when the side travelled to South Wales to take on Swansea three days later. He went on at half-time with the scoreline goalless and promptly hammered a hat-trick past Wolves' former keeper Mark Kendall to announce loud and clear: I'm back!

Bull then scored two beauties in the space of a minute after Wolves had flown to Belfast to play a friendly against Robbie Dennison's old club Glenavon, and his quick return to the groove had considerably eased Turner's apprehensions.

"We were worried how Steve would react with playing so long into the summer, especially in the heat of Italy," the manager said. "That's why we gave him another couple of weeks off when he came home. But, if anything, being with the best players in England and talking to the top players on the Continent has done him the world of good. He has come back sharper than ever. He is making more good runs and it seems he has learned a lot from

111

being with England. He looks full of goals again."

Turner continued on an optimistic note after Bull had taken his tally of pre-season goals to six in five matches with another strike, this time at home to Chelsea. He said: "There's no reason why he can't go on to establish himself as a permanent fixture in the England set-up. What he has to do is set his sights on continuing to score goals for Wolves. His record in the past has proved that, when he does, international football comes his way, and I'm sure that will not change in the future."

Bull, who had a horse race named after him on the day he attended a meeting at Wolverhampton's Dunstall Park course, had already been sounded out by Taylor as part of the new national coach's efforts to become "the most track-suited manager England have ever had."

The ex-Villa boss had made it known he would like to see and at times work with players in their club environment and said: "Obviously with someone like David Platt, it isn't important because we have worked closely together. But I have never had the chance to do that with Bully and he is on my list."

Turner was armed with a five-year contract from the appreciative Haywards when he took Wolves into their second season back in the Second Division. And there were familiar noises from the man at the sharp end of his side. "The targets don't change," said Bull. "Twenty-five goals, promotion and a few more goals for England. I would be the happiest man in football if that little treble came off."

The campaign was barely five minutes old when Molineux's most familiar scenario was re-enacted; Bully had scored! The striker was on the mark again an hour or so later in the same home clash with Oldham to take his tally for the club to exactly 150 in 199 games but a spectacular hat-trick by Ian Marshall at the other end ensured kick-off day went wrong for Wolves as it had frequently done in the late 1980s.

As Bull clocked up his 200th League and cup appearance for Wolves in the following midweek,

GOAL-COUNT

149 - *Cook controlled cleverly and lofted a pass over the Oldham defence for Bull to bring down and steer right-footed into the far corner from 15 yards.*

150 - *Thompson laid off a short ball for Roberts to cross deep into the area, where Bull controlled and turned in at Hallworth's near post.*

Aug 25, 1990: Wolves 2 Oldham 3

WOLVES: Stowell, Roberts, Venus, Bellamy, Hindmarch, Downing, Thompson, Cook, Bull, Mutch, Dennison. Subs: Bennett, Paskin.
Goals: Bull (6, 47).
Att: 20,864.

so the side clicked with a win from behind at Port Vale, the striker making it three goals in two games but lamenting afterwards: "I might have scored eight."

Amid his double century, he still had not missed a single game through injury for the club because, of the nine matches he had sat out in nearly four years, six had been through suspension, one through an international call, one because he was ineligible for the FA Cup and one through illness.

Bull was again on the team-sheet, but not the score-sheet, when a Paul Cook goal direct from a corner earned a laboured Wolves team a draw at Brighton at the start of September, and the outcome was the same when Bristol Rovers escaped with a point after falling behind to Dennison's early goal.

After their high-octane start, Bull and Wolves had quickly gone off the boil but a boost had already come the striker's way from Lancaster Gate. He was in Taylor's first England squad - for the Wembley friendly against Hungary - with the managing declaring despite the naming of Ian Wright as a stand-by man: "There was no reason not to stick with Bull.

"It's encouraging that he has opened the season by scoring goals again for Wolves and he fully deserves his chance. I'm a believer in loyalty but not to the point of being foolish. Players will get selected for the England squad by their performances for their clubs. But they will stay in by what they do for me internationally."

Bull was in a squad now deprived of the retired Terry Butcher and Peter Shilton, and had been cheered by the opening weeks of the new regime. "I was impressed that Mr Taylor took time out to come and see me and I feel I will get a good chance to establish myself with England. While Bobby Robson might well have had his tried-and-trusted players, I think the new manager wants to gradually put a bit of youth into the team and won't be frightened of experimenting. The message to me was clear: keep scoring goals at club level and I will get my chance to do it for England. That's fair enough and I can't wait to get cracking."

The striker had the additional boost on match-night of being selected in the starting line-up alongside Lineker. And he produced a robust performance

113

in a 1-0 win secured by his strike-partner's goal.

Taylor, who had said before the match it was time "the fella had a chance," extended a consoling arm round Bull's shoulder when he withdrew him in favour of Waddle after 73 minutes. But there were more mixed reviews from a critical London audience, who had another glimpse of what this curious Black Country upstart was capable of three days later when he fired his side's equaliser at West Ham in a third successive 1-1 draw.

The trip to claustrophobic Upton Park brought a debut for Kevin Ashley, who had become Wolves' costliest-ever defender when he moved for £500,000 from neighbours Birmingham. And the quiet right-back played his first full game when he lined up in the side beaten at Swindon three nights later.

How's that then? Tim Steele is first with the congratulations for one of two goals against Plymouth in front of a delighted South Bank.

114

A 1-0 defeat not only left Wolves firmly in the lower half of the table but also brought home to Bull the extra "baggage" he was having to carry now he was a national figure. He was the blameless challenger in a County Ground clash which left defender Colin Calderwood with a bad knee injury, and was subjected to taunts of "Where were you in Italy?" from the Wiltshire club's fans. But he was unperturbed.

"One thing I am finding this season is how the World Cup experience has stepped up the amount of stick I receive from opposition fans," he wrote in his weekly Express & Star column. "But I can tell them: they only make me try harder. It only serves to wind me up even more."

Bull was sufficiently wound up to reverse Wolves' slide with two goals and an assist in the Molineux victory over Plymouth but Andy Mutch's satisfaction at scoring for the first time since March was quickly undermined by a back injury that looked likely to keep him out for several weeks.

Turner was experiencing a cruel catalogue of injuries and Bull himself had to be nursed through training with a slight foot injury either side of a Littlewoods Cup second-round first-leg draw at Hull that was secured by Stowell's penalty save from Andy Payton.

Bull had particular sympathy for his long-time partner-in-goals and said: "It may surprise a few people to hear that Mutchy and me don't see a great deal of each other

> ## GOAL-COUNT
>
> **153** - *With Cook providing the perfect pass behind Plymouth's defence, Bull ignored the time available to take the ball on and struck from the corner of the penalty area. It was the most difficult finish imaginable but the ball flew powerfully and with measured perfection into the opposite corner.*
>
> **154** - *A Cook corner was flicked on by Hindmarch at the near post for Bull to head the second.*
>
> Sep 22, 1990: Wolves 3 Plymouth 1
>
> *WOLVES: Stowell, Ashley, Thompson, Bellamy, Hindmarch, Downing, Steele, Cook, Bull, Mutch, Dennison (Paskin 76). Sub: Westley. Goals: Bull (35, 43), Mutch (44). Att: 15,137.*

off the field. But we appreciate each other's company on it. He has certainly helped me make my name and I hope I have helped him do the same." Of the first month of the season, he added: "I am typical of the team at the moment. I have times when I feel just right and others when I wonder what I am doing on the field at all."

Wolves clocked up yet another 1-1 draw when a Dennison equaliser rescued them on a miserable afternoon at Oxford, where Bull failed to impress in front of watching England No 2 Lawrie McMenemy. But he had good reason not to have made much impact. He wasn't fully fit and was being used on his own up front because of injuries to Mutch, Paskin and McLoughlin, and the fact that Colin Taylor - thrown on as sub at Hull in midweek for his debut - wasn't yet considered ready.

But, as September gave way to October, so the dry spell turned to a rich harvest for Bull. On the day of the launch of a "Wolves Greats" book that devoted a chapter to him, he scored twice against Charlton and hit the woodwork, then followed up in style at home to Bristol City four days later.

His 14th Wolves hat-trick should have been evidence enough it had been his day but he wasn't satisfied and even had the bonus of collecting £14 from the dressing-room sweep after choosing Thompson as the afternoon's first scorer! It was the second time in two games the old pals had shared all the goals and Bull's latest treble created some more astonishing statistics. In making Bristol City the first side against whom he had reached double figures over his career, he had also sprinted to the 11-goal mark in 11 games in 1990-91. Despite his earlier lack-lustre efforts, his goals added up to the best start he had ever had to a season and, as he once more looked down

GOAL-COUNT

155 - *Dennison curled over a free-kick from the left that was delightfully glanced over keeper Salmon by the head of Bull.*

156 - *Knocking on substitute McLoughlin's through ball and then realising he was running out of space, Bull turned brilliantly on to his right foot, left two defenders in a crumpled heap just outside the area and finished with the sweetest of low drives from 20 yards.*

Oct 2, 1990: Wolves 3 Charlton 0

WOLVES: Stowell, Ashley, Thompson, Bellamy, Hindmarch, Westley, Steele (McLoughlin 70), Cook, Bull, Downing, Dennison. Sub: Bennett.
Goals: Bull (10, 90), Thompson (58).
Att: 14,363.

GOAL-COUNT

157 - *Bellamy's measured through pass was taken in his stride by Bull before he steered a left-foot shot low into the far corner as the keeper raced out.*

158 - *Steele's far-post cross was controlled by Bull on his thigh and tucked gently to keeper Sinclair's left from close range.*

159 - *Bull cut in past David Rennie from the Wolves left and his low 20-yard shot somehow squirmed through Sinclair's fingers and trickled over the line.*

Oct 6, 1990: Wolves 4 Bristol City 0

WOLVES: Stowell, Ashley (Bennett 80), Thompson, Bellamy, Hindmarch, Westley, Steele (McLoughlin 85), Cook, Bull, Downing, Dennison.
Goals: Thompson (3), Bull (16, 67, 80).
Att: 17,891.

Getting in some more "flying hours" ... a victory roll after the completion of another hat-trick, this time against Bristol City.

proudly from the top of the country's marksman charts, he was described by Bristol manager Jimmy Lumsden as: "Something else. Brilliant."

Sadly, the scoring deluge did not extend to the Rumbelows Cup return at home to Hull, who went through on the away goals rule after equalising Tim Steele's early breakthrough. And there was further disappointment the following Saturday when they were denied victory in the Meadow Lane sunshine by the last-minute Notts County strike that nullified Shane Westley's only League goal for Wolves.

For Bull, however, there was compensation in the form of another link-up with his country. He was in the squad for the European Championship qualifier at home to Poland and was unconcerned by the rival claims of Wright and Beardsley. "All I'm doing is trying to put a few goals in for Wolves to make sure I'm knocking on the door," he said.

"Graham Taylor seems to like a big man in attack and I obviously hope that's me again. I have had a bit of a tough time with an injury or two but I feel fine now."

Bull, the only member of the squad in action on the pre-international Saturday that had been designated as a day-off for the top-flight representatives, felt even better when told he was in the starting line-up. And, as Player of the Year Mark Venus joined Mutch back at Molineux in facing the likelihood of a long lay-off with back trouble, Bull received pressure-easing words from his national boss in the wake of a newspaper attack on him by former England manager Sir Alf Ramsey.

The man who led the nation to World Cup glory in 1966 was reported as saying Bull should be dropped - an opinion that briefly took the player aback. "That's enough to make your confidence wobble," he said. "But they are only words, aren't they? What really matters is what the current England manager believes and he has made me feel I belong."

Taylor, who had watched Bull in the second leg of the cup-tie against Hull, said: "Steve has scored plenty of goals, yet, because he plays in the Second Division, he feels he has to justify himself. He believes he must score all the time for England and that people are waiting to step in. That's wrong. Goals aren't the be-all-and-end-all."

But Bull's more relaxed frame of mind - for the first time he was in the senior side for a second consecutive game - was not reflected in his performance. He had a poor game, missing one good chance with a first-half header before being part of a double substitution in the 57th minute. It didn't help his cause that his replacement, Beardsley, secured a 2-0 win with a beauty in the last minute, Lineker having kick-started England's night.

Bull left the stadium amid some dejection and clearly had a big battle to prevent his 13th senior cap being his last. Some were already writing him off and Taylor said: "If people want to think Bull has blown it, that's what they must think. Of course he was disappointed but disappointment is part of football. I'm disappointed for Bull but delighted for Peter Beardsley, who reacts so well to being in the squad and not always in the team."

The player himself returned to Molineux determined to earn another chance and said: "I don't think things have changed dramatically just because of this night." And, of the national Press, who seemed ready to pull down the curtain on the Bull era at international level, he added: "They build you up just to knock you down.

"Everybody wanted me in before the World Cup. Now they want me out. I suppose that's football and I have to live with it. At Wolves, I hardly have to think about where and when to run for passes from players whose minds I can read after playing with them for so long. It's nowhere near that stage yet with England. I'm not sure when Paul Gascoigne or David Platt or John Barnes are going to pass because we don't play together often enough."

Bull, who had confessed to some mental and physical tiredness in the opening weeks of the season, took out his frustration with a goal in Wolves' first win at Hull in 60 years - a revenge success that left the side fifth with 20 points from 12 matches. And they climbed another place with a Bull winner at home to Middlesbrough that Turner called "a class goal."

The club's longest unbeaten run in 1989-90 had been four matches. Now, they had quietly gone nine and their manager said: "We are better equipped for the Second Division this season." But he was forced to

GOAL-COUNT

160 - *Downing and Dennison challenged for Steele's cross and keeper Hesford's mistake allowed Bull to tap into an empty net.*

Oct 20, 1990: Hull 1 Wolves 2

WOLVES: Stowell, Ashley, Roberts, Bellamy, Hindmarch, Westley, Steele, Cook, Bull, Downing, Dennison. Subs: McLoughlin, Jones.
Goals: Bull (7), Dennison (55).
Att: 7,144.

GOAL-COUNT

161 - *After striding on to McLoughlin's flick-on to Downing's defence-splitting pass, Bull got close enough to see the whites of keeper Stephen Pears' eyes and then stroked a shot of Gary Lineker subtlety and delicacy into the bottom corner.*

Oct 23, 1990: Wolves 1 Middlesbrough 0

WOLVES: Stowell, Ashley, Roberts, Bellamy, Hindmarch, Downing, Steele, Cook, Bull, McLoughlin, Dennison (Thompson 85), Sub: Taylor.
Goal: Bull (61).
Att: 17,285.

119

remind his squad of a few home truths after a charitable home defeat against struggling Blackburn had made Frank Stapleton the second visiting player to hit a Molineux hat-trick in two months.

Wolves' strength had been, not only the goals of Bull, but the increased assurance of their defence. And the rearguard were back in mean mode in a goalless draw at Portsmouth that followed some interesting revelations from the corridors of power. Club president Sir Jack Hayward, speaking at a dinner in Wolverhampton, said two bids for Bull had been rejected - one of £2.5m from Italian giants Genoa, the other (much lower) from Wimbledon. "Having just bought the club for £2.1m," he said, "it would have been easy to accept the £2.5m offer, be in profit and leave the team to flounder. But we weren't interested in selling."

Bull, about whom an in-depth authorised video had just been launched, was already more than half-way to his pre-season goal target of 25, with barely a quarter of the campaign gone. He pledged to revise the figure if necessary around Christmas but said cautiously: "Of course I would like to think I will go on and score 30 or more. But you really don't know what's round the corner in football."

After picking up the runners-up prize at the Official Wolves Supporters Club's annual awards night, the striker discovered what was round the corner - another England call. He was named in a squad surprisingly including the 32-year-old Gordon Cowans for the Euro qualifier in Dublin and prepared to depart for the clash with the Irish amid a time of Molineux upheaval.

Paul McLoughlin's dissatisfaction with reserve football finally led to a transfer request, Venus was ruled out for the season with the injury that had raised some fears about his career and Westley damaged knee ligaments in a training-ground collision with John Paskin that was to keep him out for the season. On the incoming side, Paul Stancliffe was signed on loan and made his debut in a side skippered by Keith Downing in the absence of Hindmarch as Newcastle were seen off 2-1 at Molineux by goals from Steele and Gary Bellamy.

As international week arrived again, Turner - content at his side's fifth position - beat the drum fiercely on behalf of his 13-goal No 9. "I'm totally biased and totally in favour of Bully playing for England," he said. "I think he is ready-made for this game."

He went on to repeat his message that the player was staying put, although he this time qualified it by saying: "The only thing that might change that is if Steve wanted to leave the club."

Turner's rallying call towards Lancaster Gate fell on deaf ears as Bull found himself as an unused sub at Landsdowne Road along with Gascoigne and Tony Daley. And the manager saw the danger signs for his player as he said after the 1-1 draw: "Steve now looks like facing an uphill battle to force his way back in."

Bull, who consoled himself with the knowledge that there had been so few chances going that it would have been difficult to impress Taylor anyway, was looking for a pick-me-up when he headed for Leicester with his Wolves team-mates. This time, there was no Steve Walsh to cross swords with - the defender was ruled out by injury - but the home rearguard still achieved a shut-out and had the bonus of seeing David Kelly (also unemployed as sub in the Eire v England game) snatch the winner at the other end.

Bull had suddenly gone four games without a goal and, when Paul Cook celebrated his 50th League and cup game for the club by rifling in a tremendous point-saver in the next match - at Barnsley a week later - the striker was stuck in his worst-ever drought as a Wolves player.

But a fresh breakthrough was only three days away as Wolves made an early return to Leicester's Filbert Street ground for a Zenith Data Systems Cup tie. The match - the club's first to be televised live for seven years - marked Colin Taylor's first full game, but the main satisfaction was felt in familiar quarters.

Taylor's strike partner had been stuck on unlucky 13 for the season for five weeks, and said after steering his side to a first cup win in 15 months: "I had tried not to let the

> ## GOAL-COUNT
>
> *162* - *Dennison released Steele on the right for a fine cross which Bull despatched fiercely past Mike Hooper from close range.*
>
> *Nov 27, 1990: Leicester 0 Wolves 1, Zenith Data Systems Cup, first round.*
>
> *WOLVES: Stowell, Roberts, Thompson, Bellamy, Stancliffe (Hindmarch 62), Downing, Steele, Cook, Bull, Taylor, Dennison. Sub: Paskin.*
> *Goal: Bull (10).*
> *Att: 4,705.*

pressure get to me during the five games I went without scoring. But the fans have obviously come to expect goals from me and I didn't want to let the run go on a minute longer than necessary."

John Major had been installed as Prime Minister on the day of the Leicester sequel but Wolves were having big troubles of their own at No 10. Although Bull was now moving again, the total number of goals from the club's other recognised strikers (Taylor, Paskin, McLoughlin and the injured Mutch) was a paltry one!

Going into December, Bull was again left to carry the scoring burden as he rattled in both goals in a home draw with Ipswich to nudge himself a little

GOAL-COUNT

163 - *Thompson fed through a low ball and Bull turned superbly to control and hammer a right-foot shot from 20 yards into the bottom corner.*

164 - *Cook chipped forward brilliantly from a Mutch lay-off and Bull drove powerfully past the advancing Forrest on the run.*

Dec 1, 1990: Wolves 2 Ipswich 2

WOLVES: Stowell, Roberts, Thompson, Bellamy, Stancliffe, Bennett, Steele (Paskin 46), Cook, Bull, Taylor, Dennison. Sub: Hindmarch.
Goals: Bull (4, 78).
Att: 15,803.

closer to becoming the club's second all-time leading scorer. His Wolves tally of 164 left him fifth in the Molineux charts, with three of the four who were ahead of him, Jimmy Murray (166), Johnny Hancocks (168) and Billy Hartill (170), within touching distance.

It was also becoming obvious, injury or transfer apart, that Bull - once again installed as the country's leading scorer - would one day outstrip John Richards as the club's highest marksman. And Richards, for the time being 30 ahead on 194, said: "No-one will have deserved it more.

"Steve has done so much good for the club and, if he stays out of any serious injury trouble and remains at Wolves, he can set an incredible record that would obviously take some beating. I shall not shed any tears if and when he passes my record. I have had my time and enjoyed it. Now, it has gone."

As Bull pledged to try to score more of his goals in twos and threes, Wolves battled for a way into a promotion race that was threatening to turn sour on them. They had taken only six points from their last 18 and, although still fifth, were seven points adrift of the third automatic top-flight spot.

And, after the postponement of the home game with Port Vale because of snow drifts through which keeper Mike Stowell had to dig his way to answer an England B call-up to Algeria, there was another interesting development in the career of a striker Wolves had kicked out. Stan Collymore had turned up at Stafford Rangers following his departure from Molineux but Crystal Palace manager Steve Coppell saw enough potential in him to want to take the risk.

He moved South for £200,000 in a deal which left Turner to try to defend the club's corner. "There was never any doubt about Stan's ability," he said. "He scored some good goals for us both in pre-season last year and in a couple of months at the end of the previous season. But he had left Walsall for disciplinary reasons and the problem when he was with us was his attitude to training and playing. Things came to a head when he failed to

122

turn up - and we released him."

As the 19-year-old Collymore, whose Molineux tasks had included cleaning Mutch's boots, set off towards fame, fortune and a future English record fee of £8.5m, Bull spoke again of his intention to stay put despite reported interest from Everton.

"If I moved, I would be turning my back on so much - a club I love, a great team spirit and, above all, you fans," he wrote. "It would mean starting all over again."

Wolves' position deteriorated still further with a 4-1 defeat on the Oldham plastic despite Thompson's early goal, and Turner was longing for the reunion after injury of his long-established strike-force. "Andy Mutch is not as prolific a scorer as Bully but they are a good combination and he is capable of chipping in with 12-15 goals a season," the manager said. "Fortunately, he is making very good progress."

But, following a Zenith Data Systems Cup exit against Leeds on am icy Molineux night, Wolves revived themselves with a 4-1 win of their own. Bruce Rioch's Millwall were the victims on an afternoon best remembered for the two goals driven in by England youth international Taylor in the style of another Wolves striker.....

Bully was on the mark once in that last match before Christmas but the day belonged to his colleague,

GOAL-COUNT

165 - *Somehow, Dennison was denied by the diving Horne following a through pass by Thompson but the ball ran free for Bull to scoop into the roof of the net from six yards.*

Dec 22, 1990: Wolves 4 Millwall 1

WOLVES: Stowell, Bennett, Thompson, Bellamy, Hindmarch, Downing, Paskin, Cook, Bull, Taylor, Dennison. Subs: Steele, Roberts.
Goals: Bellamy (5), Bull (43), Taylor (75, 83).
Att: 14,504.

and Turner said: "Colin has proved in the youth and reserve sides he has that knack of scoring goals. Time will tell whether he can do it in the first team as well."

As Wolves fans welcomed a starry-eyed youngster to the fold, so they were criticised by Turner for booing one or two of the more established players. Dennison was attracting some vitriolic treatment from supporters, so was Hindmarch, although the experienced defender regained some of his stripes with a scrambled injury-time equaliser in the December 29 clash at Albion.

Wolves, who had come from behind even more spectacularly through Cook and Bull to salvage a Boxing Day lunchtime draw at Sheffield

Wednesday, stabilised their form over the Christmas period and needed to build on it in the run of home matches that took them into 1991.

Sadly, the reality was very different. A turgid goalless home draw with Watford had Turner sympathising with the paying customers, then Third Division Cambridge could even afford the luxury of a missed penalty in becoming the latest club to put Wolves out of the FA Cup at the third-round stage.

The manager, still riddled with a cruel injury list, redoubled his efforts at finding new players - a chase he acknowledged as having now demanded "considerable urgency" - but was at least able to welcome back into his starting line-up for the second weekend of the year one of the old favourites.

A back injury had ensured Andy Mutch was not seen in the senior side for four months from September but he was back with a goal for the visit of bogey club Brighton. Bull also hit the target but the slide went on with a 3-2 defeat.

For Bull, there was the chance to get away from the domestic disappointment when he was named alongside the likes of Ian Rush and Dean Saunders in the Football League squad to visit their Italian counterparts. "I didn't think I would see Italy again so quickly," he said.

Unfortunately, he saw it from a familiar vantage point - from the subs' bench, getting on only for the last few minutes of the 3-0 defeat in Naples.

Turner recognised the seriousness of Wolves' slump and made a double swoop on his former club Villa, first recruiting England under-21 midfielder Mark Blake on a month's loan and then, a couple of weeks later, splashing out £400,000 on Paul Birch. And the first sign of improvement came via a

More magic under the Molineux floodlights ... left-foot finishes against Port Vale
(above) despite an opponent's efforts to put him off and Leicester (below)
before Wolves' promotion challenge petered out disappointingly.

168 - *Bishop's dreadful pass was intercepted by Mutch and pushed forward for Bull to drive in for what proved to be the winner.*

Feb 2, 1991: Wolves 2 West Ham 1

WOLVES: *Stowell, Bennett, Thompson, Hindmarch, Stancliffe, Blake, Birch, Cook, Bull, Mutch, Dennison (Steele 75). Sub: Roberts.*
Goals: *Birch (45), Bull (49).*
Att: *19,454.*

1-1 draw at Bristol Rovers that was set up by Geoff Twentyman's own goal.

Wolves took themselves off to Bournemouth for a recuperative three-day break, which had the desired effect when they returned to become only the second side in 30 games to beat runaway leaders West Ham. Birch marked his debut with a goal and Bull, in joining Johnny Hancocks as the club's third all-time highest scorer, took his season's tally to the 20 mark during a period of fluctuating personal fortunes.

It was somewhat ironic that, at the time he was skippering the side for the first time - regular captains Downing and Hindmarch were injured - he should be dropped from the senior England squad for the first time under Taylor. Instead of being selected for the Wembley clash with Italia 90 sensations Cameroon, Bull was picked for the B international against Wales at icy Swansea.

On the captaincy issue, he revealed he had never even skippered a school team before. His international handling, meanwhile, left him quite philosophical. "I think I need proper games to establish myself at that level and what better way of doing that than playing for the B team and perhaps getting a goal or two? I have been assured I have not been forgotten."

Bull had rattled in seven goals in four previous trips to Vetch Field and his enduring popularity among England supporters was reflected in the extra cheer he was given when the teams were read out before kick-off. But he chose this occasion not only to draw a blank but to have a generally unimpressive game.

"It's frustrating and disappointing not to have done more and not to have scored but I didn't think I had much chance," Bull said. "I still get a buzz out of playing for England, though, and have to keep plodding on and hope things go my way."

Bull and his team-mates had to wait three weeks to try to build on their win over West Ham, a snowy blast keeping them sidelined until they made their first return to Newcastle since the historic trip there on the first day of the decade. This time, though, with Blake having gone back to Villa after his loan, it was a much more sedate affair that finished goalless.

Turner was in charge for the 250th game when Port Vale visited Molineux three days later and Bull scored twice to make the Potteries side the second against whom he had a double-figure tally in his Wolves career. The side came from behind to win well and ensure their manager had exactly twice as many victories as defeats (124 against 62) with the club.

Bull's brace, which left him alongside Billy Hartill in the club's goal-scoring list, meant only John Richards (194) now stood ahead. And the rampaging No 9 said: "I'm flattered when I'm described as one of the greats, even if I'm being compared with players I never knew and have hardly heard of."

Seventeen of Bull's 22 goals in 1990-91 had come at Molineux and he drew another away-day blank as Wolves were held 0-0 at Ipswich - the fifth successive draw on the side's travels. Wolves had fallen an astonishing 20 points behind leaders West Ham and were 11 adrift of the third promotion spot occupied by Sheffield Wednesday. But hopes of a play-off place continued to burn brightly following a scratchy home win over Leicester, in which Bull and Mutch took a little more revenge on Steve Walsh, the defender Wolves fans love to hate.

Bull's goal left him on his own as the club's second all-time leading scorer but there was nothing he could do on the following Saturday as Barnsley subjected Wolves to their heaviest defeat of the Turner era and the club's biggest at home

GOAL-COUNT

169 - *Cook spotted the first hole in Vale's defence and threaded through a pass which Mutch turned into a hard, low cross for Bull to slide in from close range.*

170 - *Cook added to that "assist" with the game's outstanding moment, receiving a half-clearance on the edge of the area and bringing the ball under control before lobbing superbly over a crowded area on to Bull's left foot. The rest was a formality.*

Feb 26, 1991: Wolves 3 Port Vale 1

WOLVES: Stowell, Bennett, Thompson, Hindmarch, Stancliffe, Downing (Steele 40), Birch, Cook, Bull, Mutch, Dennison. Sub: Clarke.
Goals: Bull (30, 42), Mutch (69).
Att: 15,919.

GOAL-COUNT

171 - *Stowell's big kick brought a misplaced header by James, leaving Bull to outpace Walsh and produce a fierce shot. Keeper Muggleton beat it out but the striker followed up to crash home with his left foot.*

Mar 5, 1991: Wolves 2 Leicester 1

WOLVES: Stowell, Bennett, Thompson, Hindmarch, Stancliffe, Steele, Birch, Cook, Bull, Mutch, Dennison. Subs: Clarke, Taylor.
Goals: Bull (5), Mutch (61).
Att: 15,707.

since Watford also won 5-0 there in December, 1983.

Mark Burke was drafted in from Middlesbrough for £15,000 and Turner recruited Mark Todd on loan from Sheffield United after a host of missed chances had cost his side a second successive defeat, this time under lights against Charlton at Selhurst Park in Mutch's 200th League game.

Wolves' season was at the crossroads but Bull had a massive double boost, by being recalled to the England squad for the European Championship qualifier at home to the Republic of Ireland and with another astonishing afternoon's work.

With a whirlwind 14-minute hat-trick in the first half of the home game against Oxford, he appeared to have blown away the gloom that had resulted in a gate of only 11,357, the club's lowest for two and a half years. Yet Wolves faded so alarmingly after the interval that they turned a 3-0 lead into a 3-3 draw that contained two Oxford goals in the last four minutes and caused an awful lot of bad feeling among fans.

It was a disastrous hammer-blow to morale and, after an angry fan had showered a depressed home dressing-room with glass by putting his fist through the window, the mood became gloomier still with a midweek defeat at home to Notts County.

> ## GOAL-COUNT
>
> **172** - *Cook set up the opener with a superbly-struck 30-yard pass to Bull, who rose perfectly to head across keeper Veysey.*
>
> **173** - *Bull's second was just as dramatic as he headed in a Thompson cross.*
>
> **174** - *With the Oxford defence still ruffled, a poor pass from skipper Steve Foster let in Bull and he rounded Veysey to score easily with his left foot.*
>
> *Mar 16, 1991: Wolves 3 Oxford 3*
>
> *WOLVES: Stowell, Bennett, Thompson, Hindmarch, Stancliffe, Todd, Birch, Cook, Bull, Mutch, Burke (Steele 69). Sub: Clarke.*
> *Goals: Bull (11, 16, 24).*
> *Att: 11,357.*

Although a Dennison free-kick rescued an unlikely point at Bristol City, where Cook was sent off for dissent, there was further disappointment in the camp when Bull was overlooked even for a place on the subs' bench for the following Wednesday's 1-1 international draw with the Irish. He took up the option to leave for home before the game even kicked off and said: "It came as a blow to miss out completely." Once more, there was nothing else for it but to submerge himself in Molineux matters.

Turner challenged his side to play like champions to achieve the 70-point target he thought might still be good enough for a play-off place - and saw them stockpile three of them with a thrilling Easter Saturday win over Ron Atkinson's Wednesday. Mutch put Wolves on the way with a goal after only

Highs and lows ... Bully completes his 15th Wolves hat-trick (above) but
his joy against Oxford is in stark contrast to the injury misery he
started to experience with this ankle injury against Swindon
(below) and a good old-fashioned remedy.

29 seconds and Bull hit the target for the 27th time in a season in which the team had taken four points off Wednesday and twice kept the 25-goal David Hirst off the score-sheet.

It was on the road, however, that Wolves needed to improve, their record of 12 away draws already a club record for a season and the highest anywhere in the country in 1990-91. And, despite an early free-kick goal by Cook, their wait for an away win stretched close to six months when Teddy Sheringham's 30th goal of the season condemned them to defeat at Millwall.

Bull, booked at The Den but an ever-present with the season five weeks from its conclusion, reached another milestone in the return match against Albion. This time, it was an appearance landmark - his 200th League game for Wolves prompting a time for reflection. "I could easily have been doing all this for Albion," he said. "It was their decision to sell me."

In a dramatic rain-hit derby in which Wolves had Tom Bennett in goal for the final 44 minutes after Stowell had been stretchered off with a knee injury, the striker was again close to a last-gasp winner. But his "goal," after Dennison and Mutch had earlier been matched on the score-sheet by Don Goodman and Tony Ford, was disallowed for offside.

A disappointing defeat at Plymouth three nights later in Tony Lange's first outing for 19 months, confirmed Wolves would be staying put for another year and the slide continued at second-from-bottom Watford, where the side's first penalty in 15 months - converted by Cook - was rendered academic by a Paul Wilkinson hat-trick.

Bull, pictured with John Major on the Prime Minister's visit to Goodyear, had gone four games without a goal and suddenly had problems of a different kind. He hobbled off after a collision with Ross MacLaren 23 minutes into his team's third successive defeat - this time at home to Swindon - and was doubtful for the weekend visit of Hull.

At the same time, Turner was effectively pulling the curtain down on the direct style on which Wolves had relied for so many of the goals in the magnificent Bull-Mutch partnership. The manager now accepted it would take something a little different to continue the ascent of the divisions and said:

"We have been very effective with a certain style geared to feeding the front two. But now is the time to change things a bit. Against better-quality defenders, I recognise we have to vary things, be more patient and pass the ball more, so we will use the last few games to experiment for next season."

A crowd of 9,799 - Wolves' lowest for nearly three years - watched the Swindon match and there were a few hundred fewer for the weekend visit of Hull. By then, Bull had suffered another international blow when left out along with Cowans, Beardsley and Waddle of the squad to travel to Turkey.

"I'm disappointed but not surprised," was his ever-honest appraisal. "I have not been used in the last few internationals and I have to admit I have not scored enough goals recently. I have lost some of my sharpness and my workrate has to improve."

Graham Taylor confirmed the player's England career was on indefinite hold and said: "Someone like Bull needs a run in the side but I have not been able to give him that. If you analyse his goals, it is amazing how many come from 15-20 yards with the power of his right foot. But those chances don't come along as often at international level."

Bull, predictably, passed himself fit for the Hull game, only to limp out of a dire goalless draw with a first-half injury. And, this time, his number was up. A pulled hamstring put him out of the following Saturday's defeat at Middlesbrough - the first time in nearly five years he had missed a game through injury. "It had to happen some time," he said. "My record of missing very few games because of injury is something I'm very proud of and I should perhaps be grateful it has come at a time when we are not involved in a crucial promotion or relegation match."

Bull also sat out the next two games as a season Turner admitted had gone "horribly wrong," ended with a point at Blackburn and a home win over Portsmouth. Wolves had finished an unsatisfactory 12th, a daunting 24 points off the final automatic promotion place, and Bull's haul of 27 goals (identical to 12 months earlier) left him third behind Sheringham and Hirst in the Second Division. The momentum of the club's rise had been lost.

BULLY'S 1990-91 STATISTICS:
Played 48 (43 League, 2 Rumbelows Cup, 2 Zenith Data Systems Cup, 1 FA Cup). Goals 27 (26 League, 1 Zenith Data Systems Cup).
CUMULATIVE WOLVES CAREER:
Played 246 (204 League, 12 League Cup, 18 Freight Rover/Sherpa Van Trophy, 5 FA Cup, 3 Zenith Data Systems Cup, 4 play-off).
Goals 175 (136 League, 26 Freight Rover/Sherpa Van Trophy, 7 League Cup, 4 FA Cup, 1 Zenith Data Systems Cup, 1 play-off).

RECORD-BREAKER AGAIN

1991-92

No sooner had the last ball been kicked in Wolves' ultimately unhappy 1990-91 campaign than there were more significant developments in Steve Bull's Molineux career.

The player had already described as nonsense reports that he had met Kenny Dalglish and then George Graham for transfer talks but the stories linking him with a move to neighbours Aston Villa refused to go away. Bull's response was to do all he could to underline his commitment to the gold and black cause. He signed a two-year extension to his contract that effectively ensured he would see out his playing days at the club.

"The fact is that Steve is perfectly happy with Wolves and wants to stay," said his agent and father-in-law Gene Dace. "He is determined to play his part in getting the club to the First Division."

His re-signing was announced on the morning - two days after Albion had been relegated to the Third Division for the first time in their 112-year history - that Wolves revealed they had lost £1.5m on their latest financial year. But it was one problem solved as far as chairman Jack Harris was concerned as he reflected on tying up the club's star player. "Steve wants to finish his career at the club," he said. "The deal takes him to 1996 and was the easiest negotiation I have ever had."

Bull was still a God at Molineux but his international career remained deadlocked. Not only was he left behind from the senior summer tour of Australia, New Zealand and Malaysia, during which Graham Taylor equalled Don Revie's all-time national record of nine opening games without defeat, but he was overlooked for the B international against Switzerland at neighbouring Walsall.

"It looks as if I'm out of the picture for the moment," he acknowledged. "Things couldn't have finished on a more depressing note for me and the Wolves team last season but I shall come back bursting for more goals."

The upshot to the alarming spring fade-out was that Wolves handed free transfers to six players, including midfielder Paul Jones and veteran defender Paul Stancliffe. Coach Barry Powell also departed - but for reasons left undisclosed by Turner. His leaving was a messy business, one certainly not

New team off the field ... lining up on the happy day of the Haywards' takeover are (from left) chairman Jack Harris, his son John, president Sir Jack, his son Jonathan and Billy Wright.

befitting the dignity of a man who had loyally served the club during three spells.

Welshman Chris Evans was recruited in Powell's place and Turner's low-key summer of signings was kicked off by the capture of his son Mark, an 18-year-old former Paget Rangers midfielder. There was an £80,000 splash on Kidderminster keeper Paul Jones after the patient Vince Bartram had decided to seek first-team opportunities with Bournemouth, and Andy Mutch, like his strike-partner, agreed a new two-year contract.

For Paul Birch, there was a particularly sweet prelude to the new campaign as a 17,612 gate - boosted by the return to England for the night of Bari's £5.5m signing David Platt - turned out to see his Wolves side visit and beat his ex-club Villa 3-2 in a friendly. Wolves also filled their boots on a five-match tour of Sweden, during which Bull's goal tally climbed to six. But their domestic warm-up form was unconvincing.

Injuries quickly raised their ugly head and the loss of Shane Westley for several months with a fresh knee injury prompted the free-transfer capture, two days before the start of the season, of the veteran former Sheffield

133

Wednesday stopper Lawrie Madden. Wolves' central defensive turmoil continued when captain Rob Hindmarch - destined not to play for the club in his last nine months with them - asked for a move after a bust-up with Turner.

Bull, who had married his long-time sweetheart Julie Dace in June and severely toned down both his personal appearances and his media profile, went into the 1991-92 programme haunted by not having scored in his last six appearances in the previous term. And he quickly made his mark as goals by he and Mutch from Paul Cook set-pieces inspired Wolves to a cracking win at Watford that gave the club their first opening-day success for nine years and their first away League win since October.

Bull, who had profited at Vicarage Road from the sending-off of defender Joe McLaughlin and plundered his first away goal of 1991, struck again in a home draw with Charlton. And, when he followed up by sharing three goals with Mutch in a high-powered draw at Brighton, the old firm were back in full swing.

The gauntlet was again being thrown down to other attacking partnerships but Turner countered: "I don't know if they are the best pair of strikers in the Second Division and I don't really care. As long as they score 50 goals between them, I shall be happy." But the

GOAL-COUNT

176 - *Cook was again the creator with a curling free-kick and Bull was on hand to find the net with a glancing header.*

Aug 17, 1991: Watford 0 Wolves 2

WOLVES: Stowell, Ashley, Venus, Bennett, Madden, Downing, Birch, Cook, Bull, Mutch, Dennison. Subs: Steele, Thompson. Goals: Mutch (61), Bull (71). Att: 13,547

GOAL-COUNT

177 - *Bull prevented Wolves' homecoming becoming a total letdown with a magnificent knockdown and right-foot volley which equalised Robert Lee's shock opener.*

Aug 24, 1991: Wolves 1 Charlton 1

WOLVES: Stowell, Ashley, Venus, Bennett, Madden, Downing, Birch (Steele 83), Cook, Bull, Mutch, Dennison. Sub: Thompson. Goal: Bull (33). Att: 16,309.

GOAL-COUNT

178 - *When Venus again chipped over Brighton's defence, Bull was breathing down the neck of O'Reilly and he won the tussle for possession before beating Digweed with a low left-foot shot.*

Aug 31, 1991: Brighton 3 Wolves 3

WOLVES: Stowell, Ashley, Venus, Bennett, Madden, Downing, Birch, Cook, Bull, Mutch, Dennison. Subs: Thompson, Steele. Goals: Mutch (24, 74), Bull (33). Att: 10,621.

134

GOAL-COUNT

179 - *After a square pass by Venus, Downing flighted an immaculate ball over Foster for Bull to overcome a poor challenge by Melville, cut inside and hammer in a fierce rising drive from 15 yards.*

Sep 7, 1991: Wolves 3 Oxford 1

WOLVES: Stowell, Ashley (Bellamy 70), Venus, Bennett, Madden, Downing, Steele, Cook, Bull, Mutch, Dennison. Sub: Paskin. Goals: Dennison (2), Bull (8), Steele (42). Att: 12,549.

GOAL-COUNT

180 - *Bull's goal was more straightforward - a thumping finish after Madden had flicked on Dennison's corner.*

Sep 14, 1991: Newcastle 1 Wolves 2

WOLVES: Stowell, Ashley, Venus, Bennett, Madden, Downing (Birch 82), Steele, Cook, Bull, Mutch, Dennison. Sub: Bellamy. Goals: Scott (og, 49), Bull (73). Att: 20,195.

GOAL-COUNT

181 - *Bull made amends for an earlier glaring miss by tucking a one-on-one chance past keeper John Vaughan.*

Sep 17, 1991: Cambridge 2 Wolves 1

WOLVES: Stowell, Ashley, Venus, Bennett, Madden, Downing, Steele, Cook, Bull, Mutch, Dennison (Birch 61). Sub: Bellamy. Goal: Bull (76). Att: 6,552.

manager, acknowledging what was their best combined start to a season, added: "Mutch is looking very sharp while Bully seems all the stronger for his summer's rest. If they continue as they are, we will be up there with the best."

The first down-turn came in a home defeat by Port Vale - the Potteries club's first win at the ground in 64 years - but the following Saturday's Molineux victory over Oxford confirmed Wolves' place in the top half of the table. The win was sparked by two goals in the first eight minutes, one of them from Bull, but the side flirted with the throwing-away of a 3-0 half-time lead against Brian Horton's side for the second time in a few months.

There were more encouraging noises when Wolves won at Newcastle a week later, not least because the St James's Park crowd included England manager Taylor. He saw Bull score his fifth goal in six matches and was also highly impressed by the performance of Mike Stowell in goal. The striker had already been left out of the season's first international squad - for the Wembley defeat against Germany - but continued to do all he could at club level to support his case.

He struck once again in the disappointing midweek defeat at Cambridge and superbly hit one of the two goals that overcame visiting

Swindon on an afternoon when the absence of Mutch through injury was more than offset by Stowell's penalty save from Micky Hazard. Victory over the Wiltshire club kept Wolves on the fringes of the early promotion pacesetters but Bull's contribution to it brought a mixed reaction from the man marking him for part of the game, Glenn Hoddle. "His goal-scoring record speaks for itself but, for international football, there are other aspects he needs to work on," said the Swindon player-manager.

Closer to home, Bull was lavished with unqualified praise after hitting two of the six goals which made up Wolves' biggest win in the League Cup. Their 6-1 crushing of Shrewsbury in the home leg of a second-round tie eclipsed their 5-1 wins over Millwall and Exeter in 1968 and 1973 respectively and had Gay Meadow boss John Bond in raptures.

Bond, whose side had boasted the country's second best defensive record before the game, admitted: "I used to watch Bully playing for Albion's Reserves and think he couldn't play. He was rubbish and I used to say that. But, for the life of me, I can't understand why First Division clubs don't clamour for him. If Liverpool can pay £2.9m for Dean Saunders, someone can pay £5m for Bully. The massive difference between the sides was Bull."

The striker, like two-goal Paul Birch, went desperately close to completing a hat-trick against the Third Division side and was still being spoken of as an England possible. But he said in a TV interview: "I don't think I have ever got anything to prove. I'm here to do a job. I had a break in the

137

summer and that did me a world of good. Having a break of six weeks has made me feel better."

Bull welcomed a new partner in the aftermath of the slaughter of Shrewsbury - Wayne Clarke. Turner had responded to the loss of Mutch by recruiting a member of one of British football's most famous families, initially on a month's loan. The talented striker, 30, who had left the depressed Molineux of the mid-1980s to seek his fame and fortune with Birmingham, Everton, Leicester and Manchester City, was delighted to be back in the West Midlands and said: "I can't wait to play alongside Steve Bull. His record is phenomenal and I think we should make a good combination. It's time to come home but I know I have to raise some eyebrows while I'm here to bring that about."

The only emotion Clarke aroused was sympathy. His "second coming" with his home-town club was restricted to a paltry 20 minutes at Southend before he was led off with a fractured rib and collapsed lung. It quickly became likely he would not figure in action again in his month's stay. Nevertheless, Wolves climbed to fifth place by winning at Roots Hall with a combination of another cracker from Birch, Kevin Ashley's only goal for the club and Stowell's latest penalty save.

Turner was a contented man but voiced an unfamiliar complaint following the 1-0 Zenith Data Systems Cup defeat at Grimsby three days later. He had said several months earlier it was time a more cultured passing game evolved at Molineux but the tame exit at Blundell Park left him convinced his orders had been taken too far. "With the make-up of our side, it's no use making half a dozen or even ten passes and then still not getting someone through," he said.

The October 5 visit of Barnsley had a strong parallel with the 1990-91 clash of the two sides. Each time, Wolves went into the game in fifth spot, only to lose and hit the slippery slope. Unlike the 5-0 crash of a few months earlier, there was the boost of an early lead but Cook's first goal of the season was overturned by two from the struggling Yorkshiremen in a game in which Keith Downing was stretchered off to hospital with severe concussion. It was a miserable way for Turner to mark his 44th birthday, Wolves' defeat being sufficiently surprising for Graham Taylor to name Barnsley as winners of the Barclays Team of the Week award.

Bull, still without experienced support because of the injuries to Mutch and Clarke, had suddenly gone three matches without scoring. But that didn't stop the transfer stories. Manchester City were reported to have lined up a £3m bid for him but Turner retorted: "I have not had a bid from Manchester City. In the past five years, I have had a number of inquiries about Bull but he is still here. There's no change in our position and clubs know full well Steve is going nowhere."

For the first time in 1991-92, Bull's name was off the team-sheet when Wolves headed across the Shropshire border to complete the formality of progress in the League Cup competition now sponsored by Rumbelows. He was absent with a bruised heel and replaced by 17-year-old debutant Shaun Bradbury in a second leg Wolves were thankful to lose only 3-1. But the colourful Bond still made him the main theme of his post-match address.

"If we had had Bully, we would have won 6-1," he argued. "We could have gone in four up and they weren't half-chances. They were great chances, some with just the keeper to beat. Bully would have sneaked three or four of them in, no danger."

Bull recovered in time to turn out four days later at Middlesbrough in a repeat of one of the fixtures he had missed at the end of 1990-91. Neither he nor his side scored but the point they gained raised their spirits after three straight defeats and put a dent in the run of ten successive Ayresome Park League victories which had given early leaders Boro the country's best home record.

Another international date came and went without Bull when England took on Turkey in midweek but there was a boost for the striker shortly afterwards on his own doorstep. Mutch returned in the reserves after injury and his first hat-trick for the club had him pencilled in for duty for the following Saturday's first-team trip to Leicester. The Filbert Street duel was the duo's first game together in a month but the experience was an unhappy one with a 3-0 defeat and an early return to the treatment table for both players.

They were back in harness for the disappointing home draw with promoted Tranmere a week later but these were trying times for both they and the club. Wolves had drawn two and lost four of their last six matches in a run in which Bull's sequence without a goal had become his longest since he left Albion. He had again gone six games without hitting the target but this time the goal-less minutes he had actually spent on the pitch stretched to 603, rather than the 508 that marked his unhappy end to 1990-91.

Bull, in contrast to the 19 goals already managed by Tranmere's John Aldridge, was stuck on nine while Mutch had not scored in six outings going back to the second Saturday of the season. It all provided an unhappy backcloth to Wolves' third-round Rumbelows League Cup trip to Everton, where the satisfaction of a first-half Bull equaliser was quickly lost in a 4-1 defeat. The tie was billed as the clash between two of Taylor's early England casualties and, with Peter Beardsley wriggling through brilliantly near the end to follow Bull to the ten-goal mark for the season, individual honours at least were even.

Wolves, eliminated at or before the third round of the competition for the 12th successive season since they won it in 1980, broke more unwanted ground when they headed for Plymouth three days later. On the afternoon of England's defeat in the rugby union World Cup final, they were without both Bull and Mutch through injury - and the performance from the side in their absence was a dismal one.

Wolves' 1-0 defeat against the division's bottom club sent them plummeting to 16th place in the table and was enough to have some of their disillusioned travelling fans chanting "Turner must go" as they filed out of Home Park. It was the biggest show yet of discontent but chairman Jack Harris said: "Twelve months ago, Graham was the best and everyone was screaming at us to give him a long-term contract. We have recently lost a few matches and this was a lamentable performance. But it's time for keeping our nerve and remaining strong."

Turner recognised the seriousness of the plight and called on his chastened players to display their character as he said: "There's pressure on us now. We can all play football when the goals are flying in and we are playing well. But, when the chips are down, it sorts the men from the boys."

GOAL-COUNT

185 - Bull swept home a right-foot shot from near the penalty spot after Birch had sent Mutch away to provide an intelligent early cross.

Oct 30, 1991: Everton 4 Wolves 1, Rumbelows Cup third round.

WOLVES: Stowell, Ashley, Venus, Bennett, Madden, Downing, Birch, Steele, Bull, Mutch, Dennison. Subs: Bellamy, Thompson.
Goal: Bull (22).
Att: 19,065.

Back in business ... Bull celebrates his Rumbelows Cup equaliser at Everton - his first goal for seven matches.

The manager described the result of the forthcoming home game against the new occupants of the bottom spot, Bristol Rovers, as "absolutely vital." And Molineux had an unusual look for the Bonfire Night clash because the much-loved North Bank - closed for safety reasons since the 1985 Bradford fire disaster - had been demolished.

Sir Jack Hayward, finally recognising there was no-one to finance the stadium's much-needed redevelopment but himself, had duly acquired ownership from previous landlords Wolverhampton Council and had promised Wolves fans a stadium to be proud of. But the team were a different matter as, despite two specials from a partially-fit Bull, they slid to a miserable defeat in front of their smallest crowd for three and a half years.

The club's multi-millionaire president flew back to the Bahamas next day but not before firing a warning shot across Turner's bows. He used adjectives like disastrous and devastating to describe the nosedive from fourth place to 17th and the exit from two cup competitions over the same 36-day spell. "I'm sure everyone else in Wolverhampton feels the same," he said. "It's frightening to lose at home to the bottom-of-the-table club as we did, especially as we had lost as well at Plymouth on Saturday. I saw that game and our display was pathetic. The manager has got to meet us and explain what's happening on the field."

Wolves' nine-game sequence without a victory was their worst since Tommy Docherty's side had suffered a trot of 21 successive win-less matches in 1984-85. Turner, having recalled Paul McLoughlin from a fruitful loan spell at Walsall and put into motion plans to borrow Derek Mountfield from Aston Villa, declined to comment on the security of his position, but debate was starting to rage over whether Bull - now nearing five years at the club - would grow tired of playing in a side whom he had clearly outgrown.

At the Bristol Rovers game, Villa had Dave Sexton and Brian Whitehouse watching from the John Ireland Stand, along with a Manchester United representative, and fans started to worry whether one of the many

141

inquiries for the striker would lead to something more concrete. One extremely prominent ex-Wolves player argued it was time for Bull to seek fresh pastures if the club missed promotion again while popular former defender George Berry said: "The decision has to be made whether to sell Steve Bull for £2m-plus and build a new team or take the plunge and spend money perhaps they don't have to give Bully the support he needs. One thing is certain: they can't stay as they are."

Those of us who suggested the striker would be seen as unambitious if he didn't pursue top-flight football while he was in his prime, were soon made fully aware of the powerful views of the majority. An Express & Star readers' vote on the issue came down six-to-one in favour of the player staying. But, with neither Bull nor the rest of the side able to stave off further punishment when Derby scored twice in the last five minutes to run out 3-2 winners of a Molineux thriller marred by the sending-off of Madden, the spotlight swung back towards Turner.

And the manager was relieved to hear the increasingly strong voice of Jonathan Hayward in the aftermath of an eighth loss in ten games. Not only did the vice-chairman repel the growing calls for Turner's departure but gave him a massive vote of confidence by insisting: "There's no-one better equipped to take us to the First Division.

"Graham Turner has led this club from the depths of despair. We are engaged in a long-term project to rebuild Wolves but people should realise there's not another £8.5m round the corner for the team. There's a lot of hard work to be done and nothing that happened in this game indicated to me that Graham should not be the man to do it."

Turner's transfer market forays were being severely restricted by the huge outlay on the stadium redevelopment but he didn't lack support in the dressing-room. Bull was a known ally of his manager while popular midfielder Downing said: "We are well aware of all the comments that have been made. The boss has handled it all very well, kept himself to himself and not shown any signs of being worried by the pressure. His job may be on the line but everyone is working hard for him."

At the end of a week marked by the late Gary Lineker equaliser in Poland that took Taylor's England into the European Championships finals in Sweden, Wolves slumped one more place in the table to 20th with their odd-goal defeat at Millwall. After their long wait for a penalty, they had now been awarded two dodgy ones in successive weekends - this second one converted by Cook at the second attempt. But still the slide went on.

The anti-Turner brigade based their arguments not only on the current run of nine defeats in 11 games but on the broader picture provided by

Wolves' form over 46 League games stretching back a year. That cross-section of "progress" showed an abysmal record of 11 wins, 17 draws and 18 defeats - results that made the club the second worst Second Division side after Plymouth over a full year.

Bull's fifth anniversary was marked by Wolves slipping into the bottom four, courtesy of Newcastle's midweek victory over Southend, and the gloom deepened with a home defeat against Ipswich despite the early boost of Birch's goal. It was the signal for Sir Jack - now back in the Bahamas - to make an unscheduled return and convene an emergency session with his board.

"I feel very deeply about what is happening and do not want to be seen to be doing nothing thousands of miles away," he said as he prepared to fly into Gatwick prior to the midweek home game with Grimsby. And he carried to unusual lengths his wish to see the crisis as it really was, donning his brown raincoat to watch an uninspiring 2-1 victory from the sparsely-populated South Bank terraces.

The multi-millionaire paid his £4 admission and pushed his way through the OAPs' turnstile to witness the end of the slump at the expense of the side who had started it. He admitted after seeing Birch's late winner that the game still hadn't been very good and then explained why he had held a lengthy talk-in with a dozen supporters afterwards. "They know far more about football than I do. But I don't think they knew who I was until someone came up and starting taking photographs," he said.

With Sir Jack's son Jonathan having stressed a decision on Turner's future would be taken on the strength of what had happened over many months, not just a few weeks, the manager's prospects seemed as bleak as the November weather before the following day's board meeting.

But the smiles on the faces of the arriving central characters in the plot suggested a vote of confidence was on the way. Turner spotted his former midfielder Robert Kelly among the waiting Press corps as he entered Molineux and even joked to the fledgling Express & Star news reporter: "Make sure you get my age right!"

Turner, who won the admiration of the assembled board by taking all the criticism himself and deflecting it away from his under-fire coach Garry Pendrey, duly survived a five-hour meeting with a "Must do better" warning - but promptly missed out on a £250,000 signing as Leicester striker David Kelly chose Newcastle ahead of Wolves and Sunderland. At the time local boy Nicky Clarke was sold to Mansfield, Turner landed Darren Simkin from Blakenall before seeing the side's plight worsen again with a 1-0 defeat at Portsmouth.

Face in the crowd ... Sir Jack Hayward surveying the on-field crisis after flying in from the Bahamas to pay to watch from the South Bank terraces.

Bull missed the match at Fratton Park through heel and ankle injuries but Turner quickly played down fears of a lengthy absence. "To suggest Steve will be missing for three months is wide of the mark," he said. And, to underline the point, the ever-popular No 9 was pencilled in for a return soon after Wolves had conjured up a late Cook winner at home to a nine-man Sunderland side in which Don Goodman was making his debut after a £1m move from Albion. The pitiful struggle to break down a team hit by the sendings-off in the first 11 minutes of John Byrne and Gordon Armstrong brought out the anger in the Molineux crowd but there was an up-beat mood in the follow-up match at rain-lashed Port Vale on the last Saturday before Christmas. Bull ended his 46-day famine with an early breakthrough and the home side's late equaliser would have been no more than a consolation had Cook not seen a second-half

GOAL-COUNT

188 - *Bull gave Wolves the lead with a powerful right-foot shot on the run.*

Dec 21, 1991: Port Vale 1 Wolves 1

WOLVES: Stowell, Ashley, Venus, Bennett, Madden, Mountfield, Birch, Cook, Bull, Mutch, Thompson. Subs: Burke, Taylor. Goal: Bull (13). Att: 8,480.

144

penalty saved by Mark Grew.

Wolves had at least broken a distressing sequence of five successive defeats and they carried their improved form into a Boxing Day 0-0 draw at home to Kenny Dalglish's Blackburn table-toppers, whose spending spree was being called incredible even then, although it was still in its infancy around the £5m mark.

Wolves were still bogged down in the lower reaches but finally made a serious upwards move as goals by Burke and Mutch - the latter scoring his first at Molineux in 1991-92 and his first anywhere in 15 appearances - helped them to their first-ever League win over Brighton, at the 14th attempt. It was the team's first win by more than the odd goal for three months and, when they went into the New Year with a victory at Grimsby by the same scoreline, they were sitting comfortably in mid-table.

> ## GOAL-COUNT
>
> *189* - *By his standards, Bull has had a bad run but fiercely despatched a chance teed up by Steve Gatting's carelessness and Birch's quick thinking.*
>
> *Jan 15, 1992: Charlton 0 Wolves 2*
>
> *WOLVES: Stowell, Ashley, Venus, Bennett, Madden, Mountfield, Birch, Cook, Bull, Mutch, Thompson. Subs: Dennison, Burke. Goals: Bull (42), Bennett (85). Att: 5,703.*

Turner repeated his belief that his side were potentially a top-six outfit and, after granting former skipper Gary Bellamy's transfer request, saw them produce a heroic performance in defeat in their FA Cup third-round tie at Nottingham Forest.

Bull was guilty of a couple of glaring misses at the City Ground but, following the side's 11-day lay-off, exploded back into life with the first of the two goals that saw off Charlton in an impressive team display at neutral Upton Park. While Tom Bennett used a happy evening to score his first goal for the club in three and a half years, Bull was nudging ever closer to his 150th League goal and the 195th Wolves goal that would sweep him past John Richards' tally.

His totals clicked on to 149 and 190 respectively as he hooked in one of Wolves' three that saw off

> ## GOAL-COUNT
>
> *190* - *Venus set up Thompson for a left-wing centre which Bull chested down and turned past Waugh from close range.*
>
> *Jan 18, 1992: Wolves 3 Watford 0*
>
> *WOLVES: Stowell, Ashley, Venus, Bennett, Madden, Mountfield, Birch, Cook, Bull, Mutch (Burke 74), Thompson. Sub: Dennison. Goals: Cook (63), Bull (76), Holdsworth (og, 80). Att: 14,175.*

visiting Watford, his goal not only helping his side to a fifth successive League win without a goal against, but also putting him on the score-sheet in consecutive matches for the first time since September.

The day had sparked a curious response, though, from Turner, who tore up the protocol and insisted on receiving his January Manager of the Month award in private and not in front of fans now warming to his side's revival.

The out-of-sight ceremony was a sign of the rift that had developed between manager and fans but there was further celebration when a Leicester side managed by Turner's Molineux predecessor Brian Little were sent packing after Wolves had returned from a mid-season sunshine break in Gibraltar. They followed up a 5-2 romp over a representative side on The Rock with a narrow win in Turner's 300th League and cup game - yet another victory to be secured by Bull's finishing power.

It was the 16-goal striker's 150th League goal for the club, and a brilliant effort into the bargain, but there was a reminder of how far he had fallen from international favour when England manager Taylor spoke on Sky TV about the likely partners for Lineker in the forthcoming finals of the European Championships in Sweden. Answering a question about the claims of Rangers' Mark Hateley, Taylor hinted that David Hirst, Ian Wright, Alan Smith and Alan Shearer were the challengers, although he qualified his remarks by saying no player of international potential would be forgotten.

Bull, who had been watched by Dave Sexton in the completion of the double over Watford, received his usual pick-me-up from Turner, who reflected at length on his star asset's season to date.

"I would like Steve to be in the England squad but my main priority is to have him doing well for Wolves," the manager said. "Whatever happens above that is a bonus. If he can score a dozen goals between now and the end of the season, it will enhance our chances of finishing in the top six and, at the same time, help his England prospects. Steve has been nowhere near his best but he has just scored in consecutive games and that will have done his confidence a power of good."

GOAL-COUNT

191 - *With a brilliant example of his strength and single-mindedness, Bull brushed aside about four Leicester challenges in a packed goalmouth before rifling home a characteristic low right-foot shot.*

Feb 1, 1992: Wolves 1 Leicester 0

WOLVES: Stowell, Ashley, Venus, Bennett, Madden, Mountfield, Birch, Cook (Rankine 72), Bull, Burke, Thompson. Sub: Dennison.
Goal: Bull (36).
Att: 18,574.

As well as Bull's goals, Wolves had been lifted by a defence now figuring £150,000 former Villa and Everton stalwart Mountfield. Six League clean sheets in a row emphasised his impact alongside the admirable Madden and there was another addition to the playing staff when Doncaster midfielder Mark Rankine was recuited for £70,000.

But the wheel came off the revival when mid-table Tranmere scored both in the first few seconds and the last few seconds of a spectacular 4-3 win at Prenton Park.

It was the end of Wolves' 547-minute run without conceding a Second Division goal and, although Bull, Cook and Burke all scored gems at the other end, the repercussions of the setback were anxiously awaited.

Wolves had a recent history of turning good runs into poor ones and they could ill-afford the fortnight's break they now had between games. In the meantime, Bull was presented with Wolverhampton Sporting Club's Midland Sports Personality of the Year award and was given another nudge by his Molineux employers. Sir Jack Hayward had a chance meeting with Graham Taylor at Inverness Airport and reported later: "I took the opportunity to remind him both that Steve Bull has started scoring goals again and that Mike Stowell hasn't been letting any in recently."

Wolves' hopes soared even higher when Mutch, sidelined for five weeks with an ankle injury, returned as sub for the home clash with Portsmouth. And he said of his attacking spearhead with Bull: "For one reason or another, Steve and I have not fulfilled our potential as a partnership since we came into the Second Division. But we have had a good understanding in the past and it can work again. I firmly believe we can get into the play-offs."

Sadly, after the out-of-favour John Paskin had gone to Wrexham in part-exchange for midfielder Jimmy Kelly, Wolves did their best to undermine Mutch's prediction with a disappointing draw against Portsmouth at windy Molineux - and then in a wasteful 1-0 defeat at Sunderland, where they were sunk by a disputed penalty and Bull's unusual charity in front of goal.

By this time, the striker had been called up for yet another trip to Italy, as part of Glenn Hoddle's Second Division Select X1 to take on their Serie B counterparts in Caserta. But, to any hovering talent-spotters - scouts from

Milestone accomplished ... Paul Birch and Mark Burke join in during a familiar scenario, this Bully winner coming on a special day for the striker and manager Graham Turner.

Torino and Genoa were reported to be monitoring Bull's performance in the Italians' 3-0 win - there was a familiar message.

"They are wasting their time because Steve is not interested in playing abroad," said his father-in-law and agent Gene Dace. "It just doesn't appeal to him. He feels having his family and friends near him is important, especially as he is about to become a father in a couple of months. He is thrilled to bits at that prospect and is as committed as ever to Wolves."

March dawned disappointingly for Wolves with tepid draws against the two Bristol clubs, although Bull scored equalisers in both to equal John Richards' all-time club record goal tally of 194. Bull was the only Wolves player to have scored in a damaging five-and-a-half-week period and the club's defensive meanness had also become a thing of the past as they yielded their first goal at home for three and a half months.

Dissatisfaction was again filling the Molineux air and Wolves' players were on the end of some vitriolic blasts from their manager. Turner admitted the prospect of even a play-off place was slipping away and, with the relegation slots as close as those being occupied by the chief promotion-chasers, the main point of interest among the club's dwindling support was when and how Bull would make his next piece of club history.

He saw skipper Mark Venus drive in a second-half winner at home to struggling Plymouth before an unhappy quartet of matches against West Country opposition ended with a defeat away to an Andy Cole-inspired Bristol City. All Bull got for his labours at Ashton Gate was a booking but his big day came in the sunshine of Derby's Baseball Ground the following Saturday.

Wolves seemed destined for

GOAL-COUNT

193 - *Having squandered a host of easier chances in the previous match and a half, Bull latched on to Bennett's chip, capitalised on a rare slip by Osman and flashed a terrific angled rising drive past Welch with his feared right foot.*

Mar 7, 1992: Wolves 1 Bristol City 1

WOLVES: Stowell, Ashley, Venus, Bennett, Mountfield, Downing (Rankine 78), Birch, Cook, Bull, Mutch, Dennison (Burke 78). Goal: Bull (45). Att: 12,542.

GOAL-COUNT

194 - *In one telling thrust of his head, the otherwise subdued Bull directed home Ashley's excellent right-wing cross.*

Mar 11, 1992: Bristol Rovers 1 Wolves 1

WOLVES: Stowell, Ashley, Venus, Bennett, Mountfield, Madden, Birch, Cook, Bull, Mutch (Rankine 72), Downing. Sub: J Kelly. Goal: Bull (77). Att: 6,968.

---

defeat at the hands of Derby's newly-assembled £4m strike-force but, for the first time in more than a year, they came from behind to win, Birch clipping home a penalty equaliser and Bull hooking in his milestone 20th goal of the season less than a minute later.

It was only the second time in nearly 60 years the club's all-time goal-scoring record had changed hands, and Richards said: "The honour is Steve's for keeps. I don't think the record will ever be broken. The way football is going, there will be precious few players who stay at one club long enough to score this many goals. What Bully has achieved since he arrived at Wolves is absolutely amazing. The only surprise is that, considering his earlier rate of scoring about 50 goals a season, it has taken so long to reach 195. He has done everything expected of him - and more."

The Baseball Ground had become a notable venue for both strikers. Richards, as a County player, scored his last Football League goal there in

Right, that's the record ... history is made at Derby on March 21, 1992.

150

December, 1982, while Bull's solitary away goal for Albion also flew in away to the East Midlands club. The comparison in scoring rate was also interesting; Richards had taken 486 Wolves games to score his 194 goals as against Bull's 283 to rattle in one more. The present-day folk-hero had clearly benefited, statistically, from playing his matches outside the top flight but it was still a fantastic feat.

Turner, while naturally proud of the man in whom he had invested a meagre £64,000 five and a half years earlier, was angered by a Sunday newspaper story which suggested over the same weekend that a deal had been done "in principle" between Wolves and Villa over Bull. But his mood lightened slightly when told the report earmarked Mark Burke as one of the players who might be heading for Molineux in part-exchange. Burke had been a Wolves player already for over a year!

As Bull lined up in an awful goalless draw at home to Millwall on his 27th birthday a week later, I predicted he would take the goal mark to almost 300 if he saw out the remaining four years on his contract. And the Sporting Star that night contained an image of the man it would take to overhaul that type of figure.... "He would need to be blessed with the predator instincts of Jimmy Greaves, the skill of Gary Lineker, the height of John Fashanu and the single-minded dedication of.....well, Steve Bull."

Behind Bull's ascent into the record books, the season had turned dull. Five home games had yielded a grand total of only four goals - for or against - and it had become more exciting watching the growth of the new Stan Cullis Stand than it had the on-field fare. But that changed spectacularly when Mutch was credited with the first hat-trick of his senior career as Kevin Keegan's relegation-threatened Newcastle were run out of town 6-2 on a magical evening.

Mutch had scored only once in 27 appearances since August and was initially too embarrassed to claim his third goal after Cook's free-kick had gone in off his shoulder. But he was cajoled into accepting it by team-mates who had earlier taken the mickey to such an extent over his famine that he sent Andy Thompson to the bookies before the game to put £10 on him

GOAL-COUNT

196 - *Just when everyone was asking when Wolves last hit five without Bull scoring, the club's record marksman rounded it all off with a fine angled drive on the run.*

Mar 31, 1992: Wolves 6 Newcastle 2

WOLVES: Stowell, Ashley (J Kelly 87), Venus, Bennett, Madden, Mountfield, Birch, Cook, Bull, Mutch, Downing. Sub: Steele.
Goals: Mutch (6, 11, 85), Bennett (26), Cook (49), Bull (87).
Att: 14,480.

151

to score the first goal. At odds of 7-1, Mutch cleaned up and left Molineux that night with £80 as well as the match-ball!

Bull, who had scored the last of the goals against a Newcastle side whose attack were headed by David Kelly, was still seeking his first hat-trick of 1991-92, and Mutch said: "Bully takes a lot of keeping up with but I've never been known as a prolific scorer. Even so, I've scored 90-odd goals for Wolves now and I'm happy I've been a good servant to them."

True to form, Wolves came down to earth with a bump, beaten by a late goal at Oxford in what Turner called an inept performance and then pipped by a last-gasp penalty after Mutch's late equaliser had apparently salvaged a point away to Second Division leaders Ipswich. They were firmly back in mid-table.

Late goals by Rankine and Mutch then pulled a victory out of the fire at home to second-placed Cambridge. And Wolves gave their fans something else to cheer when they again hit back from a goal down to squelch to an Ewood Park win against a Blackburn side suddenly in danger of missing even the play-offs. Bull, emerging from a wasteful spell, took his career League and cup tally with his two clubs to exactly 200 with his sharply-taken equaliser.

No.201 followed as visiting Southend were comfortably beaten on Easter Monday but Wolves had, in the meantime, followed up their £20,000 signing of Burton striker Darren Roberts with their usual defeat at Swindon. And the last mathematical chance of reaching the play-offs disappeared when Bull and Mutch were unable to trouble the scorers in a defeat at Barnsley which marked their 250th and 249th Football League appearances respectively.

The impressive Mountfield was sent off at Oakwell and, when the curtain

---

GOAL-COUNT

197 - *Mountfield pumped forward a deep free-kick, Mutch flicked on and Bull turned brilliantly to rifle home a low right-foot shot.*

Apr 14, 1992: Blackburn 1 Wolves 2

WOLVES: Stowell, Ashley, Venus, Rankine, Madden, Mountfield, Birch, Cook, Bull, Mutch, Downing. Subs: Steele, Simkin. Goals: Bull (55), Birch (90). Att: 14,114.

GOAL-COUNT

198 - *Bull put Wolves ahead by turning well and driving home a low right-foot shot from inside the area.*

Apr 20, 1992: Wolves 3 Southend 1

WOLVES: Stowell, Ashley, Venus, Burke, Madden, Mountfield, Birch, Cook, Bull, Mutch, Downing. Subs: Steele, Thompson. Goals: Bull (37), Mountfield (52), Birch (60). Att: 10,953.

finally came down on the club's campaign, it did so in sensational fashion, arsonists causing £100,000 worth of damage to the Waterloo Road Stand and leaving 32 explosive booby-trap devices in the Molineux pitch the night before the home game against Middlesbrough. The attack was to be repeated two nights later as secretary Keith Pearson's office was destroyed and Boro's promotion-clinching victory - after Mutch had given Wolves the lead and defender Nicky Mohan had been sent off - became a secondary issue.

Wolves owner Sir Jack Hayward offered a £10,000 reward for information leading to the attackers' arrest but the search for them was to drag on in vain for years.

The same could be said about the club's search for the elusive promotion formula. Their defeat against Boro was their first at home for nearly six months but they had now had three frustrating years in the middle of the Second Division, and the Premier League was about to be launched without them. Bull had added another 23 goals to his haul - his lowest for the club in a full season - and a final placing of 11th in the table satisfied no-one.

The striker's impatience for top-flight football was understandable.

BULLY'S 1991-92 STATISTICS:
Played 47 (43 League, 2 Rumbelows Cup, 1 Zenith Data Systems Cup, 1 FA Cup).
Goals 23 (20 League, 3 Rumbelows Cup).

CUMULATIVE WOLVES CAREER:
Played 293 (247 League, 14 League Cup, 18 Freight Rover/Sherpa Van Trophy, 6 FA Cup, 4 Zenith Data Systems Cup, 4 play-off).
Goals 198 (156 League, 26 Freight Rover/Sherpa Van Trophy, 10 League Cup, 4 FA Cup, 1 Zenith Data Systems Cup, 1 play-off).

A CRISIS OVERCOME

1992-93

For the first time in more than half a decade of astounding success, Steve Bull seriously considered his Wolves future in the summer of 1992. But the doubts didn't last long.

At 27, the player, who became a father for the first time in the close season, realised the time for a big-money move to an established top-flight club would soon pass him by - and asked for a meeting with Graham Turner. It was one of football's worst-kept secrets that Villa manager Ron Atkinson would buy Bull given half a chance. And the striker, if not swayed by the interest and by Wolves' lack of progress on the pitch, was at least considering his options. Not for long, though.

A day later, on Thursday, May 28, he made it clear he was going nowhere and his father-in-law Gene Dace emerged from the tense talks to say: "Steve has given the matter an awful lot of thought and he's quite happy to stay. He's still very popular here, not only with the fans but also the rest of the staff, and the club have always made it clear they don't want him to go. He's very happy with the situation."

Bull subsequently signed improved, but not extended, terms while, off the field, Wolves suddenly parted company with commercial manager Keith Butler. Gary Leaver was upgraded to the post, David Clayton was drafted in as director of marketing and public affairs, Keith Pearson graduated to company secretary and a directorship, and, following the surprise standing-down of Jack Harris in favour of a routine seat on the board, Jonathan Hayward became one of the Football League's youngest chairmen. "The name may change but the aims remain the same - to make this club a major force in football again," said the 35-year-old.

Express & Star reporter Robert Kelly returned to the club as a coach and Wolves strengthened a strong link with the more distant past by giving former manager Stan Cullis a testimonial game against Villa at which he cut the ribbon in front of the stand now bearing his name.

Bull, typically, used the happy Sunday lunchtime occasion to further endear himself to Wolves fans with two goals in an exciting draw. It was fitting, with the North Bank end of Molineux populated again after the seven-year gap that followed the Bradford fire tragedy, that all four goals should be scored in that net, the last two of them by the man Villa were prepared to break the bank for.

Until then, Wolves' build-up had been unimpressive. They lost at Shrewsbury and, in a testimonial for Kenny Hibbitt, went down at Walsall after returning home from a mixed tour of Scotland. There was also a home defeat against Arsenal for a squad who had cast off Brian Roberts and Tony Lange since the end of 1991-92.

But the glut of season ticket sales, many of them for the Stan Cullis Stand, enabled the club to recruit left-back Paul Edwards from Coventry and central defender Paul Blades from Norwich in loan deals that were to lead several weeks later to permanent moves of £100,000 and £325,000 respectively.

And, when it really mattered, Wolves got it right. Bull, who had invested in one of Molineux's £8,000 John Ireland Stand boxes for the match-day comfort of his family and friends, came haring out of the starting stalls as usual as his side kicked off with a 2-0 win at newly-promoted Brentford.

200 up ... Steve Bull slides his shot round keeper Carl Muggleton and into the net to open the scoring against Leicester in Wolves' first home League game of 1992-93. It completed his double century of goals for the club.

GOAL-COUNT

199 - *Downing pushed the ball into the inside-right channel, where Bull needed no further invitation to unleash a fierce right-foot shot from 15 yards that beat Benstead at his near post.*

Aug 15, 1992: Brentford 0 Wolves 2

WOLVES: Stowell, Ashley, Thompson, Downing, Westley, Blades, Birch, Cook, Bull, Mutch, Dennison. Subs: Roberts, Edwards.
Goals: Dennison (47), Bull (54).
Att: 9,069.

Bull and Robbie Dennison plundered the second-half goals that saw off the reigning Third Division champions on an afternoon when Shane Westley returned after an absence of nearly two years with knee trouble. Sadly, Wolves had been deprived of Tim Steele and would-be skipper Mark Venus because of knee injuries for several months, the latter missing out on a tremendous Molineux night against his former club Leicester.

Bull, again made captain, shook hands with his old adversary Steve Walsh before kick-off and promptly capitalised on the defender's attempted clearance to become the first member of Molineux's 200 Club. His double century of Wolves goals had come in only 295 matches and his menace so riled Walsh that the Leicester skipper aimed an off-the-ball blow that brought him a red card.

Wolves stylishly turned the screw on opponents against whom Bull had scored six goals in four Molineux meetings, although Mike Stowell had to make his second penalty save in two games before their best start to a season in 13 years was guaranteed. Bull, who described Walsh as a gentleman for going into the home dressing-room afterwards to apologise for his misdemeanour, was already on a high as he set himself another 25-goal target. "This is one of the best starts I've had and one of the best starts the club have had," he said. "But I don't take any notice of records. It's my job just to score goals."

GOAL-COUNT

200 - *Walsh succeeded only in heading on Thompson's pass and Bull chested down and squeezed the ball left-footed under Carl Muggleton.*

Aug 18, 1992: Wolves 3 Leicester 0

WOLVES: Stowell, Ashley, Thompson, Downing, Westley, Blades, Birch, Cook, Bull, Mutch, Dennison. Subs: Roberts, Simkin.
Goals: Bull (19), Mutch (38), Birch (90, pen).
Att: 15,821.

Turner had a glint in his eye as he looked forward to what he believed "could be a very good season for us," and said of Bull's latest milestone: "We should not be surprised by anything he does. It's a brilliant record in such a short space of time and we hope there are another 200 goals in him."

Wolves' players were enthusing over the new-look Molineux, where fans were now assembled on three sides while work began on rebuilding the Waterloo Road structure as the showpiece Billy Wright Stand. But, on a pitch that was a credit to groundsman Bill Pilbeam, Glenn Hoddle's elegant Swindon side ended Wolves' 100 per cent record in a 2-2 Molineux draw salvaged by equalisers from Andy Mutch and Keith Downing.

For the first time, Bull had been off-target but, with the first England squad of 1992-93 due to be named, the No 9 received a massive vote of confidence from Oxford manager Brian Horton. Hednesford-born Horton saw his side scrap their way to a 0-0 Manor Ground draw with the deposed First Division leaders but said of Bull's claims to a recall in the national side: "Why not?

"We're crying out for a replacement for Gary Lineker and a front two of Bull and Alan Shearer doesn't sound bad to me. His record is phenomenal. It goes before him. I don't see why being out of the Premier League should stop him being selected."

But Graham Taylor again overlooked Bull for the friendly in Spain and the player was left to find consolation in his club's first win at Barnsley for more than 50 years. Paul Birch's superb goal and the frequent intervention of the woodwork trawled in three more points on a night when manager Turner dented egos by dropping three players, including Paul Cook.

Landmarks and records came thick and fast in the opening weeks, with Turner's best start to a Wolves campaign marked by a treble milestone in the exciting home win over Peterborough. Mutch's first goal of the afternoon took his combined goal tally with Bull to exactly 300 while his second not only made him the 15th player to achieve a century of Wolves goals but also confirmed Turner's 150th win as manager.

Wolves, with Bull on target again, were back up to third but drew a blank in a goalless return match at Leicester in the former Albion striker's 300th game in the famous gold and black.

> ## *GOAL-COUNT*
>
> *201* - *Cook's diagonal pass from the left was beautifully weighted and Bull took advantage of a rebound off Ronnie Robinson to hammer a close-range shot past the helpless Bennett.*
>
> *Sep 5, 1992: Wolves 4 Peterborough 3*
>
> *WOLVES: Stowell, Ashley (Thompson 46), Edwards, Downing, Madden (Westley 57), Blades, Birch, Cook, Bull, Mutch, Burke. Goals: Bull (6), Burke (45), Mutch (48, 49). Att: 14,532.*

157

On its way ... Steve Bull is a study of concentration as he directs a header
out of reach of Watford keeper Perry Suckling for Wolves'
late equaliser in the September draw at Molineux.

Mutch led the club's scoring charts at this stage with four goals to Bull's three but, before sitting out an unnecessary Anglo Italian Cup defeat at Tranmere, predicted: "It won't last." And his words started to come true as Bull plundered two headed equalisers at home to Watford to scrape another point. The game proved a Molineux swansong for Westley, who was caught on video commiting a heat-of-the-moment misdemeanour and was subsequently sold to Brentford for £100,000.

Bull, by contrast, was rolling on and on, hitting the target again in a Coca Cola Cup tie first-leg defeat at Notts County before welcoming at his side Darren Roberts, a 22-year-old who made the most spectacular of full League debuts for Wolves for decades.

Roberts, who had combined non-League football at Armitage and Burton with fitting shutter-doors, stepped in for the televised Sunday derby at Birmingham because of an injury to Mutch, and promptly scored a 31-minute first-half hat-trick as Wolves blitzed their newly-promoted neighbours 4-0. It was only the third hat-trick scored by a Wolves player on a full Football League debut and the first to achieve the feat in nearly half a century, but he was in no doubt where most of the credit should go.

"The biggest help of all was playing alongside Steve Bull," Roberts said. "He never stopped encouraging me. Training with him has improved my game 100 per cent and to play alongside him is an honour. The Blues defenders were far more interested in marking him because nobody had heard of me. Bully never moans or talks about the England situation but I'm

GOAL-COUNT

202 - *Bull climbed to meet Cook's curling free-kick and headed home from close range.*

203 - *Bull came to Wolves' rescue when Dennison crossed well from the left and provided him with a virtual open goal to head into.*

Sep 19, 1992: Wolves 2 Watford 2

WOLVES: Stowell, Ashley, Edwards, Downing (Dennison 72), Westley, Mountfield, Birch, Cook, Bull, Mutch, Rankine (Roberts 81).
Goals: Bull (38, 87).
Att: 13,497.

GOAL-COUNT

204 - *Bull, having already brought a save from Cherry, hooked a left-foot shot past the former Walsall keeper following a fine build-up between Mountfield and Mutch.*

Sep 22, 1992: Notts County 3 Wolves 2, Coca Cola Cup second round first leg.

WOLVES: Stowell, Ashley, Edwards, Downing, Madden, Mountfield, Birch, Cook, Bull, Mutch, Rankine (Dennison 79). Sub: Roberts.
Goals: Bull (12), Cook (89, pen).
Att: 4,197.

surprised and shocked he has been overlooked for so long."

Roberts' immediate reward for his heroics was to be dropped for the meaningless midweek Anglo Italian Cup win over Peterborough. But he went on for the last quarter of an hour in place of Colin Taylor, who marked his last appearance in the starting line-up with his third and final goal for the club. Taylor's demise from an international youth career of rich promise was a sobering reminder to Roberts, the new pretender to the goal-scoring crown worn by Bull and Mutch for the best part of a decade.

Roberts was back in the starting line-up for the ugly goalless home draw with West Ham - a match that had the TV pundits questioning Bull's part in a flashpoint incident for the second successive Sunday. Criticised in some quarters for the typically full-blooded lunge that had ended Blues keeper Andy Gosney's participation at St Andrew's, the striker followed up with a running feud that ended in a yellow card for him and a red one for Julian Dicks.

By comparison, the subsequent Coca Cola Cup exit against Notts County at Molineux was a tame affair and Wolves had entered Turner's seventh year as manager on a faltering note. Although still unbeaten in the First Division and boasting their longest undefeated run at the start of a League programme for 30 years, they had slipped out of two cups at the first hurdle and had gone two games - both at home - without scoring, or threatening to score.

Mutch returned to League duty after injury to head Wolves' goal in a seaside draw with Southend and, when Birch followed up his ten-goal heroics of 1991-92 with his fourth of the new term, the side salvaged the home draw with Portsmouth that equalled the club's all-time best start to a season (12 League games without defeat).

Bull had not scored in four matches, though, and was facing another handicap - a recurrence of a heel injury. It was enough to cause his withdrawl from the Football League squad to face Italy's Serie B representative side at Bristol City. It was now more than two years since he had played for England and, hot on the heels of a glowing tribute from West Ham striker Clive Allen, Turner felt the time was right to promote his star

160

striker's international claims once more.

"Maybe he was discarded too early," said the manager. "If you look at his international record, it is excellent. Recent events have proved how difficult it is for front men to prove themselves at full international level. You look at the other strikers used over a number of games, even those who have played against Australia and teams in the Far East, and see they have found it very difficult."

Bull's club form had dipped since his exciting start to the season but Turner added: "I'm not unduly worried - and I don't think he will be. What he has to do is have a consistent run of performances and pop a few in. It has been suggested the captaincy is not helping him but it's nothing like that. He's just going through one of those patches."

For player and team alike, things got worse before they got better. Having become the last unbeaten team in all four divisions as a result of runaway First Division leaders Newcastle's shock home defeat against Grimsby, Wolves succumbed tamely on a waterlogged Millwall pitch 24 hours later. Then they completed a hat-trick of successive 2-0 defeats by going down against Derby and Sunderland, Don Goodman sealing their fate on an early-November night in the North-East with his 100th career goal.

Chairman Jonathan Hayward, having been elected to the Football League board of directors, wore a worried look as he departed on the short journey home from Roker Park to the Border Country, and two other men had particular reason for concern. Keeper Stowell had undergone an operation on his knee while, at the other end of the pitch, Bull - after his second successive wayward visit to Wearside - was in his worst goal-less run for the club.

Typically, he exploded out of his drought in eye-opening fashion, his two Molineux goals in Wolves' first win over Bristol Rovers in nine attempts making him the club's highest-ever scorer in the Football

GOAL-COUNT

206 - *Cook had Rovers back-pedalling with a headed through ball but it was Dennison who opened the visitors up with a neat diagonal pass. Bull raced to the edge of the area before driving a right-foot shot low past the advancing Parkin.*

207 - *Burke chipped in a neat cross which Bull despatched past Parkin with a brilliantly controlled first-time left-foot volley.*

Nov 7, 1992: Wolves 5 Bristol Rovers 1

WOLVES: Jones, Ashley, Edwards, Burke, Mountfield, Blades, Birch, Cook, Bull, Mutch (Roberts 58), Dennison. Sub: Rankine.
Goals: Dennison (8), Bull (28, 62), Burke (48, 56).
Att: 12,163.

History unfolding … (above) Steve Bull strikes one of the two goals at home to
Bristol Rovers that confirm him as the player to have scored more League
goals for Wolves than anybody else. Below: Robbie Dennison tries to
coax a smile out of the man of the moment during the celebrations.

League. With his first strike of the afternoon against the First Division's bottom club, he equalled Billy Hartill's 57-year-old record of 162 - then he beat it.

In 15 minutes against Rovers, Wolves had bettered their goal output of the previous seven matches and the following weekend's throwaway draw at Notts County showed they had rediscovered their striking powers. Bull and Dennison were again on target at Meadow Lane during a period of the season marked by modest transfer activity, the popular Gary Bellamy being lined up for a move to Orient while Lee Mills was recruited from part-time football in Sheffield.

Bull was back in the shadows as Wolves' season showed encouraging signs of an uplift with successive home wins over Charlton and Grimsby, the unsettled Mark Burke scoring in both to become joint second leading scorer with five and extend his record of having found the net in all the home games he had started in 1992-93.

Wolves were back in touch with the promotion-chasing pack and stretched their unbeaten run to five games as Bull's 11th goal of the season salvaged a point at Cambridge. "We're still in the top four or five, we're doing well and we're hoping to be up there so we can push for the Premier League," said the contented striker.

But Wolves' recent past was littered with false dawns and another was exposed when struggling Luton arrived at Molineux to overturn Paul Blades' first goal for the club and register a shock win. Then, a John Aldridge hat-trick at Tranmere and David Kelly's brace at Newcastle either side of

Christmas Day brought back all the old doubts. Kelly's goals - after Cook had put Wolves ahead in front of a Boxing Day full house at St James's Park - was particularly poignant as Turner had almost bought him 13 months earlier.

There were the loudest calls yet for the manager's dismissal during a dreadful goalless home draw with Bristol City while Bull, now replaced as skipper by the fit-again Venus, was in a poor run of form. "I know Steve enjoyed being captain and he has said he would be happy to take it on again at any time in the future," Turner added. "We have obviously seen him play better, especially in front of goal, but he will come through it."

For the first time, Bull's struggles were beginning to test the patience of fans consumed with the disappointment at the team's slide. But, as 1993 dawned, he was back in the old routine on the day Wolves recorded their first FA Cup victory since December, 1988. He scored one of the four goals that sank Watford at Vicarage Road, his record of 51 Wolves appearances in knock-out football bettered only by 11 players, headed by Kenny Hibbitt and Derek Parkin (108 each).

> ## GOAL-COUNT
>
> *210* - *Bull had a simple finish into an empty net after Blades had gone round Suckling following a through ball from Downing.*
>
> *Jan 2, 1993: Watford 1 Wolves 4, FA Cup third round.*
>
> *WOLVES: Jones, Madden, Edwards, Rankine, Mountfield, Blades, Downing, Cook, Bull, Mutch, Venus (Birch 32). Sub: Burke.*
> *Goals: Holdsworth (og, 13), Downing (69), Mutch (75), Bull (86).*
> *Att: 12,363.*

The third-round tie marked the first game together for Bull and Mutch for two months, the No 10 having recovered from injury and smiling afterwards: "It was just like old times. Steve and I really enjoyed terrorising a defence again, especially after the club's dismal record in the competition over the last ten years."

Wolves were back at Watford a week later on League duty and, as was their wont, promptly dismantled the optimism. On the afternoon Lawrie Madden (37 years and 103 days) succeeded Derek Dougan as the oldest player ever to appear in a senior Wolves match, the side crashed 3-1.

Bull, quickly restored as skipper because of a fresh knee injury to Venus, welcomed one of his former England squad colleagues to Molineux before the following weekend's Sunday win at home to Birmingham. Chelsea keeper Dave Beasant checked in on a month's loan and made his debut in preference to the unlucky Paul Jones in a game in which late goals from Burke and Mutch - the latter his first at home since September - gave Wolves their first League win for two months.

As injury-hit Wolves jetted off for a few days in the Lanzarote sun, they had seen the prospect of a mouth-watering Cup clash with Liverpool snatched away from them by Second Division Bolton's shock replay win at Anfield. But Bruce Rioch's emerging side still proved Wolves' masters as they rode their luck on a grim Sunday afternoon at Molineux.

Bull and Mutch, having survived a potential threat to their partnership when a move for Middlesbrough striker Bernie Slaven broke down, suffered more than anyone. Chance after chance eluded them, Bull in particular, and the saddest aspect of a desperately disappointing day was the booing heaped upon the striker in his own kingdom.

It was as though a little bit of love died for Bull that day but, in his admirable up-and-at-'em style, he quickly underlined his passion for the club. Asked whether he would brood over the reaction of elements of a near-20,000 crowd, he said: "I go home and think about it all the time and have grey hairs. But I take no notice and the next game is another day. I have three years of my contract left and I hope to have another couple of years on top of that and see my career out here."

Against a background of reported interest from Newcastle, Turner was adopting a kid-glove policy with a star some were convinced was starting to fall. The manager was again on the receiving end of calls for his own departure but said of a man who had scored a staggering 210 goals in 324 games for the club: "He has been absolutely brilliant here for six years and to turn against him would have a detrimental effect on the whole side. I think he can carry this and get over it. He is big enough and strong enough in character and it will turn for him."

Bull, whose booking in the Bolton game earned him a two-match suspension for February, admitted in the club programme his form had not been up to scratch in 1992-93 but qualified it with a remark that no-one could question: "I'm always trying hard."

Players and management alike were apprehensive at stepping back into the Molineux spotlight so soon but the 11,342 who watched the home game with Barnsley three nights after the Cup defeat lifted their spirits. They chanted Bull's name several times and, while they couldn't help him back on to the score-sheet, they at least saw him tee up Mutch's second-half winner.

Two successive League wins had reopened the door leading to the play-offs, only for misfortune and misery to return very quickly. Bull had another off-day in an ill-deserved defeat at Swindon and was then denied by good goalkeeping as a one-sided home game against Brentford somehow turned into a 2-1 defeat despite Mutch's breakthrough goal.

165

Wolves, having scored 23 goals in their first 12 games of the season, had managed only 25 more in the next 23, with Bull stuck on 12 and Mutch next on nine. It was with heavy irony therefore that the floodgates opened with a 3-2 win at Peterborough in mid-February on the day Bull started his ban. Burke, an own goal and Roberts made up the tally, the latter appearing on the score-sheet for the last time - with the first goal by a Wolves No 9 other than Bull since 1989.

The side promptly fell flat on their faces with defeat at home to mid-table Oxford a week later - their seventh loss in 11 League games - and a post-match 15-minute sit-in and march up Waterloo Road by several dozen supporters reflected Turner's demise.

At least Bull was now available again but the striker admitted in the club's newspaper before his return: "I've started wondering where the next goal is coming from. Deep down, it does worry me. When I thought about the crowd booing me against Bolton, it hurt. But I couldn't blame the fans. I might have scored over 200 goals for the club but, when they saw me blow ten chances in one match, it was understandable how they felt."

Behind the self-analysis, though, there was still confidence it would all come right again, and Bull added: "Once I get one goal, I'll get more. And I don't care how that first one comes. It can go in off my shin or my elbow for all I care."

As it happened, in the following Saturday's home game against Southend, it went in off his right foot in regulation fashion, and he sunk to his knees in relief in front of

> ## GOAL-COUNT
>
> *211* - *Cook's through ball sent Bull clear to lob cleverly over the advancing Sansome.*
>
> *Feb 27, 1993: Wolves 1 Southend 1*
>
> *WOLVES: Jones, Blades, Edwards, Burke, Mountfield, Madden, Rankine, Cook, Bull, Mutch, Dennison. Subs: Venus, Roberts. Goal: Bull (50). Att: 11,563.*

the Stan Cullis Stand. But Wolves threw away two more points, another demonstration followed at full-time and Molineux was a bitter place.

There was also sadness in the air when 1940s and 1950s star Roy Pritchard died at 67 at the start of March, his passing-away following close behind that of England World Cup-winning captain Bobby Moore. And, having drawn with the only League club Moore managed (Southend), Wolves then travelled to East London to face the side for whom he played for most of his glittering career.

Upton Park was awash with choking emotion and colourful tributes as Wolves and West Ham did battle in a match that somehow seemed irrelevant against its backdrop. Bull, however, used the occasion to score his 14th goal of the season before the claret and blue tide took over.

Bull confirmed his return to form with two goals in the midweek Molineux mauling of Notts County and, after his mid-season slump, had scored in three games in a row. "It's nice to see him back on the mark," said a relieved Turner. "He could still end up with 24 or 25 goals despite everything."

Mutch had been relegated to sub for the previous two games but was back in the starting line-up as Bull struck again in Wolves' usual 1-1 draw against Bristol Rovers at Twerton Park. Stowell had also been restored after his 20-game injury absence, with Beasant sent back to Chelsea, while, from the boardroom, came solid backing for the under-fire Turner.

"Removing Graham Turner is something I have not even contemplated," said chairman Hayward after a family holiday in his father's island paradise in the Bahamas. "And I have no intention of doing so. As far as we are concerned, Graham is the best man for the job. He is under no

GOAL-COUNT

212 - *Rankine pulled the ball back from the left and Bull let fly with a well-struck right-foot shot which flew just inside Miklosko's post.*

Mar 6, 1993: West Ham 3 Wolves 1

WOLVES: Stowell, Blades, Venus, Burke, Mountfield, Madden, Rankine (Mutch 75), Cook, Bull, Thompson, Dennison. Sub: Edwards.
Goal: Bull (57).
Att: 24,679.

GOAL-COUNT

213 - *Cherry and Palmer got in each other's way and succeeded only in prodding the ball down to the lurking Bull, who gratefully accepted the gift with a right-foot shot from ten yards.*

214 - *Burke combined with Cook and Mutch before his cross to the far post was precision itself and gave Bull a close-range header he gleefully accepted.*

Mar 9, 1993: Wolves 3 Notts County 0

WOLVES: Stowell, Rankine, Edwards (Mutch 59), Burke, Blades, Madden, Downing, Cook, Bull, Thompson, Dennison. Sub: Mountfield.
Goals: Bull (66, 89), Johnson (og, 78).
Att: 11,482.

GOAL-COUNT

215 - *Dennison delivered a superb 30-yard pass into the path of Mutch, who took the ball on before crossing to the far post - and there was Bull to head home from close range.*

Mar 13, 1993: Bristol Rovers 1 Wolves 1

WOLVES: Stowell, Blades, Thompson, Burke, Downing, Madden, Rankine (Mountfield 58), Cook, Bull, Mutch, Dennison. Sub: Edwards.
Goal: Bull (7).
Att: 5,982.

167

pressure at all from the board."

There was good and bad news for Bull in the aftermath of the game at Bath. His booking against Notts County was confirmed as being sufficient to take him to his second two-game ban in a few weeks but talks over an extended contract taking him to the summer of 1999 were at an advanced stage.

"Steve has agreed the contract and is happy about it," said the player's trusty father-in-law Gene Dace. "He wants to stay in the Midlands and he wants to stay at Wolves to what will effectively be the end of his playing career. There have been offers and, only a few weeks ago, a third party came to me saying Newcastle were interested. I put the offer to Steve, he had two or three days thinking about it and then said he wanted to stay at Wolves."

Bull, who could expect to be challenging the one-club totals of players like Dixie Dean (377 League goals for Everton) and John Atyeo (350 for Bristol City) if he saw out what was now the remaining six years on his contract, agreed the deal at a time when the Haywards' commitment to Wolves was reflected in a loss of more than £550,000 on the latest financial year and in the spiralling cost of the Molineux redevelopment - now something like £14m and approaching double the £8.5m originally touted.

Of Bull's deal, Hayward Jnr said: "I know it is a gamble and it could be a considerable burden. But this seems the natural thing to do. I want Steve to be playing for Wolves until 1999 and the combination of that and him being happy to stay led to the extension being agreed. He deserves to be looked after." Bull continued to make a mockery of his earlier troubles by scoring for the fifth successive game when Cambridge visited Molineux. Only once before (early in 1987-88) had he scored in more games in a row but Wolves' latest shock defeat plunged the side to 12th.

With their leading scorer suspended, the side produced a dour backs-to-the-wall performance at Charlton but had the bonus of an undeserved late winner from Dennison just before Birch was sent off for dissent. Then, Dennison and Mutch struck to send Sunderland home empty-handed in the game that

---

GOAL-COUNT

216 - *A left-wing corner by Dennison was deflected to Bull, who stuck out his right foot and netted through a crowded six-yard area.*

Mar 20, 1993: Wolves 1 Cambridge 2

WOLVES: Stowell, Blades (Mountfield 46), Edwards, Burke, Ashley, Madden, Rankine, Cook, Bull, Mutch, Dennison (Thompson 73).
Goal: Bull (66).
Att: 11,473.

marked Cook's 150th Wolves appearance and Birch's 100th.

After Stowell had signed an extended contract, there was more good news when Jonathan Hayward hinted at a multi-million pound summer spending spree. It was accompanied by the more coolly-received news that Turner would be the man to indulge in it, the chairman writing in his programme notes: "I sympathise with those fans who are used to the normal reaction in football that, when things get tough, you sack the manager.

"Unfortunately, you have inherited a chairman who does not believe in this philosophy. We have a talented team who, with the addition of a few quality players, will make the grade into the Premier League, and we have a manager I have the greatest confidence will bring all our dreams to reality."

Although Bull was back in the side at Grimsby a week later, Wolves' performance was one of which nightmares, rather than dreams, are made. A 1-0 defeat merely emphasised what a long run-in it was going to be now promotion was out of reach, and Bull's own campaign ended sadly at draw specialists Luton four nights later.

After scoring his first-ever goal against the Hatters to rescue a point on Darren Simkin's debut, the striker was led off by physio Paul Darby with the recurrence of an Achiles injury Turner said could take some weeks to heal. But, despite Bull's absence, Wolves collected their annual big-name spring scalp when they not only curbed the menace of Newcastle's David Kelly, Andy Cole, Robert Lee and Co, but also beat the leaders and country's top scorers with Mutch's tenth goal of the season.

GOAL-COUNT

217 - *Bull set off in what looked to be a futile pursuit of Mutch's flick-on to a long Venus free-kick. The home players complained bitterly that Dreyer was dumped in the mud illegally but Bull sidefooted gently under the advancing Chamberlain.*

Apr 7, 1993: Luton 1 Wolves 1

WOLVES: Stowell, Simkin, Venus, Downing, Mountfield, Blades, Rankine, Cook, Bull (Thompson 86), Mutch, Dennison. Sub: Madden.
Goal: Bull (81).
Att: 7,948.

Madden made the 450th League appearance of his career as Keegan's side were surprisingly outplayed but Wolves' attempts at a follow-up were pathetic. They lost to a late goal at Bristol City two days later, then collapsed at home to Tranmere to leave them closer - in terms of points - to third-from-bottom Birmingham than the sixth-placed Merseysiders.

When Wolves slipped to an utterly predictable third successive defeat - unable to prevent promotion-chasing Portsmouth from making it 11 wins out of 12 on a sun-splashed afternoon at Fratton Park - they were left 27 points off the second automatic promotion spot.

But two goals by youngster Shaun Bradbury on a dream League debut gave Wolves fans something to cheer when the South Bank terraces were occupied for the last time on May 1, 1993. Burke and Millwall's Malcolm Allen also scored in front of the massive bank that was due to go under the bulldozer in the summer and, when Wolves lost at Derby on the last day of the campaign on Mark Turner's debut, fans were hoping the same sort of demolition and overhaul could be administered to the team.

Bull had missed the last six matches of a desperately disappointing season and had fallen short of 20 goals in a full campaign for the first time as a Wolves player. But he was still top scorer for a record seventh successive year and the comings-and-goings in the wake of a miserable final placing of 11th would go on around him in the summer. After his mid-winter crisis, he was still King of Molineux.

BULLY'S 1992-93 STATISTICS:
Played 42 (36 League, 2 Anglo Italian Cup, 2 Coca Cola Cup, 2 FA Cup).
Goals 19 (16 League, 1 Anglo Italian Cup, 1 Coca Cola Cup, 1 FA Cup).

CUMULATIVE WOLVES CAREER:
Played 335 (283 League, 16 League Cup, 18 Freight Rover/Sherpa Van Trophy, 8 FA Cup, 4 Zenith Data Systems Cup, 4 play-off, 2 Anglo Italian Cup).
Goals 217 (172 League, 26 Freight Rover/Sherpa Van Trophy, 11 League Cup, 5 FA Cup, 1 Zenith Data Systems Cup, 1 Anglo Italian Cup, 1 play-off).

GT MARK II

1993-94

Despite a summer-time heel operation, Steve Bull was perky and very optimistic as he reported for pre-season training in July, 1993.

He hadn't played since early-April because of the injury and Wolves took advantage of the close-season by sending him for surgery on the body that was becoming bruised and not a little battered by his near-seven years of heroic front-line service.

When he checked in for duty, there were several new team-mates to meet and the departure of others to discuss. Popular Keith Downing, one of the mainstays of the climb from the Football League basement, had headed a quintet of free-transfers, with Lawrie Madden, Tim Steele, Colin Taylor and Rob Hindmarch also released. Others, like Andy Thompson, Andy Mutch and Robbie Dennison, had been made available for offer.

It was a summer of massive hope at the club. The showpiece Billy Wright Stand was close to completion and the Haywards, not wishing to see the bricks and mortar become their only concern, also invested more heavily than ever before in players.

Rumours had been rife that David Kelly would be on his way back to the West Midlands in the summer, and the 28-goal hero of the Geordies' spectacular promotion season was duly signed by Graham Turner for £750,000 in early June.

Within a couple of weeks, the cheque-book was out again with a deal that really turned heads. Crystal Palace and England midfielder Geoff Thomas, having almost joined Blackburn for £3m a year or so earlier, pulled out of a proposed move to Manchester City and opted instead for Wolves for £800,000. A jubilant Jonathan Hayward supervised the second eye-catching deal and said boldly: "I think we already have the basis of a championship-winning squad."

Both fees easily exceeded the previous highest amount Turner had splashed out as Wolves manager (£500,000 for Kevin Ashley) and showed the club meant business. Big business. "If the fans can still get 20-1 on Wolves winning the title, I would urge them to wager a bob or two," the chairman added. "Signing a player of Geoff's quality will, I believe, prove a landmark in the club's history."

When midfielder Kevin Keen arrived from West Ham in July for £600,000, Wolves had pumped over £2.1m into their 1993-94 promotion challenge. And, after Cyrille Regis had been recruited on a free transfer, there was clearly plenty more in the pot because a long-running pursuit of QPR centre-half Darren Peacock included at least one bid of around £1.5m. "It looks like I will keep throwing money at it until I am taken away by the men in white coats," said president Sir Jack Hayward. "I was 70 a few days ago, so I'm running out of time. But my ambition is to see a Wolves captain hold aloft the FA Cup and for us to be up there competing with Manchester United, Arsenal and Liverpool, and beating them."

In the wake of the big spending, Mutch, Dennison and Thompson were omitted from a typically goal-filled trip to Sweden. But the treatment they received when excluded from the annual team picture back at Molineux seemed shabby for players who had given such loyal service. Mutch looked particularly crestfallen off-camera and it was for the best when, after a Wolves career of 338 appearances and 106 goals, he joined Premiership newcomers Swindon for £250,000 a couple of weeks later.

So long, pal ... Steve Bull and Andy Mutch, seen here in their late-1980s
hey-day, now parted by the Liverpudlian's move to Swindon.

Thompson would have left as well - to Huddersfield in the autumn - had the Yorkshire club been able to raise the £50,000 asking price, while Dennison was to endure one of the troughs of his Molineux stint with a stretch out of favour. But, despite the sorrow, the photo-call was by no means a sombre affair, and Bull - temporarily lifting his self-imposed interview ban - told a collection of reporters of his big plans for the season.

"I have never given up hope of playing again for England," he said. "I accept Wolves would probably have to be in the Premier League but, if I can bang in 30 goals before Christmas, Graham Taylor would have to look at me again, even if I am a First Division player. That is the sort of mood I am in at the moment. I am 28 but Gary Lineker is a perfect example of a player who scored goals regularly into his 30s. I have a few good years left in me. David Kelly works as hard as Mutchy and his goals last season speak for themselves.

"I always set myself a target of 25 goals and, if David matches that, we will be up. With the new signings, nobody is even thinking about the play-offs. We are all thinking about the championship. The mood is that positive. It has always been my dream to get into the Premier League with Wolves and I really think we are going to do it this season. I have not looked forward so much to a season since I first signed for the club. The fans did not see the real Steve Bull last season. For the last 18 months, this Achiles problem has been nagging away at me but I can really feel the difference now it has been cleaned up. The new signings and the ground have given everyone a lift. The past couple of seasons have been a bit flat but now there is such a buzz about the place, I can't wait to get cracking."

Bull had scored on kick-off day for the previous three years and an experienced observer in the Press Box confidently predicted the player would have Wolves ahead inside 15 minutes in their curtain-raiser at home to Bristol City. The feat was

GOAL-COUNT

218 - *A long clearance from Stowell landed midway inside the visitors' half but hesitant defending allowed Keen to knock the ball forward and Bull showed tremendous strength and determination to go round to or three opponents before slamming home a superb rising drive from 20 yards.*

219 - *Bull delightfully turned home a close-range left-foot shot from a lovely low centre by Keen.*

Aug 14, 1993: Wolves 3 Bristol City 1

WOLVES: Stowell, Rankine, Venus, Cook, Mountfield, Blades, Birch, Thomas, Bull, D Kelly (Regis 77), Keen. Subs: Burke, Felgate.
Goals: Bull (9, 85), Mountfield (69).
Att: 21,052.

173

accomplished with six minutes to spare and a vibrant Molineux - a capacity 21,052 were watching in splendour in a stadium now all-seated for the first time - witnessed a comfortable win. The three points came despite Mark Venus's late sending-off, with Bull striking again in the second half.

With the three summer signings in action and the rebuilt Waterloo Road side of the ground open again after eight years, it was a tremendous day for the club. And another new signing, 32-year-old Sheffield Wednesday central defender Peter Shirtliff, was signed for £250,000 before the side headed off

You beauty ... Steve Bull is hugged by new skipper Geoff Thomas as Paul Cook prepares to add his congratulations after the striker's first goal in the redeveloped Molineux.

to surrender two points in a televised derby at Birmingham after leading 2-0 through goals from Venus and Thomas.

Chants of "Champions" had begun with indecent haste at the end of the first half at St Andrew's but Wolves were third after Bull had been joined for the first time on the score-sheet by Kelly in a one-sided Molineux triumph over Millwall - the game marking both the official opening of the Billy Wright Stand and Bull's 150th League and cup goal at the ground.

Pacesetters Middlesbrough spiked the early confidence by plundering three points on their visit to the West Midlands on the day Thompson was welcomed back to the fold. Thomas and Kelly were again among the goals and three more flew in during the midweek Anglo Italian Cup clash with Stoke, the last two of them salvaging a draw when all seemed lost. For the first and so far only time in his Wolves career, Bull started a game as substitute when the club's old Staffordshire rivals came calling and, even in a 45-minute appearance, there was a certain inevitability about him becoming the first player to step off the bench and score for the side in more than three years.

Bull had once more shot out of the starting stalls in double-quick time with four goals in five games and he celebrated in front of an exasperated Birmingham Road End as he soon opened the scoring in the Sunday derby at Albion. But this was to prove one Hawthorns return too many and Keith Burkinshaw's side hit back in a cracking game to record their first win over the old rivals for 11 years.

Just as seriously for Wolves, Bull had pulled up sharply in the second half, painfully clutching the hamstring that was to rule him out for a sizeable

GOAL-COUNT

220 - *Kelly's persistence earned him a second chance to cross following Blades' long ball down the right and Bull did the rest with an open goal beckoning.*

Aug 25, 1993: Wolves 2 Millwall 0

WOLVES: Stowell, Rankine, Venus, Cook (Burke 84), Blades, Shirtliff, Birch, Thomas, Bull, Kelly, Keen. Subs: Felgate, Regis.
Goals: Bull (32), Kelly (62).
Att: 19,570.

GOAL-COUNT

221 - *It paid off handsomely as Bull blasted home at the far post from Cook's right-wing corner.*

Aug 31, 1993: Wolves 3 Stoke 3, Anglo Italian Cup preliminary round.

WOLVES: Stowell, Rankine, Thompson, Burke, Blades, Venus, Birch (Cook 68), Thomas, Regis (Bull 46), Kelly, Keen. Sub: Felgate.
Goals: Kelly (44), Bull (79), Keen (90).
Att: 9,092.

Different number, same result ... Bully marks his first-ever substitute appearance for Wolves with a late Anglo Italian Cup cracker against Stoke.

slab of autumn. And his season took another down-turn shortly afterwards as a delayed result of a misdemeanour in a pre-season friendly at Wrexham. The aggressive striker had been unpunished and apparently unnoticed by referee John Lloyd when aiming a retaliatory swing at marker Mel Pejic but a video of the offending incident was later sent to the FA, and Bull was handed a three-match ban by a hearing at Shrewsbury.

Wolves, not for the first time, fared poorly in the striker's absence. There were a few calls for Turner's dismissal during a dismal midweek defeat at Watford and, despite an overwhelming vote of confidence from chairman Hayward after the following Saturday's scrappy home draw with Portsmouth, the pressure remained from supporters.

An inconsequential Anglo Italian exit at Birmingham on the night Lee Mills appeared (and scored) for the first time in the starting line-up was followed by the loan signing of West Ham striker Mike Small and the injustice of a victory at Sunderland that had serious undertones. Thomas, having struck in the North East with a brilliant fourth goal in ten matches, was caught by a bad injury-time tackle from substitute Lee Howey and stretchered off into a future of uncertainty.

Turner's future wasn't much rosier after his dwindling popularity suffered a blow it could ill-afford in the first leg of a Coca Cola Cup second-round match at Swindon. He produced a four-letter outburst from the dug-out in the dying minutes of a 2-0 defeat and fans who suspected the abuse was aimed at them put it down as another black mark.

Andy Mutch headed one of the goals at the County Ground and Wolves' ills continued with a defeat on the afternoon of an aborted Bull comeback in the League at Grimsby. A home draw with Charlton did little to lift the gloom and, after a late flurry had almost salvaged Coca Cola Cup progress at the expense of Swindon, the season was in some turmoil.

Jonathan Hayward had already received a weighty post-bag after his comments that Turner would never be under pressure while he was chairman. But Sir Jack started to seriously address the manager issue in a lengthy open letter to the Express & Star. "Surely, the time to judge Graham Turner is when he has all his team fit and playing together again," he wrote from the Bahamas. "Until then, he has to have the board's loyalty and support. Obviously, they (the directors) will have to review the situation if winning results do not come and when there can be no excuses. The Hayward family have kept all their promises to Wolverhampton so far. We will not let you down in the future."

The Molineux crowd were split over Turner, who was the fifth longest-serving manager in the country. Some had wanted him out for three years while others were sympathetic to an unfortunate catalogue of injuries and grateful for the excellent work he had done in the late 1980s. He was under no illusions, though, after admitting pre-season: "It would be fair to say we have stood still for two or three seasons and now there has got to be another big push."

Kelly's early goal took a surprise point off leaders Crystal Palace at Selhurst Park and the striker hit the target again to set up a winning position against Stoke that was frittered away partly because of a rare penalty miss by Thompson. Then came another remarkable outbreak of Bullymania.

Injury and suspension had sentenced the striker to nearly two months without completing a first-team game, so Turner was anxious to ease him back in; first through a goal-scoring appearance in a private friendly against Nottingham Forest, then with an outing against Manchester United's talented second string at Molineux. And what an outing it was!

Bull scored twice against a side captained by Darren Ferguson as a crowd of 9,000, 10,000 or even 12,000 poured in. Advance publicity had informed the masses that United would not field their big names, so the massive turn-out had only one plausible explanation. The King was back holding court.

Wolves officials, caught totally on the hop by the turn-out, realised the number of turnstile operators was inadequate and eventually resorted to flinging open the exit gates to let in the gathering thousands. Normally, only the upper tier of the Billy Wright Stand was used for reserve matches but I recall seeing startled players and coaches watching hordes of fans walking round the perimeter track while play was in progress to take up seats in the Stan Cullis and John Ireland Stands. Amid the first team's troubles, it was a refreshing and welcome night.

With Sir Jack then flying in from the Bahamas in the absence of his holidaying son, Wolves had Bull back for the end-of-October trip to Southend after missing six matches out of seven through injury and then three through his ban. But it needed Paul Cook's late penalty to rescue a point at Roots Hall, and the team were flattered by the margin of a follow-up midweek victory over struggling Notts County that restored Bull to the score-sheet for the first time in two months.

Once again, the determined Turner had come back from what was seen as the brink of the sack and sat back proudly at the Baseball Ground the following Sunday to witness his side's best performance for years. It was all too much for high-riding Derby, who were blown away by Bull's brilliant first hat-trick in 62 outings going back to March, 1991.

The heroics took the striker alongside Billy Hartill as the scorer of a club record 16 hat-tricks and restarted the "Recall him for England" campaign. Despite his problems, he had scored nine goals in nine starts in 1993-94 and, as he savoured the golden moment afterwards, he clutched the match-ball and said proudly: "This one's for my son Jack. I've been trying to get one for him all season. I should have had five goals but three will do." Of the wider implications of his performance, he added: "The gaffer is trying hard. They were chanting for his neck but he is doing his job and we're getting it together. We'll be there at the end of the season."

Like Turner, Graham Taylor,

GOAL-COUNT

223 - *The final act was played out when Bull drove Keen's pass in off the underside of the diving Cherry.*

Nov 2, 1993: Wolves 3 Notts County 0

WOLVES: Stowell, Simkin (Thompson 46), Venus, Edwards, Mountfield, Shirtliff, Cook, Birch, Bull, Kelly, Keen. Subs: Regis, Jones.
Goals: Birch (10), Keen (67), Bull (86).
Att: 15,989.

GOAL-COUNT

224 - *Bull thrust the first dagger-blow into Derby's chests with a right-foot lob from Birch's incisive through ball.*

225 - *Then he lashed in No 2 after a Kelly head-down to Edwards' cross.*

226 - *Finally, he sank to his knees in celebration of his hat-trick goal - a header over the shell-shocked Taylor from Edwards' brilliant long through ball.*

Nov 7, 1993: Derby 0 Wolves 4

WOLVES: Stowell, Thompson, Venus, Edwards, Mountfield, Shirtliff, Cook (Rankine 73), Birch, Bull, Kelly, Keen. Subs: Regis, Jones.
Goals: Bull (18, 60, 68), Keen (89).
Att: 14,310.

who overlooked Bull for his swansong as manager away to San Marino, was having major problems winning over the masses and there was another similarity. While the Wolves manager's Swindon outburst was merely picked up on Central TV's highlights programme, the national boss was party to an in-depth video that homed in on his accusations of a German referee during England's fateful qualifying defeat against Holland in Rotterdam.

179

First of a hat-trick ... Bull is the toast of the three Pauls (Edwards, Cook and Birch) after opening the scoring in Wolves' stunning 4-0 win at Derby in November, 1993.

227 - *Kelly nodded on Keen's cross from the left for Bull, at the far post, to direct a superb downward header past Ward's left hand.*

228 - *Again, it was finishing of the highest calibre as Bull ran on to Cook's through ball, held off a challenge by Hill and buried a superb low right-foot drive in at the near post.*

Nov 27, 1993: Leicester 2 Wolves 2

WOLVES: Stowell, Thompson, Edwards, Venus, Simkin, Shirtliff, Birch (Dennison 77), Cook, Bull, Kelly, Keen. Subs: Regis, Jones.
Goals: Bull (29, 34).
Att: 18,395.

Over the next few weeks, the fortunes of the two beleaguered managers moved in opposite directions. Taylor resigned in November while Wolves hit a good vein of form, the following four matches all bringing score-draws that took their unbeaten run to 11 games and suggested the corner was being turned. But the first of them - a Molineux cracker with Nottingham Forest - was preceded by the sad news that Thomas would be out for the season because of a cruciate knee injury suffered in his comeback against Derby Reserves.

Kelly scored with headers both against Forest and visiting Barnsley before Bull found another trip to the East Midlands fruitful, launching his eighth year at the club by bagging a brace on an afternoon at Leicester on which Wolves almost turned a 2-0 half-time lead into defeat.

The side, having switched to a five-man defence, remained barely in the top half of the table and, despite the joy of Kelly's last-gasp equaliser in a stormy Sunday re-match with Derby, were still struggling for victories. Bull, in his 300th Football League appearance, scored again before being helped off injured following one of several flashpoint incidents.

His only absence, though, was from the prestige midweek friendly against Honved, the Hungarian giants who had graced Molineux in one of the famous floodlit matches of the 1950s and who had been chosen as opponents on the night Wolves officially opened their redeveloped stadium. The club's biggest crowd for 13 years, 28,041, were plunged into semi-darkness by a pre-match electricity fault but the

GOAL-COUNT

229 - *Wolves built up a promising head of steam and Bull turned in the equaliser with his left foot from close range.*

Dec 5, 1993: Wolves 2 Derby 2

WOLVES: Stowell, Thompson, Venus, Edwards (Regis 78), Blades, Shirtliff, Dennison, Birch, Bull (Simkin 90), Kelly, Keen. Sub: Jones.
Goals: Bull (45), Kelly (90).
Att: 16,900.

reunion between Billy Wright and Ferenc Puskas, and an open-top car tour round the edge of the pitch by Sir Jack, still made it a wonderful evening.

Jack Harris was the proudest man in the West Midlands as he cut the ribbon to open the new stand bearing his name but it was perhaps to be expected that Wolves would be held to another draw despite the goal with which Thompson celebrated his removal from the transfer list and his signing of a new 18-month contract. Bull was back, with a goal, in a straightforward Molineux win over Watford the following Saturday - his 350th League and cup appearance for Wolves. And there was a hint of irony, in the wake of what was to happen, as disillusioned Watford fans chanted for the return of Graham Taylor to Vicarage Road.

No sooner had Wolves raised their supporters' hopes, though, than they lowered them with a miserable pre-Christmas defeat in the rain at Bristol City. And it took a Bully blockbuster to rescue a draw from a Boxing Day visit to their bogey ground, Tranmere, on the afternoon left-back Neil Masters made his debut following a £350,000 move from Bournemouth. It was another reminder of how heavily Wolves relied on their record-breaking marksman and he said before the visit of lowly Oxford as he reflected on his earlier absence from the side: "I sat down in those weeks and looked very hard at myself. I'm 28 now, the age where a lot of footballers are at their peak. If that's right, I've got to make the most of my time left in the game.

"Maybe I got into a rut last season without realising it. But I decided during those eight weeks that I would come back with all guns blazing and keep it going that way. I've got 230 goals for Wolves but I

GOAL-COUNT

230 - *A hail-storm had left the pitch greasy and, when Bull ran on to Dennison's through ball to unleash a low drive from 25 yards, Sheppard lost his footing as the shot skidded past him.*

Dec 12, 1993: Wolves 2 Watford 0

WOLVES: Stowell, Thompson, Edwards, Venus, Blades, Shirtliff (Bennett 46), Birch, Cook, Bull, Kelly, Dennison. Subs: Regis, Jones.
Goals: Bull (25), Dennison (34).
Att: 17,460.

GOAL-COUNT

231 - *Cook sent forward a long ball, new boy Neil Masters diverted it back in-field with his head and Bull thrashed a bludgeoning first-time right-foot shot that scorched past Nixon and almost lifted the net off its hooks.*

Dec 27, 1993: Tranmere 1 Wolves 1

WOLVES: Stowell, Thompson, Masters, Venus, Blades, Shirtliff, Birch, Cook, Bull, Kelly, Keen. Subs: Regis, Bennett, Jones.
Goal: Bull (62).
Att: 15,603.

**Well done, partner ... David Kelly lifts Steve Bull to his feet after Wolves'
first goal in the pre-Christmas victory at home to struggling Watford.**

want to make it well over 300 before I've finished. I've got a few years left in me yet and I want to fill them full of goals."

Bull stressed his two big aims were the same as ever - top-flight football and the reclaiming of his international jersey. "I know that, if I came to the end of my career without playing in the Premier League, I would grieve about it, especially after seeing Andy Mutch up there and playing quite well. And I'm as determined as ever to get back into the England squad. If Gary Lineker can play for England at 32, why can't I get back in the side? The European Championships are coming up and I would love to be in the squad."

There was a feeling Wolves had been short-changed from a run of bright performances. But that altered over the other three holiday games. Cook (penalty) and Keen each scored in the last five minutes to pull an undeserved victory out of the fire against Oxford in front of Molineux's biggest League crowd for over a decade. Then Cyrille Regis came up with his first Wolves goal at the 12th attempt to deliver another last-gasp winner, this time at bottom club Peterborough.

When Wolves clung on to Dennison's early goal to beat Bolton on a waterlogged surface, the side's fortunes really had appeared to change, and they proceded to slip into top gear despite the surprise absence from the goals columns of Bull. The striker was again led off injured in a Kelly-secured FA Cup win at home to First Division leaders Crystal Palace and, despite being fit for the Molineux League clash with the same opponents a week later, had to be satisfied with one of the assists on the day Thompson's first goal of the season and Keen's sixth delivered a highly impressive win.

Wolves had finally clicked and expectations soared even higher following the arrival of midfielders Chris Marsden and Darren Ferguson for £150,000 and £250,000 respectively. Both were in the side who performed valiantly in a thrilling goalless draw in front of the Sunday TV cameras at Forest and, when Second Division promotion-chasers Port Vale were accounted for by goals from Paul Blades and Keen in a fourth-round Cup-tie in the Potteries, Wolves really were on the march. They had won six games out of seven, had not conceded a goal in six matches since the turn of the year and were looking at their most convincing since their return to this division five years earlier.

There was the additional incentive of a paid trip to the Bahamas if they won the Cup while Bull had greeted news of Terry Venables' appointment as national coach by sounding a familiar theme: "I don't see why I can't get back in. I enjoyed every moment when I played for England and I want to be there again. If I'm not good enough, fair enough. But I want to score

184

goals and get him here to have a look at me."

Sadly, that winter's afternoon in Burslem proved a watershed occasion. With 16 minutes left, Bull was caught by a bad tackle from behind and hobbled off for the third time in less than two months. This time, there was to be no quick comeback and he was found to have ruptured ligaments and a torn cartilage in his left knee.

The much-loved striker, now only a few weeks short of his 29th birthday, had come in for a cruel battering from his markers over several weeks and was to miss nearly three months' football - a period that not only effectively cost the club their promotion chance but also brought the curtain down on the Turner era.

Not that there was any immediate down-turn as Blades' second goal on successive Saturdays earned a useful point at Stoke. Wolves had at one time clipped the gap between themselves and the leaders to a mere five points but they were again drawing too many games - and then allowed Southend to become the first visiting side since Middlesbrough in August to win at Molineux. On the same afternoon, Turner chose to receive his January Manager of the Month award in the privacy of the dressing-room rather than on the pitch.

The follow-up was a 1-1 Cup draw at home to Premiership strugglers Ipswich on the day 1950s star Johnny Hancocks died, then came an easy win in the snow against Barry Fry's sliding Birmingham - both marked by Kelly goals. That 3-0 romp made up some of the lost ground but a surprise home defeat against a languishing Albion side now containing Molineux old boy Paul Edwards had a massively damaging effect.

It was the first time Wolves had suffered a League double at the hands of their neighbours in 12 seasons and it was the defeat that hurt more than any other. The manager's popularity was again waning.

To tighten the noose even further, Turner was the hands-down loser of an unnecessary skirmish with the Express & Star. The relationship had, at best, been frosty for a couple of years and he broke off all connections after an article that appeared in the newspaper's columns on February 24.

In an interview for Wolverhampton-based radio station Challenge FM shortly before, Turner had said he hoped to be given another season to win Wolves promotion even if the 1993-94 campaign ended in failure. The newspaper reported his comments, only to find themselves on the end of a vitriolic attack from the manager on BBC Radio WM. Turner appeared to imply he hadn't realised the radio interview he had given was to be broadcast - and said he was surprised to see parts of it appear in print.

Radio WM rounded off their on-air link with Turner by saying his comments had "put the record straight" on the matter but the Express & Star were sufficiently angered by that assertion as to carry a back-page opinion piece two days later under the headline "Putting the record a little straighter." The newspaper stood its ground, having merely reported comments that had appeared in the public domain, and had spoken to Graham Turner, Wolves manager, for the last time.

The manager's sense of PR with supporters had been poor for many months and, for a man who had done so much for the club in his earlier years, it was sad he had to endure the indignity of a slow death in the job. In hindsight, and it must be said a lot of observers thought so at the time as well, it would have been better for him to have left a year or two earlier with his head held higher and without the endless "Turner must go" chants that infested home games for well over 12 months.

The Haywards had been extremely loyal to him and there was one final defiant twist before the inevitable parting of the ways. It came as Wolves produced a stunning performance to win their fifth-round Cup replay at Ipswich - their first cup win over a top-flight club for 13 years and their first time in the FA Cup quarter-final since 1981. First-half goals by Mills and Thompson thrilled the live Sky audience and booked a last-eight visit to Chelsea.

In the meantime, though, despite the belated signing of a replacement for Bull (Guy Whittingham on loan from Villa), Wolves lost a scruffy League game at Middlesbrough to a late goal and, when the Stamford Bridge clash finished with the same score, the end was near for Turner.

It came in the wake of a shocking performance in a 3-0 midweek defeat at Portsmouth. Jonathan Hayward, who had consistently backed the manager in the face of mounting criticism, sat stony-faced throughout the journey home from the South Coast, then snapped as the coach pulled into Wolverhampton and delivered a few home truths in a manner that showed he was very much a frustrated supporter as well as an ambitious chairman. Turner refused to accept the powerful words, which he probably saw as an undermining of his authority, and, after a meeting with reserve-coach Garry Pendrey well into the early hours, decided to resign.

Pendrey, who had felt the fans' fury for years too - he left the club for the two seasons in which promotion was won in 1988 and 1989 - went as well. Wolves were 13th in the table and, despite the excellent form of a few weeks earlier, were as far away from promotion as ever.

A cloud of depression hung over Molineux following the departure of a man with a record of 179 wins, 110 draws and 123 defeats from his 412 matches in charge, and Wolves - under the caretaker management of the

Scourge of the East Midlands ... following up a hat-trick at Derby with two goals at Leicester.

inspirational Shirtliff - lost the impressive Marsden with a broken leg and damaged ankle ligaments in a turgid 0-0 home draw with Grimsby.

QPR's Gerry Francis was first to be offered the vacant manager's job and then Manchester United and England legend Bryan Robson was interviewed. But Francis said no because he didn't want to leave London while Robson's chances appeared to be dented by the number of big-name backroom colleagues he had in mind.

At the same time, though, Wolves were giving strong consideration to Graham Taylor, who had resigned as England manager a week after a 7-1 victory away to San Marino. That win in Bologna came too late to salvage the country's World Cup qualifying campaign, and the former Villa and Watford favourite had a few weeks of recuperation before seeking a route back into employment.

One duly materialised at Molineux three days after Wolves had revived their season with a 1-0 win at Charlton, the on-loan Whittingham scoring their first goal in five games. Taylor, only the second national boss to go back into English club management, immediately spoke of channelling all his energies towards the "11 cup finals" that might just lift Wolves into the play-offs from their current 15th place.

Taylor had been blamed in some quarters for not using Bull more at international level but quickly stressed his high regard for a player he had once tried to sign for Villa. "I want to help him into the Premiership with Wolves," he said. "If people think I don't rate Steve Bull, they must be crackers. We're looking forward to getting him fit as soon as possible."

Bull's replacement, Whittingham, got the manager off to a winning start with two goals, either side of one from Thompson, at Bolton, then the Villa striker opened his Molineux account to set up a home win over Tranmere that was secured by Mills' late goal. The door to the play-offs had been pushed slightly ajar but a nightmare 4-0 trouncing at Oxford on Easter Monday, followed by a poor home draw against relegation-bound Peterborough, checked the impetus.

Taylor had made quick inroads with winning over fans opposed to his appointment and was deriving real value from Whittingham, the striker scoring in the 2-0 midweek win at Luton and in the victory by the same score at Notts County four days later. That was on the afternoon Bull, after a two-goal comeback in the reserves in front of a crowd of 3,300, was finally back after a damaging 16-game absence. "He has been as miserable as sin to live with for eight weeks but now he is beaming," said his father-in-law Gene Dace. "He lives for the job and is itching to play - everyone knows that."

Wolves were again knocking on the door and followed up a 1-0 defeat at promotion rivals Millwall with the completion of an April double over Luton thanks to Whittingham's eighth goal in nine games. Midweek results went favourably, too, and, after five frustrating years in this division, a play-off place was Wolves' if they could win their last three matches. They failed horribly.

A dismal performance saw them well beaten at Barnsley, then Bull's first goal since Boxing Day - he had played 11 games in that time despite his injury - was cancelled out by a Don Goodman equaliser for visiting Sunderland. The play-offs were finally out of reach and, at home to Premiership-bound Leicester on the last afternoon of the season, Kelly's first goal since a six-week absence with an ankle injury accomplished nothing more than Anglo Italian Cup qualification.

It had been an eventful campaign but another disappointing one, not least for Bull. Despite finishing top scorer for an eighth successive season - far and away a club record - he had managed only 15 goals, mainly because he had played only 30 games out of 55. He

---

GOAL-COUNT

232 - *The outside of Cook's boot brilliantly bore a hole down the centre of Sunderland's defence and Bull shook off Ball's challenge to blast in a vintage left-foot shot from 16 yards.*

May 3, 1994: Wolves 1 Sunderland 1

WOLVES: Stowell, Thompson, Rankine, Bennett, Blades, Shirtliff, Birch, Cook, Bull, Whittingham (Kelly 72), Keen. Subs: Burke, Jones.
Goal: Bull (31).
Att: 25,079.

---

had missed nearly half the games but maintained a good 50 per cent strike-rate in the others while Kelly had mustered a moderate 14 in 44.

Wolves had not had a single player among the First Division's top 22 marksmen but the late rush under Taylor had taken them to their highest Football League placing for nearly a decade (eighth) and to within three points of the play-offs. If anyone at Molineux deserved Premiership football - and nobody doubted that lovable Sir Jack Hayward warranted reward for his enormous backing - it was Bull. But time, sadly, was beginning to run out.

BULLY'S 1993-94 STATISTICS: Played 30 (27 League, 2 FA Cup, 1 Anglo Italian Cup). Goals 15 (14 League, 1 Anglo Italian Cup).

CUMULATIVE WOLVES CAREER: Played 365 (310 League, 16 League Cup, 18 Freight Rover/Sherpa Van Trophy, 10 FA Cup, 4 Zenith Data Systems Cup, 4 play-off, 3 Anglo Italian Cup). Goals 232 (186 League, 26 Freight Rover/Sherpa Van Trophy, 11 League Cup, 5 FA Cup, 1 Zenith Data Systems Cup, 2 Anglo Italian Cup, 1 play-off).

PLAY-OFF HEARTACHE

1994-95

Steve Bull was still under contract for five years as Graham Taylor embarked on his busy first close-season as Wolves manager. By the end of it, the striker was tied only for another three years after a mutually agreed deal which offered Bull the chance to make the same money up to 1997 that he was due to make up to 1999.

It meant the 29-year-old would have time to seek another club at the end of his deal if he wished while Wolves would still be entitled to ask a fee for him, as a 32-year-old, if he went. It suited both parties, not least Bull because he still had a testimonial year written into his contract, and the two parties went their separate ways for a few weeks as all around them changed.

Out went ten players on free transfers - including Derek Mountfield, Cyrille Regis, Kevin Ashley, Mark Burke, Darren Roberts, Shaun Bradbury and Graham Turner's son Mark - along with physio Paul Darby and chief scout Ron Jukes, the man at Molineux credited with having spotted Bull kicking his heels in Albion's Reserves eight years earlier. In came two big-money Villa wingers, Tony Daley and Steve Froggatt, and Millwall centre-half Neil Emblen while Bobby Downes, Steve Harrison, Stuart Gray and Barry Holmes were added to the coaching team.

It was a massive overhaul in such a short time and Taylor, who restricted himself to one week off over the summer, also devoted what hours he could to finding a new training ground - a project he believed was of the utmost importance. "It's a sign of Graham's long planning that he would probably rather splash out an extra £1m on a training ground than on another new player," said chairman Jonathan Hayward.

As had become the norm, Wolves travelled to Sweden early in their pre-season countdown and filled their scoring boots in the usual way, with Bull leading from the front. He blasted five goals during one sun-baked afternoon against the part-timers of Smedby and struck twice when the squad made the short hop over to Copenhagen to beat Peter Schmeichel's former club Hvidovre.

And he was equally impressive after returning to home soil, giving his side a lead they couldn't hold in an entertaining sell-out friendly against

Back in the old routine ... Bully savouring a pre-season Molineux goal.

double winners Manchester United and scoring one of the goals which saw off visiting Coventry. But, when kick-off day came, it all went cruelly wrong for the striker.

Having suffered a hamstring injury against the Sky Blues, he aggravated the problem when helping set up Froggatt's debut winner at home to Reading and lasted only 12 minutes. The man who hadn't missed a single game through injury for his first four and three quarter years at the club, was now the periodic limping casualty of his own bravery and his ever-present red-blooded determination to play.

"What we now have to do with Steve is make sure we don't rush him back too early," Taylor said. "He has to learn to look after himself and tell us if he isn't properly fit. He has probably played at times when he hasn't been quite right and that has had a knock-on effect. We don't want him to risk doing further damage if it isn't necessary."

Wolves had a mixed bag of results in Bull's absence, Andy Thompson's penalty rescuing the club's first away draw for nearly seven months from an untidy performance at Notts County and then, after a David Kelly winner away to Lecce in the Anglo Italian Cup, Thompson and Kelly again providing the goals in an impressive and joyously acclaimed revenge win at home to Albion.

Wolves were third but the follow-up left Taylor in no mood to sample the hospitality extended by his former club Watford after a goal by Emblen - suddenly playing well in midfield after a nightmare debut against Reading at centre-half - had failed to stave off defeat at Vicarage Road. Mark Venus's first goal for more than a year - on the sad September day on which Billy Wright lost his fight against illness - earned a point at Sunderland but the season was stuck in second gear after Ascoli's antics in victory at Molineux started to question what Wolves were doing in the Anglo Italian Cup.

Then, with Bull returning after a month's recuperation, exciting things began to happen. With Daley yet to kick a ball for the club because of a knee injury picked up on tour, Paul Stewart and Mark Walters had been recruited on loan from Liverpool, the former preceding Emblen on to the score-sheet in a solid home win over Tranmere. The win over the Merseysiders marked the return of Bull and Froggatt after injury and was a suitably happy outcome to an afternoon which had started with the most moving of tributes to Billy Wright.

Although Stewart quickly fell victim to the club's chronic injury problems, Wolves were immediately to turn on another performance of which their 105-times-capped former centre-half would have been immensely proud. The day after a massive turn-out in the town in Wright's memory, Wolves' fourth home League win out of four, without a goal against, took them top of the table.

Southend were the hapless victims of Wolves' biggest League victory in four and a half seasons as Bull, having suffered his longest start-of-season wait for a goal, finally got on the score-sheet with his side's fifth goal of a night that sent them top of the table for the first time in two years. Bull, having struck only his second goal of 1994, scored his first away goal since Christmas as Wolves hung on for three points at Burnley to regain the leadership they had lost to Middlesbrough in midweek.

The campaign was progressing nicely and Bull struck twice in a Coca Cola Cup first-leg success at Chesterfield - the 71st Football League club against whom he had scored. Goals by Walters and Kelly ensured the winning run reached five games on the visit to Portsmouth and, after the irrelevance of a second-leg draw at home to Chesterfield as Wolves reached the third round of the Coca Cola Cup for only the second time in ten

GOAL-COUNT

233 - *A quick throw by Stowell set Froggatt off on another full-throttle dash down the left and the perfect cross that followed was rolled in off the post by a grateful Bull.*

Sep 13, 1994: Wolves 5 Southend 0

WOLVES: Stowell, Smith, Thompson, Emblen, Venus, Shirtliff, Walters, Ferguson, Bull, Kelly, Froggatt. Subs: Blades, Jones, Birch.
Goals: Emblen (8), Kelly (11), Froggatt (40), Walters (64), Bull (68).
Att: 23,608.

GOAL-COUNT

234 - *One goal from the head of an erratic Bull was all it needed, the striker nodding home after Kelly had helped on Ferguson's right-wing corner.*

Sep 17, 1994: Burnley 0 Wolves 1

WOLVES: Stowell, Smith, Thompson, Emblen, Venus, Shirtliff, Walters, Ferguson, Bull, Kelly, Froggatt. Subs: Blades, Birch, Jones.
Goal: Bull (59).
Att: 17,766.

GOAL-COUNT

235 - *Bull sidefooted the equaliser into an empty net from a Birch-Froggatt link-up.*

236 - *Bull went off on a solo run that ended with a ferocious low right-foot shot in off the post - his 48th goal in 56 cup appearances for the club.*

Sep 20, 1994: Chesterfield 1 Wolves 3, Coca Cola Cup second round first leg.

WOLVES: Stowell, Smith, Thompson, Emblen (Blades 18), Venus, Shirtliff, Birch, Ferguson, Bull, Kelly, Froggatt. Subs: Keen, Jones.
Goals: Bull (63, 85), Kelly (76).
Att: 5,895.

193

years, two Thompson penalties condemned Port Vale to defeat at the start of October and underlined the side's position at the top of the tree.

Taylor, named Endsleigh League Manager of the Month for September, was irritated but not perturbed by the odd-goal defeats that followed away to Venezia in the Anglo Italian Cup and Swindon in the League, the latter ensuring they left the County Ground empty-handed for the seventh time in a row. Confidence was still high as an unconvincing home win over Grimsby in Stowell's 200th Wolves appearance was followed by the building of a 3-1 lead against visiting Millwall. Bull scored two of the three

Graham Taylor ... monthly award.

and the impending celebration of three more points was further fuelled by Daley's debut appearance as a 76th minute sub. But the following 14 minutes turned into some of the blackest of the season as Daley pulled up sharply at the end of his first run and Wolves yielded two late goals. Two crucial points had been squandered - the club's first at home in the League - and their record signing was subsequently found to have cruciate knee ligament damage and was destined to sit out the rest of the season.

Bull's brace against the Londoners pointed him closer to another major landmark, his 250 in League and cup for his two League clubs. His tally now stood at 241 and, after a thrilling Coca Cola Cup exit at home to Nottingham Forest in front of a 28,369 crowd who smashed Wolves' gate receipts record for the second time in a few

GOAL-COUNT

237 - *Thompson's gigantic free-kick eventually found Walters, who laid it off to Smith - and the youngster's cross was headed firmly past Keller by Bull.*

238 - *Bull grabbed another early in the second half, tapping in after Keller had failed to hold Froggatt's shot.*

Oct 22, 1994: Wolves 3 Millwall 3

WOLVES: Stowell, Smith, Thompson, Venus, Blades, Shirtliff, Walters (Daley 76), Ferguson, Bull, Kelly, Froggatt. Subs: Thomas, Jones.
Goals: Bull (27, 53), Venus (79).
Att: 25,059.

weeks, he nudged even closer with a cracking equaliser in a Sunday draw at Stoke.

With the on-loan Stewart back after injury, though, and Kelly rifling in his first Wolves hat-trick in a 5-1 midweek romp at Bristol City, there was some discussion as to which two of the three made up the club's best strike-force. Bull was withdrawn near the end of his goalless appearance at Ashton Gate to allow Stewart a run and then failed to reappear for the second half of the unnerving Bonfire Night afternoon slump at home to Luton.

Taylor later confirmed the striker's withdrawal was tactical - the first time the Molineux legend had ever been taken off, in effect, because it was felt Wolves could do better without him. The shockwaves bounced around Bull's legion of fans for quite some time and, amid some of the wild rumours that followed, the manager had some calming words to the effect that he felt Wolves - beaten for the second successive home match after going eight months without defeat at Molineux - simply needed strengthening in midfield against David Pleat's away-day specialists.

Bull then picked up an injury that ruled him out of both the Anglo Italian swansong at home to Atalanta and the awful mid-November Sunday defeat at arch-rivals Middlesbrough that cost Wolves their shaky hold on top spot. In the meantime, Taylor had agreed a fee with Liverpool for Stewart's permanent move but the former England player, after failing to score in a reviving 3-1 home win over Bolton - a repeat of the victory that had launched the manager's Wolves career - was booed loudly before going off with a groin injury in the following weekend's flop at home to Derby. Taylor immediately shipped him back to Anfield, saying he was not fit and wouldn't have passed the medical.

The development left the stage clear again for people's champion Bull, whose name had been chanted repeatedly during his absence. And he returned after a four-game injury absence to play a spirited part in another Sunday flop, this time at Millwall in a game marked by the sending-off of Kelly. Wolves had lost four League matches out of five and their miserable form was causing such concern that Taylor took decisive action. He flew to Holland to set up the £600,000 signing of Dutch international John de Wolf

195

GOAL-COUNT

240 - *Smith suddenly fed in a centre from the right that Bull swept in with a first-time right-foot drive that looped beyond Cherry and into the far corner.*

Dec 10, 1994: Wolves 1 Notts County 0

WOLVES: Stowell, Smith, Venus, Ferguson, De Wolf, Emblen, Rankine (Kelly 69), Goodman, Bull, Bennett (Blades 46), Froggatt. Sub: Jones.
Goal: Bull (46).
Att: 25,786.

and then negotiated with Sunderland for the £1.1m switch South of Don Goodman.

Both made their debuts at home to struggling Notts County the following Saturday when Bull, just to remind everyone he wasn't ready to hand over star billing just yet, hooked in the only goal of the game. County had long been one of the striker's favourite sets of opponents, becoming in 1993-94 the third side against whom he had scored double figures during his Wolves career and now on the end of a Molineux goal from him for the third season running.

De Wolf's arrival had coincided with the side's first clean sheet in 18 games but Taylor's urgent team strengthening continued with the surprise £25,000 acquisition of Gordon Cowans from Derby. And, after Bull had scored again in the thrilling defeat at Reading in which Froggatt's season was ended by a bad tackle from Scott Taylor, the manager bought youngster Jermaine Wright from Millwall and signed up trialist Brian Law.

It was a considerable overhaul to make in mid-season but there were further worries over Bull, whose effort at Elm Park meant he had now scored against every other side in the 1994-95 First Division except Grimsby. He was still troubled by a heel problem and Taylor made it clear he would not be able to play the full holiday programme, which Wolves entered in second place but with sixth spot much closer points-wise than leaders Middlesbrough.

GOAL-COUNT

241 - *Bull's fine early header gave Wolves the lead from the third of their eight first-half corners.*

Dec 18, 1994: Reading 4 Wolves 2

WOLVES: Stowell, Smith, Venus, Emblen, De Wolf, Blades, Rankine, Goodman, Bull, Ferguson, Froggatt (Birch 2). Mills went on for Birch 46. Sub: Jones.
Goals: Bull (9), Quinn (og, 59).
Att: 10,136.

"With four games coming up in quick succession, it may be that we have to nurse Steve through and play him, say, in two of the matches," Taylor said. "I can't see any way he can play two games in 48 hours, for example."

Sure enough, the record-breaking marksman sat out a miserable Boxing Day lunchtime hammering at Oldham, where Cowans and Law made their debuts. A much-changed side in which Paul Jones came in for the dropped Mike Stowell and Darren Ferguson appeared in the starting line-up for the last time in 1994-95 also figured Robbie Dennison in the club's League 11 for the first time in ten months, the Northern Ireland winger scoring in a thumping defeat inflicted by Andy Ritchie's hat-trick.

Bull was fit for the visit of Charlton two days later but only as a farewell before departing for an operation on his heel. And he duly signed off with a goal to take his season's tally into double figures, Wolves' much-needed win being inspired by Jones' early penalty save.

Wolves were back among the goals after their barren spell and, after Lee Mills and the revitalised Dennison had scored in the opening four minutes of a New Year's Eve win at Barnsley, De Wolf and Emblen obliged at the opposite end of the next match-day to somehow salvage an injury-time point at home to Sheffield United.

Another spectacular fightback, this time featuring goals from Kelly, Dennison and Mills at Mansfield, staved off the probability of an FA Cup exit at the first hurdle after what Taylor had described as "one of the most disgraceful first-half performances I have ever seen." And Wolves were back in decent form by the time they saw off old Staffordshire rivals Stoke at Molineux through strikes from Kelly and Dennison in front of the division's highest crowd so far, 28,298. The win, achieved in Venus's 250th League and cup game for the club, also meant Wolves - with four months of the season left - had matched their 1993-94 record of ten home League wins.

The late postponement of a game at waterlogged Luton crossed off one of the matches in Bull's absence, and the striker was as thrilled as any of the club's supporters by the happy end to a heart-stopping FA Cup cliffhanger against Sheffield Wednesday. Keeper Jones, having saved Chris Bart-Williams' late spot-kick to keep his side alive at Hillsborough, then performed heroics to save two more in a penalty shoot-out which was somehow won by Wolves from 3-0 down.

Goodman, who rifled in the winning kick, broke his goal duck for the club in an unflattering crash at Bolton and, with Kelly confirming his good

---

GOAL-COUNT

242 - *Bull highlighted a heart-warming, all-action display with a close-range header after missing two clear openings.*

Dec 28, 1994: Wolves 2 Charlton 0

WOLVES: Jones, Blades, Venus, Emblen, De Wolf, Law, Goodman (Masters 67), Mills, Bull (Bennett 79), Cowans, Dennison. Sub: Stowell.
Goals: Bull (38), Chapple (og, 43).
Att: 26,738.

---

form with one of the goals in a 2-0 home win over Bristol City and then a magnificent winner on Cup fifth-round day at home to Leicester, there was the question of whether the fast-improving Bull would regain his place.

But a crucial Molineux defeat against title favourites Middlesbrough in a game which saw Brian Law sent off, prompted Taylor to devise the most popular team selection of the season. Bull had not even had a reserve game at the end of his two-month absence nor been named in Wolves' squad but so wary was the manager of allowing any gloom to develop after the Boro defeat that he acted boldly for the incident-packed late-February visit to Port Vale.

He had a quiet word with the striker after training on the eve of the match and, under a veil of secrecy, told him he would be leading the attack at Vale Park. "I was so conscious of a mood of depression settling on the players that I decided to put Steve in," said Taylor after the game. "But I decided no useful purpose would be served by announcing it in advance because of all the hype that goes with him." In typical fairytale fashion, Bull not only got through satisfactorily but scored one goal and had a hand in two others in a morale-boosting win that restored Wolves to fifth spot after they had briefly slipped out of the play-off places for the first time in five and a half months. It seemed all the sweeter that his happy comeback was in the first repeat of the fixture that had led him to miss a big chunk of 1993-94 through a knee injury.

Despite Bull's successful return, most of the headlines at muddy Vale Park went to De Wolf, who marked

> ### GOAL-COUNT
>
> *243 - De Wolf's through ball was helped on by Goodman for Bull to expertly lob the out-rushing Musselwhite for his 11th goal of the season.*
>
> *Feb 25, 1995: Port Vale 2 Wolves 4*
>
> *WOLVES: Jones, Blades, Thompson, Rankine, De Wolf, Shirtliff, Goodman, Kelly, Bull (Venus 77), Cowans, Dennison. Subs: Smith, Stowell.*
> *Goals: De Wolf (2, 43, pen 68), Bull (45). Att: 13,676.*

the handing-over of the captaincy to the fit-again Shirtliff with the first hat-trick by a Wolves defender since Ted Pheasant 93 years earlier. The club's season was right on the boil, with League gates averaging 26,000 and nearly 15 months having elapsed since a home First Division match had been watched by fewer than 20,000.

Bull was now on 197 career League goals and 243 League and cup goals, continuing to chip away towards another host of landmarks with an unusual winner against visiting Portsmouth. His renewed flurry of scoring was briefly interrupted by a first-half thigh injury in the home game with

He's back ... and delighted with his goal in a day out at Port Vale otherwise dominated by John de Wolf.

Sunderland - the side's ninth win in 14 games - and then sadly overshadowed by a season-ending knee ligament injury to the in-form De Wolf.

Wolves were as unlucky as ever with their selection problems but Bull recovered in time to play in the following Saturday's Cup quarter-final at Crystal Palace, where Cowans' steered equaliser raised the side's hopes of a third Premiership scalp. But injury worries never seemed far away for the striker and he hobbled out of the bitterly disappointing derby defeat at Albion four days later with a hamstring strain that kept him out of the draw with Watford back at Molineux.

Youngster Jamie Smith, one of the big successes of the pre-Christmas programme, and the cruelly-stricken Geoff Thomas joined the absentee list in the wake of the two unhappy results, Smith with a ban for his sending-off on a nightmare evening under the Hawthorns floodlights and the midfielder with an injury that followed his first goal for 18 months and which was to require yet another operation.

> ## GOAL-COUNT
>
> **244** - *Bull came up with a half-hit, just-about-deserved winner that somehow eluded Alan Knight at his near post.*
>
> *Mar 5, 1995: Wolves 1 Portsmouth 0*
>
> *WOLVES: Stowell, Blades, Thompson, Rankine, De Wolf, Shirtliff, Goodman, Kelly, Bull, Cowans, Dennison. Subs: Bennett, Wright, Jones.*
> *Goal: Bull (75).*
> *Att: 23,284.*

Bull launched his fifth comeback of the season on the night the Cup dream was shattered by Palace's inspired shooting - his 200th game at Molineux. And this time he was back for an unbroken spell in the manner of old. In the last game he played in his 20s, he scored one of the two goals that saw off visiting Burnley in front of a remarkable Friday night crowd of 25,703, including Stan Collymore and transfer deadline day loan signing Dean Richards.

Emblen was also back on target for the first time since January 2 but Bull, named captain in Shirtliff's absence, struck on his own in a follow-up win at Southend with another milestone goal - his 200th in the League. Wolves, third in the table, still had hopes of going up as champions after their single-goal triumph at Roots Hall and sensed their luck might be changing when an Emblen goal three minutes into injury time, added to a brace from Kelly, rescued a point in a bizarre game at Luton in which they were twice two adrift.

There was every chance the door would be nudged open a little wider when Wolves were awarded a last-minute chance to break a turgid goalless deadlock against play-off rivals Barnsley from the penalty spot. But Kelly's poor kick, following the sending-off of the visitors' player-manager Danny Wilson, was saved.

Bull endured a third successive game without a goal when the club's return to one of his happiest hunting grounds, Derby, ended in a draw and a rash of scoring for others, Richards helping himself to his first Wolves goals and Goodman ending a barren sequence of two months with his second strike for the club. Wolves were in a prolific away spell but were giving away as many goals as they were scoring and the latest in a long line of Bull

GOAL-COUNT

245 - *Bull rolled a right-foot shot on the turn after Kelly's lobbed pass had brought an ill-judged charge by keeper Russell.*

Mar 24, 1995: Wolves 2 Burnley 0

WOLVES: *Stowell, Blades, Venus, Rankine, Law, Shirtliff, Goodman, Kelly, Bull, Emblen, Dennison. Subs: Smith, Wright, Jones.*
Goals: Bull (10), Emblen (60).
Att: 25,703.

GOAL-COUNT

246 - *Bull clipped home past the advancing keeper after being sent clear by Goodman's defence-splitting header.*

Apr 1, 1995: Southend 0 Wolves 1

WOLVES: *Stowell, Blades, Masters, Emblen, Law, Richards, Goodman, D Kelly, Bull, Venus, Dennison. Subs: Birch, J Kelly, Jones.*
Goal: Bull (83).
Att: 8,522.

GOAL-COUNT

247 - *Cowans returned a left-foot cross which was superbly despatched over Ammann by the head of Bull.*

248 - *Bull revived his side again with a powerful header in off the bar from Cowans' corner on the right.*

Apr 15, 1995: Charlton 3 Wolves 2

WOLVES: *Stowell, Richards, Smith (Blades 76), Rankine, Law, Shirtliff (Wright 46), Goodman, D Kelly, Bull, Cowans, Venus.*
Sub: Jones.
Goals: Bull (43, 66).
Att: 10,922.

GOAL-COUNT

249 - *Molineux's favourite son flicked in a most un-Bully-like goal from Rankine's cross from the left.*

Apr 22, 1995: Sheffield United 3 Wolves 3

WOLVES: *Stowell, Blades (Thompson 78), Venus, Rankine, Richards, Shirtliff, Goodman, Kelly, Bull, Cowans, Dennison.*
Subs: Wright, Jones.
Goals: Goodman (58), Bull (65), Kelly (83).
Att: 16,714.

landmarks was undermined on a disappointing Easter Saturday against Charlton at The Valley. The striker marked his first appearance at the ground with two headed goals, the second taking his League tally for the club to 200, but the unfashionable Londoners inflicted a damaging defeat.

Two days later, a Kelly brace saw off defence-minded Oldham at Molineux and a play-off place at least was looking assured. But sights were once again being set higher as the side led going into the last couple of minutes of a cracking contest in the rain at Sheffield United. Bull's goal was one of three from his side in the second half at Bramall Lane and meant he had scored on no fewer than 49 Football League grounds.

But, with the tension mounting, Wolves couldn't manage even one at Grimsby a week later on the day Bull made his 400th appearance for the club. And their hopes of the title disappeared for good when Middlesbrough beat Luton the following day on the last day of League football at emotional Ayresome Park. "We have to look to the play-offs now," said Bull. "I still fancy our chances and think we'll be okay. I certainly hope so because I'm fed up of this division."

Wolves still had a bit of work to do but received a surprise helping hand when sixth-placed Barnsley were held at home by Oldham three days later. That meant Wolves needed only a point away to promotion rivals Tranmere the following night to be sure of "over-time" - and they got it. Fittingly, it was Bull's goal that did it, the striker starting his fifth century of League and cup games for the club with an historic equaliser that he celebrated ecstatically.

Golden moments ... Steve Bull drills home his 200th Football League goal (above),
this impressive finish giving his side three points at Southend on April Fool's Day.
Below: It's Wolves goal No. 250 as he steers in the equaliser at
Tranmere on the night a play-off place was assured.

After six years of trying and failing to make a serious mark on the division, Wolves had at least achieved something. And Molineux had a carnival atmosphere as they wound up their League programme with a wasteful home draw against a Swindon side who were already relegated and quickly reduced to ten men by the sending-off that preceded Thompson's ninth successful penalty of the season.

Wolves had finished with four consecutive draws - an unflattering batch of results from generally impressive form that took them into the play-offs against Bolton in optimistic mood. But, importantly, the Lancashire club's last-gasp Burnden Park equaliser at home to Burnley secured third spot, one ahead of Wolves, and meant they had home advantage in the second leg. How crucial it was to prove, although Bull and then Venus gave inspired Wolves an odd-goal lead at a noisy Molineux, the striker's thunderous header past Peter Shilton providing a poignant memory of old times. The two had been colleagues during Italia 90, at the end of which Bull asked the keeper for his gloves as a momento.

Shilton was injured for the second leg and his replacement Keith Branagan was barely tested as Wolves suffered the crushing anti-climax of aggregate defeat. Bolton goals in the first half of normal time and the second half of extra-time ended the dream and the feeling of devastation hit the Molineux camp and fans like a mortar. No-one more so than Bull, who slumped despairingly to the turf; the magnificent scorer of 251 Wolves goals, but all in the lower divisions. Would he now ever have the chance he deserved a hundred times over to play top-flight football for the club he loved?

> ## GOAL-COUNT
>
> **250** - *Bull controlled Shirtliff's pass into the area and steered a right-foot shot round the advancing Nixon for his 250th Wolves goal.*
>
> *May 3, 1995: Tranmere 1 Wolves 1*
>
> WOLVES: *Stowell, Thompson, Venus, Rankine, Richards, Shirtliff, Goodman, Kelly, Bull, Cowans, Dennison. Subs: Blades, Wright, Jones.*
> *Goal: Bull (73).*
> *Att: 12,306.*

> ## GOAL-COUNT
>
> **251** - *The tense deadlock was broken when Bull flashed a powerful close-range header past Shilton after Dennison had whipped over a tremendous centre from the left.*
>
> *May 14, 1995: Wolves 2 Bolton 1, play-off semi-final first leg.*
>
> WOLVES: *Stowell, Thompson, Venus, Rankine, Richards, Shirtliff, Goodman, Kelly, Bull, Cowans, Dennison. Subs: Law, Wright, Jones.*
> *Goals: Bull (44), Venus (51).*
> *Att: 26,153.*

BULLY'S 1994-95 STATISTICS: Played 39 (31 League, 3 Coca Cola Cup, 1 Anglo Italian Cup, 2 FA Cup, 2 play-offs). Goals 19 (16 League, 2 Coca Cola Cup, 1 play-off).

CUMULATIVE WOLVES CAREER: Played 404 (341 League, 19 League Cup, 18 Freight Rover/Sherpa Van Trophy, 12 FA Cup, 4 Zenith Data Systems Cup, 6 play-off, 4 Anglo Italian Cup). Goals 251 (202 League, 26 Freight Rover/Sherpa Van Trophy, 13 League Cup, 5 FA Cup, 1 Zenith Data Systems Cup, 2 Anglo Italian Cup, 2 play-off).

Up to August, 1995, Steve Bull's 251 Wolves goals had been scored against the following 43 clubs, listed here in the order in which he scored his first goal against them: Cardiff 5, Hartlepool 6, Bournemouth 2, Southend 6, Exeter 5, Stockport 1, Colchester 4, Orient 3, Scunthorpe 3, Peterborough 6, Lincoln 3, Scarborough 1, Notts Co 11, Hereford 5, Crewe 1, Man C 1, Torquay 4, Rochdale 1, Carlisle 1, Tranmere 4, Cambridge 4, Swansea 5, Cheltenham 3, Bristol C 13, Brentford 6, Bolton 5, Darlington 3, Burnley 3, Newport 2, Birmingham 2, Aldershot 2, Port Vale 12, Wigan 1, Gillingham 2, Huddersfield 2, Preston 4, Mansfield 4, Chester 1, Fulham 3, Blackpool 1, Bury 3, Northampton 1, Sheff U 2, Bradford 2, Brighton 3, Barnsley 3, Portsmouth 4, A Villa 1, Albion 3, West Ham 4, Hull 2, Newcastle 6, Sheff Wed 3, Ipswich 3, Watford 7, Leicester 9, Oxford 5, Oldham 2, Plymouth 2, Charlton 7, Middlesbrough 1, Millwall 4, Swindon 1, Shrewsbury 2, Everton 1, Bristol Rov 6, Derby 5, Blackburn 1, Luton 1, Stoke 2, Sunderland 1, Chesterfield 2, Reading 1.

Of that 251, 163 have been scored at home and 88 away. He has scored goals at 49 grounds and hit 16 hat-tricks: v Hartlepool, Cheltenham, Brentford, Exeter, Darlington, Preston, Port Vale, Mansfield, Bristol C (2), Fulham, Bury, Newcastle, Leicester, Oxford and Derby.

Author's P.S: At times, I have wondered how Steve Bull has remained out of reach of the big-club vultures and I was lambasted in 1991 for suggesting he would have to quit a then-languishing Wolves if he wished to play in the top flight in his prime. Had he gone, the club could have built a team out of the proceeds but it would somehow have seemed they were selling the family silver to do so. And the "vows" for the long and very happy marriage between Wolves and their most famous-ever No 9 were clearly made with a lot more than logic and mere financial interest in mind.